HUMANS AND PARAGONS

ESSAYS ON SUPER-HERO JUSTICE

HUMANS AND PARAGONS

ESSAYS ON SUPER-HERO JUSTICE

EDITED BY

IAN BOUCHER

SEQUART ORGANIZATION   EDWARDSVILLE, ILLINOIS

Humans and Paragons: Essays on Super-Hero Justice
edited by Ian Boucher

First edition, January 2017, ISBN 978-1-9405-8914-5.

Cover by Mara MacMahon and Roni Setiawan. Book design by Julian Darius. Interior art is © its respective owners.

Published by Sequart Organization. Edited by Ian Boucher.

For more information about other titles in this series, visit Sequart.org/books.

Contents

Introduction

by Ian Boucher

"He was at a loss how it should come to pass that the law, which was intended for every man's preservation, should be any man's ruin."

— *Gulliver's Travels*[1]

"They don't ask questions? They don't try to detain us? They just start shooting?"

"Welcome to the real world, Slim."

— *All-New X-Men* Vol. 1 #13[2]

We live in a time of super-heroes. They are all around us, which means the mainstream is buying beyond comics, throughout films, television, and clickbait. But the craze for super-heroics, whether through inspiration or coincidence, has also come at a time in which our own hypocrisy has been revealed more starkly (pun intended) than ever before. For as we simultaneously continue to live among atrocities, and as this book's contributors worked on their essays throughout 2015, people across the United States have grown increasingly vocal about a crucial part of the status quo festering since the 1980s. Consequently, as both super-heroes

---

[1] Jonathan Swift. *Gulliver's Travels* (London: HarperCollins Publishers, 2010). Page 242.

[2] Brian Michael Bendis (writer), Stuart Immonen (penciler), Wade Von Grawbadger (inker), Rain Beredo (colorist), Virtual Calligraphy (letterer), and Cory Petit (letterer). Eds. Axel Alonso, Nick Lowe, and Jordan D. White. Marvel Comics, Aug 2013. Page 7.

and these protests bring the fringes into the mainstream, not only we are being forced to confront ourselves in a fateful way, but, since super-heroes have exploded into the popular consciousness, their mythology provides a significant impetus for longtime fans and newcomers alike to ponder their cultural icons, giving us as members of Western society a legitimate chance to reconsider what we tell each other – for super-hero stories are not simply entertainment, but inherently communicate messages about justice. They are part of a larger cultural conversation.

The conversation about the ever elusive concept of justice has been going on for a long time, and the most well-known super-hero stories, especially in media outside comics, have been content with reacting to a peripheral status quo. The "Big Three" of DC Comics – Superman, Batman, and Wonder Woman – are culturally defined more by their personalities than their philosophies about justice. When justice does come into the picture for popular super-hero stories, the most common question presented is whether to kill or not, and further questions, such as the kinds of crimes occurring around the audience, by whom, why, and the process *after* the arrest, are not often pursued. For all their inspiration, most super-heroes in the popular consciousness are more often than not defined by antihero action archetypes, taking the path of Batman and the Punisher, focusing on capture or death.[3] How many other distinct super-hero philosophies can the casual fan legitimately name?

But we now live in a time where justice need no longer be merely taken for granted as a cultural norm, or a reinforcement – it might just *matter*. We have an opportunity to critically take a step back. As our stories entertain us, what else are they communicating? What assumptions do they support, and where do those assumptions come from? What do they do for us as a culture? What we tell each other through our stories reveals a great deal about the societies in which we live. Everything we say is relevant to what we do, especially regarding those figures that we consider so inspiring.

---

[3] The Scarecrow's ominous question – "Death or exile?" – in *The Dark Knight Rises* (2012) comes to mind.

Consider this: Wonder Woman first came to "Man's World" in 1941,[4] and yet the overwhelming majority of research reveals a horrifying maw between what we say and what we do, and it's shockingly as dystopian as *The Dark Knight Returns*.[5] Justice in the real world is a lot more complicated than Spider-Man would have us think (or is it vice versa?) when he drops criminals off at the police station. Wildeman and Western sum it up very well that crime is not solved with criminal justice policies alone, but rather "requires a greater social commitment to education, public health, and the employment opportunities of low-skilled men and women."[6]

But this is not how Western culture thinks about justice. There is a much different kind of structure operating around a significant portion of the world, very much influenced by the United States.[7] We live in a society where justice is largely synonymous with punishment alone.[8] And while the Punisher mows down mobsters – or the CW's Oliver Queen focuses on his own drama over that of "his city," for that matter – citizens in real life are convicted without being adequately represented, and plead guilty to crimes of which they are innocent.[9] Over just the last few decades, the United States has incarcerated an incredible number of its citizens,[10] and cultivated the highest incarcerated population in the world,[11] the vast majority of which is not composed of criminals like the Joker – far gone individuals from whom we need protecting – but instead low-level, non-violent drug offenders.[12] We are not simply dealing with millions of evil people who need to be locked up.

---

[4] See "Wonder Woman" in this introduction's bibliography.
[5] Originally published as *Batman: The Dark Knight* Vol. 1 #1-4.
[6] Wildeman and Western, page 157.
[7] Reynolds; Risse.
[8] Alexander; Arrigo, Bersot, and Sellers.
[9] Alexander.
[10] Geller et al.; Wildeman and Western.
[11] Campbell; Massoglia, Firebaugh, and Warner; Nichols and Loper; Vuong et al.
[12] Alexander; Bush-Baskette; Cox; Gaudio; Moore and Elkavich; Reynolds; Wildeman and Western.

The American criminal justice system has always had its share of problems, primarily in marginalizing those labeled as others,[13] especially racial minorities.[14] Madsen writes:

> It was not, however, the drug addiction of veterans, which was quietly accepted, but racist disdain that led to the first American antiopium law – the 1875 San Francisco municipal ordinance outlawing opium dens. It has been persuasively argued that these municipal provisions were part of an overall persecution of the Chinese population in northern California. The Chinese were welcomed during the Californian gold rush (1848 to 1855), when cooks and cleaners were needed. Once open-plot gold exploitation became less lucrative, and gold diggers – the so-called forty-niners – congregated in the cities, Chinese in the labor market were transformed from useful assistants to competitors, and subsequently diabolized.[15]

However, the modern explosion in incarceration is a direct result of the War on Drugs that began in the 1980s, synthesized by Republicans but ultimately a bipartisan effort.[16] The War on Drugs has used rhetoric to the extreme detriment of justice – disbursing federal funds to law enforcement prioritizing drug arrests over other crimes,[17] redirecting public funds from education and health care to prisons,[18] decreasing the discretion judges can apply in cases,[19] hurting progress in the juvenile system,[20] increasing attention on low-level offenders rather than the Kingpins of the world,[21] and exponentially adding to the difficulties of parole.[22] [23] The policies of the War

---

[13] Harcourt.

[14] Alexander; Campbell.

[15] Madsen, page 126.

[16] Alexander; Campbell.

[17] Alexander.

[18] Alexander; Massoglia, Firebaugh, and Warner; Reynolds.

[19] Alexander; Bush-Baskette; Gaudio; Reynolds.

[20] Arrigo, Bersot, and Sellers; Gaudio.

[21] Alexander; Bush-Baskette.

[22] Cox; Gaudio; Geller et al.; Massoglia, Firebaugh, and Warner; Moore and Elkavich; Rose and Rose; Schrader.

[23] Alexander writes: "About as many people were returned to prison for parole violations in 2000 as were admitted to prison in 1980 for all reasons. Of all parole violators returned to prison in 2000, only one-third were returned for a new conviction" (page 95).

on Drugs have extended far beyond the shores of the United States[24] and changed the way justice systems around the world work for the worse, actually exacerbating the problems they purport to solve.[25]

These policies have not been implemented as a result of research,[26] crime rates,[27] the effects of drugs on society,[28] or even initial public opinion,[29] but as part of a larger process of politicians capitalizing on irrational fears for support, especially among low-income white citizens.[30] As Moore and Elkavich write, "Because the US Census and other population surveys base residence on where one currently lives, as opposed to where one customarily lives, population counts in rural communities that house prisons are artificially bloated, whereas urban populations shrink proportionately," and this increases the political power of the rural areas where the prisons are.[31] Most offenders, from drug to even traffic violations, are racial minorities, and primarily African American,[32] despite a great amount of research showing that all races and classes have been found to use illegal drugs and commit traffic violations at about the same rates[33] – and actually, white people may be in the lead.[34] Laws are most enforced on people who aren't white. It would seem that we live in a world more overseen by Lex Luthor or Bolivar Trask than defended by Superman or the X-Men. Experts still have much to do in determining the most

---

[24] Reynolds; Risse.

[25] Alexander; Arrigo, Bersot, and Sellers; Bush-Baskette; Campbell; Gaudio; Madsen; Moore and Elkavich; Nichols and Loper; Reynolds; Wildeman and Western.

[26] Alexander; Arrigo, Bersot, and Sellers; Campbell.

[27] Alexander; Campbell; Cox; Harcourt; Massoglia, Reynolds; Sampson and Loeffler; Wildeman and Western.

[28] Alexander.

[29] Alexander; Campbell; Reynolds.

[30] Alexander; Campbell.

[31] Moore and Elkavich, page 784.

[32] This is not a debate in the literature. See Alexander; Campbell; Cox; Gaudio; Geller et al.; Harcourt; Massoglia, Firebaugh, and Warner; Moore and Elkavich; Sampson and Loeffler; Wildeman and Western.

[33] Alexander; Bush-Baskette.

[34] Alexander; Campbell; Gaudio; Moore and Elkavich.

accurate ways to measure and diagnose research results,[35] but even so, many strategies have been found in the meantime to be far more effective at stopping crime, decreasing recidivism, and relieving burdens on citizens' wallets, especially concerning offenders incarcerated for drug-related crimes.[36] We are not solving our problems with our current courses of action. And yet, so much energy is put into the current system, between politicians, law enforcement officials, business leaders, journalists – and storytellers of overt fiction.

This is the world we live in. Yet as much as the War on Drugs came from public relations teams,[37] it and its cultural origins have been reinforced by citizens of all walks of life and professions. How we see our world is a crucial part of how we manage it, from policies, to what we say, to what we don't say, to what we ignore, to how we are entertained. Perception affects so much.[38] Bush-Baskette even points out that the use of drugs "often leads to the psychological, social, and cultural experience of stigmatization, a negative influence that can exacerbate drug use."[39] And what is unsaid in legal proceedings is just as critical in analyzing the justice system as the rhetoric.[40]

To progress what we do, we must not only notice, but continually assess, and to do that includes looking at the assumptions around our words, what we tell each other, what media reinforces, and what it refuses to show. Super-hero comics are part of these perceptions. DeMarco argues the following about both ideals and fiction:

> Insofar as ideals may help to guide conduct and to develop institutions, clarifying moral ideals and moral exemplars is a helpful way to strengthen moral decision making... Folk heroes, religious figures, and literary creations are commonly used to promote moral behavior by presenting moral exemplars and moral heroes.[41]

---

[35] Arrigo, Bersot, and Sellers; Massoglia, Firebaugh, and Warner; Rose and Rose.
[36] Alexander; Arrigo, Bersot, and Sellers; Reynolds; Vuong et al.
[37] Campbell; Moore and Elkavich.
[38] Moore and Elkavich; Reynolds; Sampson and Loeffler.
[39] Bush-Baskette, page 921.
[40] Alexander; Arrigo, Bersot, and Sellers.
[41] DeMarco, pages 208, 213.

There have been hopeful developments in the American criminal justice system over the last few years,[42] and certainly in media. As with everything else, super-hero comics, the inspiration for the vast majority of super-hero media, have reflected on the times, sometimes in particularly encouraging ways in recent months, such as in *Action Comics* Vol. 2 #41-44,[43] *Batman* Vol. 2 #44,[44] and *Captain America: Sam Wilson* Vol. 1 #1.[45] Nevertheless, we are only at the beginning of the possibilities for something greater; there is still a lot more on our plates than purse snatchers or even Sentinels. It remains a tremendous struggle,[46] and it's most likely going to be up to us to change it.[47] But with the rise of super-hero media in recent years, as much as they are Uatu the Watcher, super-hero fans can also be more powerful than Dr. Manhattan.

This book of essays supports that further exploration and cultivation. At first glance, it may seem like nothing new. After all, much greater works, from *Gulliver's Travels* to *Watchmen*,[48] have used literature to bring to light numerous inconsistencies in Western culture's approaches to criminal justice. Certainly, essays and books have been written comparing the justice of super-hero comics with real life. But in spite of all those efforts, what has been done already is not good enough. Societies still do what they do. Even in spite of the current dialogue around these problems, the cultural framing by the mainstream goes on, and these questions are certainly not mainstream with super-heroes. We must always add to the discourse. Each essay in this book represents an individual with unique origins and experiences posing his or her own insightful questions about super-heroes and justice to others. These questions are important. Our stories are important. Carrying groups of them with us is important. Within each of

---

[42] Alexander.

[43] Whose conflict is centered on a racially diverse neighborhood and local police.

[44] In which Batman must reconsider the effectiveness of his methods in light of the shooting of a black teenager by a white police officer.

[45] In which Sam Wilson wrestles with who he is allowed to help in the midst of the current divisions and injustices within the United States.

[46] Alexander; Campbell; Reynolds.

[47] Alexander; Schrader.

[48] Originally published as *Watchmen* #1-12.

them is the possibility of realizing something new.

Although only a snapshot in the grand scheme of things – a pebble in a river, as *X-Men: Days of Future Past*'s (2014) Hank McCoy might put it – this book of essays is nevertheless a frank analysis from a variety of perspectives, topics, and comic book characters, and represents more than anything else a call to cultivation, to keep this momentum alive and conscious. It is just one reminder by fans, for fans and everyone else, to keep talking about what makes our heroes heroic, in whatever capacity the discourse ultimately needs to be; not for the promotion of super-hero comics, nor for belittlement, but because super-hero comics do so much, and it is their most fundamental element. This an opportunity to literally carry a reminder with us, to take the time to step back and think about what we tell each other for the society our heroes ostensibly defend, to start giving this conversation a permanent place among the rest of the timeless comic book questions with all of their magnificent possibilities – and even if your reminder is ultimately not contained within this book, then perhaps its essays can help lead you there. It's not enough to point out isolated flaws, or to wait for others to address them. Justice is a growing, developing, interconnected, dynamic concept that needs to retain a conscious, central awareness in our conversations that bridge the perennial ether between us and our paragons of justice.

The first two chapters of the book take a look back at the dawn of our collective justice, providing some interpretation and context about the development of super-heroes and super-villains in the mainstream consciousness. Chapter 1, "Four Color Morality," analyzes the development of super-hero comic books in conjunction with American political discourse, arguing that despite the simplistic reputation of super-hero comics, the morality of super-hero comics has in fact grown far more complex than mainstream political discourse, with significant implications for super-hero film adaptations. Chapter 2, "Keeping the Wolves at Bay," attempts to answer the famous question, "Who watches the watchmen?" with an examination into the origins of societies around the world, and determines that super-heroes, like society and the heroes passed down before them, arose from a human need to feel safe from the inexorable instability of the world, and to hope for something better.

Super-heroes, in turn, have brought forth an understanding best articulated in Judge Dredd's famous catchphrase, "I am the law." Chapter 3, "Turtles on Trial," strives to get to the bottom of the law motivating the Teenage Mutant Ninja Turtles and brings to light a mosaic of perceptions about justice around the heroes in a half shell. Chapter 4, "Those Blessed and Those Not Blessed," takes on the iconic confrontation of Batman and Superman in one of the most powerful super-hero stories of all time, *The Dark Knight Returns*, in an effort to define exactly what kind of law writer Frank Miller was advocating. Chapter 5, "Defenders of the Status Quo" grapples with the potential of super-hero stories to genuinely address social issues, from panel to screen.

Stories inform reality. If assumptions go unchecked, structures – taking a cue from Commissioner Gordon in *The Dark Knight Rises* – become shackles, and in this case, the shackles are as literal as they are metaphorical. The next three chapters bring a handful of these shackles into plain sight to further address the logic of their assumptions. Chapter 6, "Super-Heroes: Threat or Menace?" argues that super-heroes as we know them would never be able to exist in real life, even if people in real life had the resources or super-powers. Chapter 7, "Four Things You Always Wanted to Know about the Joker (but were too Afraid to Ask)," uses concepts from psychology to investigate the underpinnings of one of society's most revered super-villains, the Joker. Chapter 8, "Is the Truth Good Enough?" deconstructs the noble lie as it pertains to super-heroes as figures of justice, and explores its innovative role in the Dark Knight Trilogy.

When our assumptions are out in the open, paying homage to Charles Xavier in our own new and uncertain world, what possibilities exist for the future? Chapter 9, "Must There Be Superman Movies?" considers what tomorrow holds for inspiration as a narrative element in super-hero film adaptations. Chapter 10, "Shadows Prove the Sunshine," embarks on a journey from the personal to the historical to argue for the value of "dark" super-hero stories in inspiring people to face the adversity of the world. Chapter 11, "Honing Our Senses," argues that the most prominent discourse about justice in super-hero comics actually shrouds the tremendous complexity and diversity of justice present in super-hero comics, and that, especially in today's super-hero saturated culture, it is up to creators and fans to remember and cultivate that complexity and diversity.

A critical part of the discussion about super-hero justice is that of the perspectives and experiences of comic book creators. In the spring of 2015, Ian Boucher was fortunate to have the opportunity to interview two storytelling masters – Mark Waid, one of the most prolific comic book writers of all time, particularly acclaimed for his work on *Kingdom Come*, *The Flash*, and *Daredevil*; and Gerard Jones, writer of *Green Lantern: Mosaic*, *Martian Manhunter: American Secrets*, and such expert nonfiction as *Killing Monsters: Why Children Need Fantasy, Super Heroes, and Make-Believe Violence* and *Men of Tomorrow: Geeks, Gangsters, and the Birth of the Comic Book*. Waid and Jones have both enriched super-heroes in profound ways, using their fundamental understandings to continually find fascinating connections between humans and paragons, and their reflections in this book are invaluable to the endeavor of understanding where justice fits within our stories of super-heroes – and vice versa.

Where we all go next is up to us. Hopefully this book helps bring you to some pivotal moments in your life, and, as comics culture does so wonderfully, the lives of others.

Five Quick Notes on the Anthology:

- Spelling and grammar may vary depending on each essay. Our contributors very much represent an international gathering, and for the most part, each essay reflects the origins of its author.
- The citation style is based on the 16th edition of *The Chicago Manual of Style*, but we've adjusted it to maximize purpose, clarity, and consistency, from traditional reference sources to comic books.
- The majority of the comic book citations were verified using *The Comic Book Database*.[49]
- The dates of specific comic book issues are cover dates, not dates of publication.

---

[49] Check it out, it's awesome: http://www.comicbookdb.com/.

- Shortly after this book was first published, it was reported that Gerard Jones was arrested on suspicion of possessing and distributing child pornography. Much thought was put into whether Jones's 2015 interview and references to his previous work on super-heroes and related topics should remain in this book. Since this anthology explores issues of justice, and as proponents of the human right that a person should be presumed innocent until proven guilty, it was decided to leave Jones's interview and the references to his work as they were when this anthology was first published. This is not an endorsement of Mr. Jones, who also did not receive payment for his interview. Rather, regardless of the outcome of his case, it is meant to serve as a reflection about his work's place in culture's understandings of super-heroes and justice accordingly. Mr. Jones's case in no way whatsoever diminishes the inspiring work of this anthology as a whole.

Acknowledgements

There are many people I need to thank for their parts in this book's journey.

I thank Sequart Organization for its support, not only of this project, but of super-hero media as a whole. In a world of clickbait, we are very lucky to have them fighting the good fight for popular culture every day. They are truly an oasis in discourse, from fandom to academia. I thank them for this opportunity, for believing in this project, for standing by it every step of the way, for their guidance, and for everything they do.

I thank the contributors of this book, for their passion, collaboration, and resolution. As for this introduction's reflection about pivotal moments in life, this book's contributors certainly continue to do so for me. It has been an honor and a joy to work with them, and I would do so again in a heartbeat.

I thank my brothers Evan and Alex, for their constant strength, support, and guidance with which they always fill my life, and my wife Valentyna, for her feedback, for listening to my endless musings on super-heroes, and for truly always being there.

I thank my friend Jacoba Rock, for putting me on the path to caring about and understanding the American criminal justice system, beginning with our discussions of *Spider-Man 3* (2007) and restorative justice way back in 2008.

I thank my friend Sabina Paudel, for her expertise in football, which proved invaluable in researching one particularly relevant example of tifo.

I will be forever grateful to Gerard Jones and Mark Waid, two of the very writers whose work inspired me, for participating in this book. The insights of those who have worked in the comics industry are essential in this discussion, and their generosity in their time and attention to this book, despite their schedules, will always mean the world to me.

Most of all, I thank my friend Ryan Krumm, without whose encouragement to write about comics in the first place would I ever have thought that I would have something to contribute to the pool of ideas. I also thank him for his support beyond that, whether for this book or otherwise. The pool is ever-changing, and we all have something to say.

And finally, even more than most, I thank Wonder Woman, and Gail Simone, for the pivotal gateway that was *The Circle*.[50]

Bibliography

Action Comics Vol. 2 #41-44. Aaron Kuder (writer/penciler/inker), Greg Pak (writer), Howard Porter (penciler/inker), Hi-Fi Colour Design (colorist), Blond (colorist), Tomeu Morey (colorist), and Steve Wands (letterer). Eds. Eddie Berganza and Andrew Marino. DC Comics, Aug-Nov 2015.

Alexander, Michelle. *The New Jim Crow: Mass Incarceration in the Age of Colorblindness* (New York: The New Press, 2012). Kindle edition.

All-New X-Men Vol. 1 #13. Brian Michael Bendis (writer), Stuart Immonen (penciler), Wade Von Grawbadger (inker), Rain Beredo (colorist), Virtual Calligraphy (letterer), and Cory Petit (letterer). Eds. Axel Alonso, Nick Lowe, and Jordan D. White. Marvel Comics, Aug 2013.

Arrigo, Bruce A., Heather Y. Bersot, and Brian G. Sellers. *The Ethics of Total Confinement: A Critique of Madness, Citizenship, and Social Justice* (Oxford: Oxford University Press, 2011). PDF e-book.

Batman Vol. 2 #44. Brian Azzarello (writer), Scott Snyder (writer), Mark Simpson (penciler/inker), Lee Loughridge (colorist), and Deron Bennett (letterer). Eds. Mark Doyle, Rebecca Taylor, and Dave Wielgosz. DC Comics, Nov 2015.

Batman: The Dark Knight Vol. 1 #1-4. Frank Miller (writer/penciler/inker), Klaus Janson (inker), Lynn Varley (colorist), and John Costanza (letterer). Eds. Dick Giordano and Denny O'Neil. DC Comics, Mar-June 1986.

Bush-Baskette, Stephanie. "The War on Drugs and the Incarceration of Mothers." *Journal of Drug Issues* Vol. 30, No. 4 (Fall 2000). Pages 919-928. http://connection.ebscohost.com/c/articles/4000940/war-drugs-incarceration-mothers.

---

[50] See the trade paperback collecting *Wonder Woman* Vol. 3 #14-19.

Campbell, Michael C. "Politics, Prisons, and Law Enforcement: An Examination of the Emergence of 'Law and Order' Politics in Texas." *Law & Society Review* Vol. 45, No. 3 (Sept 2011). Pages 631-665. http://onlinelibrary.wiley.com/doi/10.1111/j.1540-5893.2011.00446.x/abstract.

Captain America: Sam Wilson Vol. 1 #1. Nick Spencer (writer), Daniel Acuña (penciler/inker/colorist), Virtual Calligraphy (letterer), and Joe Caramagna (letterer). Eds. Axel Alonso, Tom Brevoort, Katie Kubert, and Alanna Smith. Marvel Comics, Dec 2015.

Cox, Robynn J. A. "The Impact of Mass Incarceration on the Lives of African American Women." *The Review of Black Political Economy* Vol. 39, No. 2 (June 2012). Pages 203-212. http://link.springer.com/article/10.1007/s12114-011-9114-2.

DeMarco, Joseph P. *Moral Theory: A Contemporary Overview* (Boston: Jones and Bartlett Publishers, Inc., 1996).

Gaudio, Christina M. "A Call to Congress to Give Back the Future: End the 'War on Drugs' and Encourage States to Reconstruct the Juvenile Justice System." *Family Court Review* Vol. 48, No. 1 (Jan 2010). Pages 212-227. http://onlinelibrary.wiley.com/doi/10.1111/j.1744-1617.2009.01302.x/abstract.

Geller, Amanda, Carey E. Cooper, Irwin Garfinkel, Ofira Schwartz-Soicher, and Ronald B. Mincy. "Beyond Absenteeism: Father Incarceration and Child Development." *Demography* Vol. 49, No. 1 (Feb 2012). Pages 49-76. http://link.springer.com/article/10.1007/s13524-011-0081-9.

Harcourt, Bernard E. "From the Asylum to the Prison: Rethinking the Incarceration Revolution." *Texas Law Review* Vol. 84, No. 7 (June 2006). Pages 1751-1786. http://www.law.uchicago.edu/files/file/harcourt_institutionalization_final.pdf

Madsen, Frank G. "International Narcotics Law Enforcement: A Study in Irrationality." *Journal of International Affairs* Vol. 66, No. 1 (Fall/Winter 2012). Pages 123-141. http://jia.sipa.columbia.edu/international-narcotics-law-enforcement-study-irrationality/.

Massoglia, Michael, Glenn Firebaugh, and Cody Warner. "Racial Variation in the Effect of Incarceration on Neighborhood Attainment." *American Sociological Review* Vol. 78, No. 1 (Feb 2013). Pages 142-165. http://asr.sagepub.com/content/78/1/142.abstract.

Moore, Lisa D. and Amy Elkavich. "Who's Using and Who's Doing Time: Incarceration, the War on Drugs, and Public Health." *American Journal of Public Health* Vol. 98, No. 5 (May 2008). Pages 782-786. http://ajph.aphapublications.org/doi/abs/10.2105/AJPH.98.Supplement_1.S176.

Nichols, Emily Bever and Ann Booker Loper. "Incarceration in the Household: Academic Outcomes of Adolescents with an Incarcerated Household Member." *Journal of Youth and Adolescence* Vol. 41, No. 11 (Nov 2012). Pages 1455-1471. http://link.springer.com/article/10.1007%2Fs10964-012-9780-9.

Reynolds, Marylee. "The War on Drugs, Prison Building, and Globalization: Catalysts for the Global Incarceration of Women." *NWSA Journal* Vol. 20, No. 2 (Summer 2008). Pages 72-95. http://muse.jhu.edu/journals/ff/summary/v020/20.2.reynolds.html.

Risse, Mathias. *On Global Justice* (Princeton, NJ: Princeton University Press, 2012). PDF e-book.

Rose, Kristin and Chris Rose. "Enrolling in College While in Prison: Factors That Promote Male and Female Prisoners to Participate." *Journal of Correctional Education* Vol. 65, No. 2 (May 2014). Pages 20-39. http://connection.ebscohost.com/c/articles/99273293/enrolling-college-while-prison-factors-that-promote-male-female-prisoners-participate.

Sampson, Robert J. and Charles Loeffler. "Punishment's Place: The Local Concentration of Mass Incarceration." *Daedalus* Vol. 139, No. 3 (Summer 2010). Pages 20-31. http://www.mitpressjournals.org/doi/pdf/10.1162/DAED_a_00020.

Schrader, John Benjamin. "Reawakening 'Privileges or Immunities:' An Originalist Blueprint for Invalidating State Felon Disenfranchisement Laws." *Vanderbilt Law Review* Vol. 62, No. 4 (May 2009). Pages 1285-1314. http://www.vanderbiltlawreview.org/articles/2009/05/Schrader-Reawakening-_Privileges-or-Immunities_62-Vand.-L.-Rev.-1285-2009.pdf.

Swift, Jonathan. *Gulliver's Travels* (London: HarperCollins Publishers, 2010).

Vuong, Linh, Christopher Hartney, Barry Krisberg, and Susan Marchionna. "The Extravangance of Imprisonment Revisited." *Judicature* Vol. 94, No. 2 (Sept-Oct 2010). Pages 70-80. http://scholarship.law.berkeley.edu/cgi/viewcontent.cgi?article=2720&context=facpubs.

Watchmen #1-12. Alan Moore (writer), Dave Gibbons (penciler/inker/letterer), and John Higgins (colorist). Ed. Len Wein. DC Comics, Sept 1986-Oct 1987.

Wildeman, Christopher and Bruce Western. "Incarceration in Fragile Families." *The Future of Children* Vol. 20, No. 2 (Fall 2010). Pages 157-177. http://www.princeton.edu/futureofchildren/publications/docs/20_02_08.pdf.

"Wonder Woman." *DC Comics.* Accessed 1 June 2015. http://www.dccomics.com/characters/wonder-woman.

Wonder Woman Vol. 3 #14-19. Gail Simone (writer), Terry Dodson (penciler), Ron Randall (penciler/inker), Bernard Chang (penciler/inker), Rachel Dodson (inker), Jon Holdredge (inker), Lee Loughridge (colorist), Alex Sinclair (colorist), Pete Pantazis (colorist), I.L.L. (colorist), Travis Lanham (letterer), John J. Hill (letterer), and Rob Leigh (letterer). Eds. Nachie Castro and Matt Idelson. DC Comics, Jan-June 2008.

Four-Color Morality

by Paul Jaissle

The term "comic book morality" is usually used in a pejorative sense to denote a simplistic dichotomy of "good guys" versus "bad guys," derived from the simplistic tales of early super-hero comics that usually pitted heroes against evil masterminds or mad scientists bent on world domination. In these stories, the moral battle lines were clearly defined: the good guys were always right and justified in their fight against the bad guys. The "black and white" moral terms of these stories have characterized them as being overly idealistic because they ignored the complexities of everyday life, giving super-hero stories – and by extension, comic books in general – the stigma of being childish and inconsequential. This stigma has lasted for decades, as the genre conventions of super-hero stories have been parodied and "comic book morality" has been employed as a shorthand for a naïve or idealistic moral view. However, many super-hero stories have, especially in recent decades, developed a far more complex and nuanced moral view over time than popular opinion might still suggest, embracing the genre's conventions and narrative structure to explore political issues, and capturing as much of a variety of shades as the four-color printing technique that has created the stories' visual appeal.[1]

At the same time, American public discourse about political issues has increasingly been explicitly framed in the "good-guys-versus-bad-guys," "black-and-white" terms of the early days of super-hero comics, which suggests that while comics have outgrown the dichotomy of heroes and villains, most popular political discourse has embraced the simplicity of that distinction, ignoring the complexities at the heart of international conflicts. Of course, popular political debate has usually relied on simplistic language for the sake of expediency. However, since the end of the Cold War, and most notably since the turn of the 21st century, politicians have more frequently and explicitly used the language of "good-guys-and-bad-guys" to frame global politics. The popular reputation of super-hero comic books seems hypocritical when considered in this way: despite the origins of the term, "comic book morality" has little to do with contemporary super-hero comics. With super-hero stories becoming more popular in a variety of media, it is worth asking if the film and television adaptations of these characters will be able to explore such complex issues, change the public understanding of the genre, and illustrate the simplicity of current political discourse.

The disparity between contemporary super-hero stories and modern political language is more obvious when viewed alongside the history of the super-hero genre's relationship with popular culture. While the popularity of the super-hero genre and the comic book medium has grown and ebbed in reaction to changes in the cultural and political climate from the beginning – as has the popular view of so-called "comic book morality" – super-hero comic books have remained bound to the cultural zeitgeist, and as the genre evolved, so did its relationship with politics and social issues. Looking at the intertwined histories of politics and popular culture, it's clear that the moral conventions and tropes of super-hero stories have at times reflected the opinions of society at large. It's also clear that, despite being

---

[1] The four-color (or CMYK) printing process uses cyan, magenta, yellow, and black ink to create full-color images.

derided at times, the simplistic black-and-white morality associated with super-heroes and comic books has in fact not been uncommon throughout the history of American politics and culture. Indeed, the simplistic morality of "good-guys-and-bad-guys" mirrored the political climate of World War II and the Cold War. Since the late 1960s, however, comic books have engaged with complex, morally ambiguous issues more regularly, and in recent years, comic book creators have used the tropes of the super-hero genre to explore contemporary political issues from various points of view, even while the mainstream political debate on the same issues has grown more simplistic, with American political discourse increasingly couched in "us versus them" terms, from the Cold War to the "War on Terror."

Although the familiar "good-guys-and-bad-guys" trope may seem to be an intrinsic part of super-hero comics, it developed due to the unique conditions shaping comic books as an industry, and like the super-hero genre itself, the familiar conventions of heroes and villains emerged early in the history of the medium. Initially, super-hero comic book writers and artists borrowed heavily from the pulp stories that influenced them. For example, Superman emerged from the fusion of science fiction and Doc Savage ("The Man of Bronze") books, while Batman was basically the Shadow in a different costume. The focus of these early comics was usually the scourge of crime: Superman, for instance, largely used his powers to battle corrupt politicians and criminal syndicates, and quickly, the archetype of the "criminal mastermind" – another trope borrowed from pulp fiction – emerged as the main foil for costumed heroes. Ultra-Humanite, the first true super-villain, appeared in *Action Comics* Vol. 1 #13 and set the template for this new breed of criminal foe.[2] Even though Batman is usually thought of as a street-level character focused on petty criminals and mobsters, his earliest stories featured the mad scientist Hugo Strange. The introduction of Batman's most well-known nemesis, the Joker – in the same issue as one of Strange's appearances, incidentally – quickly established the

---

[2] Yes, pun intended. See Weldon.

concept of the super-villain as a main fixture of super-hero stories,[3] as well as the dichotomy of heroes and villains. Characters were defined by their opposites: each super-hero developed his or her own "rogues gallery" of colorful villains with whom he or she tangled regularly. The main reason for this was due to the high demand for new stories, titles, and characters for the rapidly growing audience. This need to churn out content meant that simplistic gangsters and bank robbers were no longer suitable foils for the heroes, and science fiction-influenced characters and stories became a part of the emerging super-hero genre that constituted the Golden Age of comic books.[4]

With the outbreak of World War II, super-heroes became a metaphor for American pride and power. The black-and-white, good-versus-evil framework of the genre clearly fit the popular understanding of the war, and like all other pop culture figures at the time, super-heroes were "enlisted" to bolster the morale of both those fighting and those on the home front. The most explicit example is clearly Captain America, created by Joe Simon and Jack Kirby in 1941. Decked out in a stylized American flag, Steve Rogers was the living embodiment of the American dream: a poor kid with unwavering determination who – thanks to the miracle of science – gains super-strength that he uses to fight for democracy, freedom, and justice. And as the cover of the first issue of *Captain America Comics* – featuring Cap landing a mighty right hook on the grimacing face of Adolf Hitler himself[5] – made it clear, the lead character and his namesake country had a real-life super-villain to fight. Nazis made an ideal foe for the ever-expanding roster of costumed heroes quickly populating the newsstands, as the implied moral distinction between the Allied and Axis countries fit the structure of the genre. Given the seemingly clear-cut nature of World War II, the parallels between super-hero comics and international politics were obvious: in the eyes of those on the home front, the Allied troops were as

---

[3] "Professor" Hugo Strange first appeared in *Detective Comics* Vol. 1 #36. He returned – this time with his Monster Men – in *Batman* Vol. 1 #1. This is the same issue in which the Joker made his first appearance.
[4] Weldon.
[5] *Captain America Comics* Vol. 1 #1.

much good guys as the costumed heroes in the comics, and as super-heroes went to war, the real-world events of the war seemed to both mirror the conventions of the super-hero genre and influence it. A stereotypical villain like the Red Skull was made more fearsome by being a Nazi, and grotesque caricatures of Japanese soldiers were regularly featured. Superman himself addressed the war by encouraging readers to buy war bonds in ads and on comic book covers, and in the pages of *Look* magazine, his creators Jerry Siegel and Joe Shuster explained how the Man of Steel would handle Hitler.[6] The collision of real-world events and super-hero stories created an even greater demand for new stories, and the emerging genre reached a whole new level of popularity and ubiquity: super-heroes became an indelible – and uniquely American – part of popular culture across demographics.[7]

However, in the aftermath of the war, the super-hero genre faded from public favor, as though the battles between brightly costumed characters seemed trivial; the colorful and exaggerated tales of good versus evil no longer appealed to a population weary from years of fighting.[8] Besides that, no super-villain plot seemed as threatening or as evil as the real-life horrors of the Holocaust. As the country tried to move on from the war, new genres like horror, romance, and crime took over the comic book industry.[9] The popularity of these new comics grew quickly, albeit briefly – for a public outcry over their seemingly subversive and violent content nearly destroyed the medium. But super-heroes – or, more correctly, the copyrights owned by the publishers – returned to save the day, ushering in the Silver Age of comic books.[10]

When super-heroes returned to comics in the mid-1950s, the familiar dynamics of the genre returned as well, and the new or reintroduced

---

[6] Which offered an admirable – if possibly naïve – pacifist solution that avoided direct American involvement in the conflict. See "How Superman Would End the War" by Siegel and Shuster, which appeared in the 17 Feb 1940 issue of *Look*, over a year before Captain America first appeared. See Weldon.

[7] Morrison.

[8] Ibid.

[9] Ibid.

[10] Ibid.

characters like the Flash and the Green Lantern had their own stables of criminal masterminds and villains with whom to tussle. With the horrors of World War II behind them, these new heroes looked toward a bright future, one driven by a unique brand of American optimism. Although the Cold War between the United States and the Soviet Union was slowly growing more tense, the political discourse of the time was in part driven by the space race between the two countries.[11] As such, the new breed of super-heroes took on a more science fiction feel: their powers were usually science-based (albeit an admittedly fuzzy pseudoscience at times), and they often had to face extraterrestrial threats. Despite this new take on the genre, the dichotomy between good guys and bad guys remained the default for super-hero comics. One-dimensional devious criminal masterminds and would-be alien invaders were routinely defeated by good old American ingenuity and know-how, and super-heroes once again became the most common comic book genre. However, since the genre and the comic book medium itself were less popular than during World War II, these stories began to be principally seen as "kids' stuff" – the simplistic nature of super-heroes and villains no longer applied to the serious threats of the real world.

But this particular simplistic dichotomy of optimistic heroes and one-dimensional villains was also the result of intense pressure to conform to the political climate of the time, defined by the increasingly tense atmosphere of the Cold War. The seemingly ominous threat of communism became the focus of American politics and culture, as the race for technological superiority – both in space and in nuclear weapons – consumed both the United States and the Soviet Union, defining them in the same black-and-white terms as the heroes and villains in comic books. Framing the relationship between the two countries in such stark political, and, at times, moral, language – such as the U.S.S.R. being atheistic and the United States "one nation under God" – made it easier to comprehend international relations, but it also created an atmosphere of unease, tension, and fear. Across all pop culture, Russian or Eastern European accents became a shorthand for nefarious intent, and the villains who

---

[11] Ibid.

schemed for world domination usually did so in the name of "Mother Russia." While comics and movies used this political tension to create entertainment, the "Second Red Scare" had dramatic – and destructive – real-life consequences, most prominently in the modern-day witch trials of Senator Joseph McCarthy, who used the fear of communist conspiracy for publicity and political blackmail. Overall, the Cold War ended up framing and defining politics and culture in a sort of existential conflict: democracy and communism became synonymous with good and evil. While the threat of atomic war between the United States and the Soviet Union loomed in politics, the tension between the two permeated popular culture, and the complexities of diplomacy were reduced to the basic narrative of "us versus them."

This climate led to the establishment of the Comics Code Authority in 1954, which regulated the content of comic books in order to mollify parents concerned about the – largely imaginary – negative influence of the medium.[12] While the Comics Code mainly focused on violent or lurid images, it also regulated how authority figures were portrayed. According to the rules of the Comics Code, "Policemen, judges, government officials, and respected institutions shall never be presented in such a way as to create disrespect for established authority," and "In every instance good shall triumph over evil and the criminal punished for his misdeeds."[13] The result was sanitized comics that avoided any sort of complex or nuanced take on ethics or morality: the good guys were unquestionably right and the bad guys could not be sympathetic. These regulations firmly established comics and super-heroes as disposable entertainment suitable only for children. The simplistic distinction between good and bad became synonymous with the super-hero genre that now dominated the comic book industry. By mandating simple, morally unambiguous stories, the Code reinforced the

---

[12] The history of this false connection between comic books and juvenile delinquency, and the public outcry and trials that followed, are expertly chronicled in David Hajdu's book *The Ten-Cent Plague: The Great Comic-Book Scare and How It Changed America*. Also see Tilley.

[13] "The Comics Code Authority (as Adopted in 1954)."

notion that "comic book morality" was unrealistic, childish, and hopelessly naïve.

The simplistic moral framework of comics continued into the 1960s, even as the genre experienced a sort of renaissance. A new breed of comic books, largely from the emerging Marvel Comics titles like *Fantastic Four*, *Spider-Man*, and *X-Men*, introduced a more nuanced take on the super-hero genre. Of course, the Cold War still loomed large and influenced these new characters. For example, Iron Man was an avowed capitalist and weapons manufacturer, and the Fantastic Four battled the Red Ghost, a Soviet scientist bent on establishing a communist empire on the Moon. But even while working within these genre and political conventions, writer Stan Lee along with artists Steve Ditko and Jack Kirby popularized super-heroes with motivations and relationships more complex than usually seen in earlier comics. The X-Men, for example, were mutants hated and feared by the public they protected simply because they were "different." The comic's parallels with the American Civil Rights Movement was subtle during Stan Lee and Jack Kirby's run on the title, but the X-Men still represented this new type of super-hero: the Shakespearean "tragic" hero whose personal struggles were as important as fighting super-villains. More radical however were the new villains that Lee, Kirby, and Ditko introduced, such as the X-Men's nemesis Magneto. Unlike previous super-villains who were driven by greed or megalomania, Magneto believed that his tormenting of humans was justified by their anti-mutant sentiment. The parallels to the American Civil Rights Movement, which again were subtle in the early years of the book, became a central part of the X-Men's appeal, even if Lee made it clear that the Martin Luther King, Jr. pacifism of Professor X was preferable to the "by any means necessary" sentiments of Malcolm X and Magneto.[14] The notion that a super-villain could believe he or she was doing the right thing was a new wrinkle in the genre that made for more compelling stories and characters as Marvel became synonymous with the growing counterculture movement on college campuses across the country,[15] resonating with an

---

[14] Howe, page 48.
[15] Howe.

The revelation in *Uncanny X-Men* Vol. 1 #150 (Oct 1981) that Magneto was a survivor of the Holocaust added depth to a character of already complex motivations. Note the strength of Magneto's conviction even before the fateful details begin to be revealed. Art by Dave Cockrum (penciler), Joe Rubinstein (inker), and Bob Wiacek (inker). © Marvel Comics.

audience that increasingly included young adults and college students who desired complex stories that offered more than the typical "good-guys-and-bad-guys" dynamic.

Despite the parallels between comics and contemporary social issues, by and large these comic books stuck to the familiar moral dichotomy; the characters may have been more nuanced, but the episodic nature of the medium lent itself to formulaic stories that had predictable plots and outcomes. Nevertheless, this new approach to super-heroes influenced the next generation of comics creators, who took these ideas and ran with them, creating whole new ways of understanding the relationships between good and evil, heroes and villains. For example, writer Chris Claremont began to reinvent the X-Men in the late 1970s with a more soap opera style approach that favored longer stories and more complex, emotional relationships between the characters.[16] Magneto became a more fully rounded and nuanced villain as Claremont introduced the idea that the character had been imprisoned in a Nazi concentration camp.[17] This detail gave the readers a greater insight into Magneto and his motivations. He may not have been an entirely sympathetic character due to his actions, but he became more than a stereotypical bad guy. The familiar tropes of super-hero comics had become even less black and white and developed new shades and nuance. The stories became more about the characters themselves as opposed to their battles with one another. Readers could understand what drove super-villains while still condemning their actions. Heroes, for their part, were forced to reconcile their commitment to the public with their personal lives, and upholding the law while working outside of its limits. However, even as creators and fans grew to explore these new types of comic book characters within the limitations of the Comics Code, the public perception of the genre was still defined by the clichés of super-hero adaptations in other media, most prominently through the 1966 *Batman* television show. Despite all of their changes, to the

---

[16] Morrison, page 175.
[17] See Morton.

American mainstream, comic books and costumed heroes were still just "kids' stuff."

Yet the ability of super-hero comics to explore moral issues has actually been one of the genre's strengths. In his book *Reading Comics: How Graphic Novels Work and What They Mean*, Douglas Wolk points out that the ongoing narrative structure of the comic book medium allows for nuanced stories and characters, claiming that the super-hero genre is "actually the opposite of the black-and-white good-guys-and-bad-guys pattern for which 'comic book morality' is still shorthand: it's an ideal framework for discussing the complexities of morality and ethics."[18] As the super-hero genre evolved, the long histories of the characters became a way for creators to explore what motivated and defined them. While stories from the Golden and Silver Ages of comics may have fallen into the general framework of good guys versus bad guys, contemporary writers have been able to add shades of grey by playing with the conventions of the genre.

The most obvious example is *Watchmen*[19] by Alan Moore and Dave Gibbons, which caused a seismic shift in what is possible – and expected – in super-hero stories. The theme of moral ambiguity raised by the story's conclusion, in which Ozymandias justifies mass murder in the name of establishing world peace, upended the typical hero and villain dichotomy of the super-hero genre. Obviously, there had been comics with morally complex characters and situations before *Watchmen*, but partially since comic books had existed outside of the prevailing popular culture for so long, *Watchmen* became a crossover success: the complexity of the narrative and the moral ambiguity of the ending came as a surprise to people who still thought of super-heroes as "kids' stuff." Notably, *Watchmen* was published without approval from the Comics Code Authority, something that had become economically viable due to the expanding direct comics market and the number of specialty comic shops.[20] While smaller publishers, along with DC's Vertigo imprint, brought more

---

[18] Wolk, page 99.
[19] Originally published as *Watchmen* #1-12.
[20] Nyberg.

"mature" comics to market without the Code, Marvel and DC continued to submit their books for approval until the early 2000s, when the Comics Code Authority – which had long outlived its necessity – had by then become effectively defunct.[21] *Watchmen*'s influence also resulted in a greater emphasis on these sorts of ethical themes in super-hero comics in general. The more nuanced motives and morals of super-heroes and super-villains have today become the central focus of the genre, which suggests that the creators and audience both desire these types of stories. By the 1980s, the stark "us-versus-them" view of the Cold War had morphed into a permanent, uneasy paranoia, reflected in such films as *War Games* (1983), *Red Dawn* (1984), and *Rambo: First Blood Part II* (1985), and moral ambiguity has since more or less become an expectation for contemporary super-hero stories.

Since the end of the Cold War, however, the language used to explain real-life political issues has continued to become more simplistic, especially in recent years. The current War on Terror is regularly framed and justified as a battle between "right" and "wrong," "good" and "evil." As Wolk points out, the "good-guys-and-bad-guys" dichotomy is "now the condescending, cynical political spin on international relations that the American government pumps out on a regular basis."[22] During the Cold War, President Reagan called the Soviet Union an "evil empire,"[23] reinforcing the notion that communism represented an existential threat to the United States, even as the U.S.S.R. was slowly going bankrupt. In 2012, the executive vice president of the National Rifle Association claimed, "The only thing that stops a bad guy with a gun is a good guy with a gun."[24] By employing the familiar language of "good-guys-and-bad-guys," the issues of gun control and self-defense are reduced to a binary, black-and-white choice, and the complexities and possibilities of debate are ignored. This narrowing of public discourse is obviously not new, but it has been an

---

[21] Rogers.

[22] Wolk, page 99.

[23] See President Reagan's "Remarks at the Annual Convention of the National Association of Evangelicals in Orlando, Florida."

[24] "Only 'A Good Guy With A Gun' Can Stop School Shootings, NRA Says."

increasingly common theme of the political conversation of the 21st century so far, as politicians make explicit reference to "good-guys-and-bad-guys." Following the terrorist attacks of September 11th, 2001, the Bush administration regularly employed terms like Axis of Evil, or phrases like "You are either with us or against us" when outlining its response to international terrorism.[25]

Certainly, the methods and goals of terrorists and despots are objectively wrong since they target innocent civilians. However, using a catchall phrase like "evil" to describe sovereign countries and autonomous groups obscures the geopolitical and historical complexities of international relations. Regardless of the fact that there is no way to justify the actions of terrorists, labeling them as "evil" prevents any way of understanding their motives, which would be useful in combating them, since "evil" has a metaphysical connotation: it cannot be reasoned with or comprehended, only destroyed by any means necessary. Of course, those means are often shortsighted, such as the Reagan administration's arming of anti-Soviet Mujahideen forces in Afghanistan, which of course led to the formation of the terrorist group Al Qaeda.[26] The old, simplistic adage of "the enemy of my enemy is my friend" is rarely a reliable basis for international policy. The label of "evil" also positions the "good guys" as unquestionably right. This "good-guys-and-bad-guys" mentality justifies any action, even if it is morally questionable. For example, the use of torture in both combat and interrogation has been repeatedly justified using the hypothetical and incredibly unlikely "ticking bomb" scenario, in which a captured terrorist has knowledge of an imminent attack and the only way to stop the attack is by torturing the suspect for information.[27] This sort of hypothetical situation is seemingly ripped right from a comic book or an action film, and in fact has been used repeatedly in entertainment media, from *24* (2001-2010) to *The Dark Knight Rises* (2012). Morally repugnant actions like torture continue to be justified, as when President Obama admitted that the United States

---

[25] "You Are Either With Us or Against Us."
[26] "Sleeping With the Devil: How U.S. and Saudi Backing of Al Qaeda Led to 9/11."
[27] "Ethics Guide: The 'Ticking Bomb' Problem."

"tortured some folks" following the attacks of September 11th, 2001.[28] Politicians and pundits have cultivated a political climate in which there is largely no middle ground or shades of grey; only good guys and bad guys, heroes and villains.

Following the terrorist attacks of September 11th, 2001 and the ensuing early years of the War on Terror, comic books, meanwhile, examined the ramifications of both the terrorist attacks and the domestic political response, with stories about the balance between safety and liberty. Writer Mark Millar used these themes as the framework for Marvel's 2006 *Civil War* crossover event,[29] which focused on the idea of a super-hero registration program that would make the personal identities of the characters public. As scores of politicians in the real world argued that potentially invasive surveillance measures such as the Patriot Act were politically expedient and necessary, Tony Stark and Steve Rogers debated how to balance the fundamental right to privacy with the necessity of public safety and protection. Even though the premise of the story had been seen before – such as the Keene Act in *Watchmen* – the Superhuman Registration Act in *Civil War* was a way for the creators to further explore contemporary issues using the familiar conventions of the super-hero genre: the powers of the characters represented a threat to the people they had sworn to protect, and it also gave the creators an excuse to have the characters literally fight over their ideological differences. By embracing both the over-the-top action of the genre along with the popular political conversation of the time, Millar demonstrated the unique ability of comic books to explore the complexities of these issues in an entertaining manner. In fact, writer Grant Morrison compares *Civil War* to a political cartoon in his book about the history of super-hero comics, *Supergods*. "The whole series, and with it a fraught moment in American history, was condensed into one supercharged image demonstrating once again that the best way to tackle contemporary political issues in a superhero story was with bold metaphor

---

[28] See Lewis.
[29] Centered around *Civil War* Vol. 1 #1-7.

and a good punch-up."[30]

Regardless of its quality as a story, *Civil War* is emblematic of the way contemporary super-hero comics have engaged with politics and culture. Even though the traditional "good-guys-and-bad-guys" formula is still part of the genre, the themes of the books are based on real-world events and concerns. Stories like *Civil War*, or DC's polarizing and controversial *Identity Crisis*,[31] didn't attempt to subvert the tropes of the genre the way *Watchmen* did, but instead used the high-stakes action and drama of super-hero comics as a backdrop for more "realistic" stories about ethical issues. As Wolk points out: "Ethical action has become Topic A in twenty-first-century super-hero comics; a lot of the best and most significant ones address the question of means and ends and where they intersect with violence and history and the notion of what constitutes moral action."[32]

By the early 21st century, seemingly every super-hero has been explored, dissected, and "deconstructed." From Superman explaining why he does not kill in "What's So Funny About Truth, Justice, & the American Way?"[33] to Wonder Woman justifying her murder of Maxwell Lord in *Infinite Crisis*,[34] contemporary super-hero comics have explored the complicated relationship between power and justice at a time when politicians have increasingly justified military invasions and drone warfare using the familiar binary moral language of good guys and bad guys, even when that simplistic language belies the devastating consequences of these policies.[35] Super-hero comic books have gone from mirroring the political and cultural zeitgeist to actively engaging with it and its ramifications. As Wolk has suggested, this may be largely due to the medium itself: comic books, unlike

---

[30] Morrison, page 353.

[31] *Identity Crisis* #1-7.

[32] Wolk, page 100.

[33] *Action Comics* Vol. 1 #775.

[34] Wonder Woman breaks Maxwell Lord's neck to stop him from controlling Superman's mind in *Wonder Woman* Vol. 2 #219. Disagreement about her actions leads to the *Infinite Crisis* storyline. *Infinite Crisis* Vol. 1 #1-7.

[35] President Obama's invocation of the "fog of war" when admitting that drone strikes had killed an American and an Italian hostage demonstrates the oft-overlooked moral complexity of foreign policy. See Collinson.

feature films, offer creators the ability to tell long-form narratives and explore many versions of the same characters over the years. The result is a rich tapestry of stories and multifaceted characters that can change with cultural and political shifts in ways that other mediums interpreting these characters and stories cannot. For example, *Watchmen* is the product of a critical reading of the super-hero genre, and one that is only possible with the historical and narrative context of previous stories. However, that story is often seen as a lone example of a mature super-hero story, rather than one among many.

Ironically, the simplistic public perception of comic books and super-heroes has made these recent examinations of real-world issues more interesting and refreshing. Because super-hero comics have not historically been taken seriously, they have eventually garnered the freedom to explore ideas that mainstream popular culture has not; after being dismissed as "kids' stuff" for decades, comics have increasingly engaged with issues of morality, power, and violence. As super-heroes have saturated the modern pop culture landscape, however, these themes that have become common in comic books seem largely unaddressed in the popular adaptations of their characters and stories. Unlike comic books, which have a comparatively small audience, these new super-hero films, often components of larger "cinematic universes," are designed and expected to generate huge sums of money for their studios, as evidenced by the fact that both Warner Bros. and Disney – the companies that own the film franchises for DC and Marvel Comics respectively – have suffused their prospective schedules with comic book adaptations. No longer relegated to specialty shops or Saturday morning cartoons, super-heroes are once again an established – and now especially lucrative – part of the pop culture landscape. However, most of these new films only scratch the surface of the rich history and culture of the super-hero genre. The costumes and the characters, faithfully recreated with the latest moviemaking magic, may be familiar, but these films tend to mimic the look and tone of typical summer blockbusters rather than capture the feel of their source material. The complex moral issues seen in the pages of the comics are replaced by the familiar predictability of action films. Even a nuanced story like *Watchmen* was reduced to a shiny-looking –

if tonally dark – CGI spectacle when it was adapted to the big screen in 2009. Obviously, translating a static comic book into a movie presents a number of obstacles, and an absolutely faithful adaptation is not possible, nor even desired. This of course raises the question of whether film adaptations of super-hero comics are really necessary in the first place, although the box office returns provide one possible answer.

Even though most of the current super-hero films merely resemble their inspirations, there are examples that try to incorporate contemporary political issues. The problem, however, is that these issues can only be hinted at in a feature film, especially one that is ultimately more focused on exciting action sequences within its running time than intellectual insight. This is another advantage of comic books and their ongoing serial narrative structure: themes and ideas can develop over time rather than be briefly mentioned. Thus, some films seem to be engaging with important issues, but rarely get deep enough to offer any worthwhile insight, presenting the illusion of importance rather than presenting a cogent debate or critique. As critic Alex Pappademas has put it, somewhat flippantly, *"Captain America: The Winter Soldier* books Robert Redford as the heavy and makes a few halfhearted allusions to our own imperiled civil liberties, and everyone calls it a ''70s political thriller' with a straight face, forgetting that actual '70s political thrillers seldom excused government malfeasance by blaming it on defrosted Nazi agents."[36]

Obviously, it may be foolish to expect a nuanced debate on public policy or ethics from a summer blockbuster. However, by limiting their message, these films offer and reinforce the same sort of "good-guys-and-bad-guys," dichotomous morality that comic books have been ridiculed for, yet simultaneously dominates the contemporary political debate. As a result, these films also serve as a sort of affirmation that any action – ethical or otherwise – is justified and expedient in the face of "evil." Christopher Nolan's Dark Knight Trilogy films are good examples of the implied political message and consequences of this approach. *The Dark Knight* (2008) hints at the issues of surveillance and privacy in modern society. In order to find

[36] Pappademas.

the Joker, Batman infiltrates the cell phones of Gotham's citizens. This invasion of privacy is justified in order to capture a dangerous criminal – much like in the so-called "ticking bomb" scenario; this scene also foreshadows the plot of *The Dark Knight Rises*, which features a literal "ticking bomb." The debate about surveillance in the film is limited to Lucius Fox expressing his unease about hacking citizens' private phones, with Batman quickly assuring him that the technology used will be destroyed. In the end, the tactic works, Batman captures the Joker, and Fox seems to accept the necessity of spying, despite his earlier protest. The invasion of privacy through surveillance of innocent citizens seems to be perfectly acceptable within the framework of this super-hero story; any concerns about the political and ethical consequences are swept away in the end. However, the current debate about CIA spying seems to be far more complex, and it's hard to imagine people willingly accepting this level of surveillance, regardless of the situation; the notion that we should trust Batman in this way, and more than our own government for that matter, has somewhat troubling implications.

While the success of super-hero films offers an opportunity for a thoughtful debate or discussion about important issues, these films seem to largely reinforce the stereotypical notions of "comic book morality," and their parameters are an indication that the current political and cultural debate is still stuck in the familiar black-and-white view of morality. While super-hero comic books, dismissed for their "comic book morality," have used their history and narrative structure to use context, revision, and reflection to explore issues with some depth, the popular view of "comic book morality" in fact largely remains the default mode for contemporary politics, and the disparity between this black-and-white morality and the more nuanced approach in contemporary comics is exasperated by the simplicity of these current films, which present super-hero stories without the historical or narrative context – the very feature that allowed the comic book medium to grow and change in ways the current political discourse has seemingly not, and made the source material iconic. Similarly, by so often operating within the familiar "us versus them" framework, contemporary political discourse lacks proper historical context as well, with the lessons of previous military conflicts or international relations rarely heeded. Although the roots of the current War on Terror can be traced to interventionist policies of the late Cold War and the first Gulf War of the 1990s, the bellicose "good-guys-and-bad-guys" rhetoric of international conflict continues to be repeated instead. Unlike comic books, which have catered to a small but passionate group of readers and have not been taken seriously by mainstream culture, big-budget super-hero films are expected to appeal to a large audience. As such, super-hero films reflect the social and political climate rather than critique it, and now that this "subculture" is suddenly mainstream, the political ideology of the day has a greater influence on it.

One hope for the future of both the super-hero genre and popular discourse is that the growing body of films will evolve, telling more complex super-hero stories within their medium, ultimately generating a commentary on the meaning of super-heroes themselves, much like what has happened in the comics. By critiquing this particular genre, now a renewed fixture of the pop culture landscape, future films may serve as a way to expand and explore the contemporary notions of ethics, politics, and justice within their universes in ways previous large-scale super-hero films have avoided. Of course, finding room in the visual spectacles and explosions may be difficult, and political expediency seems to make thoughtful debate prohibitive. Nevertheless, super-hero media, as a descendent of a medium that, as a whole, moves forward, is in a unique position for the first time in history to change that. Perhaps super-hero films, and in turn, the politics of which they are a product, can also embrace their historical narrative and break out of the familiar trope of "good-guys-and-bad-guys." Until then, there are still examples of a more nuanced, "four color" morality in the pages of comic books.

Bibliography

Action Comics Vol. 1 #13. Jerry Siegel (writer) and Joe Shuster (penciler/inker). Ed. Vincent Sullivan. DC Comics, June 1939.

Action Comics Vol. 1 #775. "What's So Funny About Truth, Justice, & the American Way?" Joe Kelly (writer), Lee Bermejo (penciler), Doug Mahnke (penciler), Wayne Faucher (inker), Jose Marzan Jr. (inker), Tom Nguyen (inker), Jim Royal (inker), Dexter Vines (inker), Wade Von Grawbadger (inker),

Rob Schwager (colorist), and Comicraft (letterer). Eds. Eddie Berganza and Tom Palmer Jr. DC Comics, Mar 2001.

Batman Vol. 1 #1. Bill Finger (writer), Bob Kane (penciler), and Sheldon Moldoff (inker/letterer). Ed. Whitney Ellsworth. DC Comics, Spring 1940.

Captain America Comics Vol. 1 #1. Joe Simon (writer/penciler), Jack Kirby (writer/penciler), and Al Liederman (inker). Ed. Joe Simon. Timely Publications, Mar 1941.

Civil War Vol. 1 #1-7. Mark Millar (writer), Steve McNiven (penciler/inker), Dexter Vines (inker), Mark Morales (inker), John Dell (inker), Tim Townsend (inker), Morry Hollowell (colorist), and Chris Eliopoulos (letterer). Eds. Tom Brevoort, Molly Lazer, Andy Schmidt, Aubrey Sitterson, and Joe Quesada. Marvel Comics, July 2006-Jan 2007.

Collinson, Stephen. "Obama Confronts 'Cruel' Reality of His Drone War." *CNN*. 24 Apr 2015. http://www.cnn.com/2015/04/23/politics/obama-drone-warren-weinstein-hostages/.

"The Comics Code Authority (as Adopted in 1954)." *Comicartville*. Accessed 1 Sept 2015. http://www.comicartville.com/comicscode.htm.

Detective Comics Vol. 1 #36 (Feb 1940). Bill Finger (writer), Bob Kane (penciler/inker), and Jerry Robinson (inker). Ed. Vincent Sullivan. DC Comics, Feb 1940.

"Ethics Guide: The 'Ticking Bomb' Problem." *BBC*. Accessed 30 Aug 2015. http://www.bbc.co.uk/ethics/torture/ethics/tickingbomb_1.shtml.

Hajdu, David. *The Ten-Cent Plague: The Great Comic-Book Scare and How It Changed America* (New York: Farrar, Straus, and Giroux, 2008).

Howe, Sean. *Marvel Comics: The Untold Story* (New York: Harper Perennial, 2012).

Identity Crisis Vol. 1 #1-7. Brad Meltzer (writer), Rags Morales (penciler), Michael Bair (inker), Alex Sinclair (colorist), and Ken Lopez (letterer). Eds. Mike Carlin, Valerie D'Orazio, and Michael Siglain. DC Comics, Aug 2004-Feb 2005.

Infinite Crisis Vol. 1 #1-7. Geoff Johns (writer), Phil Jimenez (penciler), George Pérez (penciler/inker), Ivan Reis (penciler/inker), Jerry Ordway (penciler/inker), Joe Bennett (penciler), Andy Lanning (inker), Marlo Alquiza (inker), Norm Rapmund (inker), Lary Stucker (inker), Wayne Faucher (inker), Oclair Albert (inker), Marcelo H. Campos (inker), Drew Geraci (inker), Jimmy Palmiotti (inker), Arthur Edward Thibert (inker), Sean P. Parsons (inker), Jeromy Cox (colorist), Guy Major (colorist), Rodrigo Reis (colorist), Richard Horie (colorist), Tanya Horie (colorist), Nick J. Napolitano (letterer), and Rob Leigh (letterer). Eds. Eddie Berganza and Jeanine Schaefer. DC Comics, Dec 2005-June 2006.

Lewis, Paul. "Obama Admits CIA 'Tortured Some Folks' But Stands by Brennan Over Spying." *The Guardian*. 1 Aug 2014. http://www.theguardian.com/world/2014/aug/01/obama-cia-torture-some-folks-brennan-spying.

Morrison, Grant. *Supergods: What Masked Vigilantes, Miraculous Mutants, and a Sun God from Smallville Can Teach Us About Being Human* (New York: Spiegel & Grau, 2011).

Morton, Paul. "The Survivor: On Magneto, Mutants, and the Holocaust." *The Millions*. 23 May 2014. http://www.themillions.com/2014/05/the-survivor-on-magneto-x-men-and-the-holocaust.html.

Nyberg, Amy Kiste. "Comics Code History: The Seal of Approval." *Comic Book Legal Defense Fund*. Accessed 21 Nov 2015. http://cbldf.org/comics-code-history-the-seal-of-approval/.

"Only 'A Good Guy With A Gun' Can Stop School Shootings, NRA Says." *NPR*. 21 Dec 2012. http://www.npr.org/sections/thetwo-way/2012/12/21/167785169/live-blog-nra-news-conference.

Pappademas, Alex. "Giving the Devil His Do-Rag: Why Netflix's *Daredevil* is the Least Marvel-y Marvel Property Yet." *Grantland*. 14 Apr 2015. http://grantland.com/hollywood-prospectus/giving-the-devil-his-do-rag-why-netflixs-daredevil-is-the-least-marvel-y-marvel-property-yet/.

Reagan, Ronald. "Remarks at the Annual Convention of the National Association of Evangelicals in Orlando, Florida." *The Ronald Reagan Presidential Foundation & Library*. Transcript from 8 Mar 1983. http://www.reaganfoundation.org/pdf/Remarks_Annual_Convention_National_Association_Evangelicals_030883.pdf.

Rogers, Vaneta. "The Comics Code Authority - Defunct Since 2009?" *Newsarama*. 24 Jan 2011. http://www.newsarama.com/6897-the-comics-code-authority-defunct-since-2009.html.

"Sleeping With the Devil: How U.S. and Saudi Backing of Al Qaeda Led to 9/11." *Washington's Blog*. 5 Sept 2012. http://www.washingtonsblog.com/2012/09/sleeping-with-the-devil-how-u-s-and-saudi-backing-of-al-qaeda-led-to-911.html.

Tilley, Carol L. "Seducing the Innocent: Fredric Wertham and the Falsifications that Helped Condemn Comics." *Information & Culture* Vol. 47, No. 4 (November-December 2012). Pages 383-413. http://www.infoculturejournal.org/abstracts/47.4.

Watchmen #1-12. Alan Moore (writer), Dave Gibbons (penciler/inker/letterer), and John Higgins (colorist). Ed. Len Wein. DC Comics, Sept 1986-Oct 1987.

Weldon, Glen. *Superman: The Unauthorized Biography* (Hoboken, NJ: John Wiley & Sons, Inc., 2013).

Wolk, Douglas. Reading Comics: How Graphic Novels Work and What They Mean (Cambridge, MA: Da Capo Press, 2007).

Wonder Woman Vol. 2 #219. Greg Rucka (writer), Thomas Derenick (penciler), Georges Jeanty (penciler), Karl Kerschl (penciler), David López (penciler), Rags Morales (penciler), Nelson (inker), Javier Bergantiño (inker), Bob Petrecca (inker), Mark Propst (inker), Dexter Vines (inker), Richard Horie (colorist), Tanya Horie (colorist), and Todd Klein (letterer). Ed. Ivan Cohen. DC Comics, Sept 2005.

"You Are Either With Us or Against Us." CNN. 6 Nov 2001. http://edition.cnn.com/2001/US/11/06/gen.attack.on.terror/.

Keeping the Wolves at Bay: How the Super-Hero Keeps the Wheel of Fortune from Turning

by Colby Pryor

Watchmen[1] by Alan Moore and Dave Gibbons is regarded by many to be the cornerstone of academic study on the medium of comics. *Time* magazine described it as:

> A book-length comic book with ambitions above its station – starring a ragbag of bizarre, damaged, retired superheroes: the paunchy, melancholic Nite Owl; the raving doomsayer Rorschach; the blue, glowing, near-omnipotent, no-longer-human Dr. Manhattan. Though their heyday is past, these former crime-fighters are drawn back into action by the murder of a former teammate, The Comedian, which turns out to be the leading edge of a much wider, more disturbing conspiracy. Told with ruthless psychological realism, in fugal, overlapping plotlines and gorgeous, cinematic panels rich with repeating motifs, *Watchmen* is a heart-

---

[1] Originally published as *Watchmen* #1-12.

pounding, heartbreaking read and a watershed in the evolution of a young medium.[2]

It has also won a Hugo Award and inspired a multitude of books analyzing every aspect of the work, including Sequart's own *Minutes to Midnight* anthology. One of the themes that *Watchmen* presents is encapsulated on the last page of the collected edition: "Quis custodiet ipsos custodes. Who watches the watchmen?" What gives these people in masks the right to go out and enforce laws for which they have no legitimacy or training?

The book establishes the idea that if the super-hero were to exist in the real world, the individual would be a borderline psychotic and ineffectual at establishing real change to his or her surrounding environment. In *Minutes to Midnight*, Julian Darius elaborates on this thesis:

> It was about making the super-hero realistic, because the practice of taking to the streets in costume would, in the real world, attract people prone to psychopathology. Moreover, what the super-hero sees as he encounters real-life crime could easily cause a psychotic break. Policemen encounter scenes much like the one Rorschach recalls, and like Rorschach, they often lose their faith. But theirs is an occupation with its own formalized support network that costumed vigilantes lack.[3]

Alan Moore cements this idea in *The Extraordinary Works of Alan Moore*:

> **GEORGE KHOURY:** One of the quotes I liked that I read somewhere you said, "It's dangerous to have heroes." And that was one of the things you were trying to prove with *Watchmen*.
>
> **ALAN MOORE:** Well, that's true. I think it *is* dangerous to have heroes.[4]

It may be true that a hero may be a dangerous entity, possibly disturbed, or unhinged. However, that does not change the fact that a hero serves as a scale that keeps a society in balance with itself, preventing a society from throwing away its social contract with its government and culture and turning to wanton chaos and rebellion.

Watchmen's question as to what gives the super-hero the right to uphold the laws of a people is a very good one, but it also begs the question as to what gives police officers the right to uphold the laws and not these other people? Furthermore, what gives firefighters the right to fight fires

---

[2] Grossman.

[3] Darius.

[4] Khoury, page 115.

and not the common man or woman? Or politicians to make policies and laws? The reason these people hold these positions of power in society stems from the very nature of power itself. Political power comes from one source – a symbiotic relationship with the people. This is most famously captured in the Declaration of Independence: "That to secure these Rights, Governments are instituted among Men, deriving their just powers from the Consent of the Governed."[5]

The way the government displays its given power over the people is through its symbols, such as the dress of office that the leaders of the country must wear, or the country's flag. In "The Uniform: A Sociological Perspective," Nathan Joseph and Nicholas Alex elaborate on this point further:

> The very existence of a uniform implies a group structure – at least a two-step hierarchy, the wearer and a superior individual(s) – which has granted the right to wear its uniform, which supervises conformity to group regulations and standard definitions of behavior, and to which one can resort with complaints. The uniform acts as a guarantee that an upper level in the group will control the members and, in turn, that members will conform. By permitting the use of its uniform, a group certifies an individual as its representative and assumes responsibility for his activities.[6]

Joseph and Alex state that the uniform represents the basic acknowledgment of the power dynamics between the people and the state. The person in the uniform represents everything that the state represents and enforces the agreed-upon terms of the relationship.

Both the law enforcer and the soldier share some remarkable similarities with the super-hero in that their purpose is the same. Take an archetypal super-hero from one of the major publishing houses: many people look at the uniform that Batman or Spider-Man wear and just see an outfit. However, this assumption is false. Every aspect of the uniform serves the same purpose as a police or military uniform. Batman's suit is not made out of spandex, but a special polymer that can deflect knife attacks and is resistant to gunfire. Spider-Man's uniform is designed so that it allows him

---

[5] "Primary Documents in American History: Declaration of Independence."
[6] Joseph and Alex, pages 722-723.

to swing through the skyscrapers of New York as efficiently as possible without having to worry about the glare of the sun.

However, that is not the limit of what the super-hero's uniform represents; it also serves to strike fear into the hearts of criminals and the corrupt, and can serve to help unite people. The Bat-Signal can inspire dread and fear when the criminal looks up at it, but to the citizen it can generate the same sort of comfort that police lights bring. Ironically, this innate comparison can only work if the people believe in the super-hero to do what their own governments cannot do. Two perfect examples are the ending to the film *The Dark Knight Rises* (2012) and the 12th episode of *Arrow*'s third season, "Uprising" (2015). In *The Dark Knight Rises*, Bane has conquered the city of Gotham and plunged it into a state of enforced anarchy. Bruce Wayne returns to inspire the people of Gotham to take the fight to the criminals. He inspires the people through lighting his symbol atop a bridge, and, after defeating Bane and his henchmen, ultimately saves Gotham by taking Bane's bomb out to sea. In *Arrow*, Oliver Queen is away from Starling City, and in his absence a criminal organization has taken hold of it. Oliver's friends who were inspired by his secret identity as the Arrow in turn inspire Starling's citizens to rise up against the criminals who have taken hold of Starling. This in turn builds to the point where Oliver congratulates the people of Starling and tells them that they did not fail – as Oliver has referred to it so often – "this city." In both stories, the people of each city opt to unite under the symbol of the titular hero. They give the hero the power to represent and protect the people because the government has failed in some capacity to do the same thing.

In *Politics*, Aristotle argues that humans are a "social animal."[7] A social animal is defined as:

> A group of animals belonging to the same species, and consisting of individuals beyond those in a family unit, who perform specific tasks, spend distinctly more time together, and interact much more within the group than with members of the same species outside of that group. A

---

[7] Aristotle, page 25.

social animal is defined as any animal species that typically forms into societies.[8]

Examples of other social animals are wolves, whales, elephants, and great apes. Humans, in the deepest part of their reptile brains, seek groups and want to interact with each other. Originally, this was because it offered individuals better chances of survival to have a pack or herd behind them while they went out and scavenged for food.[9] From these early groupings came simple alpha-beta relationships, in which all other animals in a social group are underneath the alpha, existing in a binary relationship between the dominant animal and the rest of the group. Early humans adopted this binary relationship in their early development as well. However, as humanity grew and changed, so did the social dynamics of the species, and the alpha-beta relationships could no longer handle the intricacies of the newly formed societies. Humanity, like all other social animals, cannot exist outside of a binary system – anarchy as a social dynamic is impossible to sustain for any long stretch of time. Hume explains it as:

> Man, born in a family, is compelled to maintain society, from necessity, from natural inclination, and from habit. The same creature, in his farther progress, is engaged to establish political society, in order to administer justice; without which there can be no peace among them, nor safety, nor mutual intercourse.[10]

Burgeoning societies needed a new form of leadership to make decisions that did not involve being the toughest or the strongest. This need allowed for different governments to be born, and while the birthing process for each primordial institution was different, the agreement between each people and their infant government was the same. Rousseau elaborates on the terms of this agreement:

> "Each of us puts his person and all his power in common under the supreme direction of the general will, and, in our corporate capacity, we receive each member as an indivisible part of the whole."
>
> At once, in place of the individual personality of each contracting party, this act of association creates a moral and collective body, composed of as many members as the assembly contains votes, and receiving from this act

---

[8] Steinberg.
[9] Immelmann and Beer.
[10] Hume.

its unity, its common identity, its life and its will. This public person, so formed by the union of all other persons, formerly took the name of *city*, and now takes that of *Republic* or *body politic*; it is called by its members *State* when passive, *Sovereign* when active, and *Power* when compared with others like itself. Those who are associated in it take collectively the name of *people*, and severally are called *citizens*, as sharing in the sovereign power, and *subjects*, as being under the laws of the State. But these terms are often confused and taken one for another: it is enough to know how to distinguish them when they are being used with precision.[11]

Philosophy calls this agreement the social contract. The contract serves to establish the terms from which all governments inevitably stem from. The key agreement is that the common people sacrifice their innate freedom to do as they please. They also agree to work for the state, obey the laws of the state, and do whatever they can to be a useful member of the state. The government agrees to protect every person who agrees to the contract from outside harm. The government also agrees to give the newly-made citizens opportunity to thrive in the newly-created sociopolitical environment, and to protect them from people inside the environment who would do them harm.

However, the contract is a fragile concept. Confucius describes this phenomenon in terms of states that can be broken if either of the two parties are dissatisfied with the service of the other party. The contract can also be discarded, if another, more appealing contract comes about.[12] To chart the lifespan of a social contract, the Rota Fortunae can be used. The Rota Fortunae, or Wheel of Fortune, is a concept used as a tool to describe the fickleness of fate:

> The wheel characteristically bears on its rim four shelves of "stages" with four human figures. The figure rising on the left is usually labeled *regnabo* (I shall reign), the one at the top is marked *regno* (I reign) and is often crowned, that descending on the right is *regnavi* (I have reigned), and the writhing figure at the lowest point is *sum sine regno* (I have no kingdom). The victim is sometimes depicted as thrown from the wheel by gravity and centrifugal force, and sometimes as crushed under a wheel fit for a heavy cart.[13]

---

[11] Rousseau.

[12] Smith.

[13] "The Iconography of Fortuna."

Fortuna, the Roman goddess of fate, is typically seen turning the Wheel, which charts the evolution of a society from its inception to collapse. The birth of a society can be considered to be *regnabo*, as the contract is just about to be finalized, with the society about to take hold and be instituted. Then comes *regno*, where society is in full swing, the government has full control, and the people are content and happy. Confucius describes the Wheel turning from *regnabo* to *regno* – the "spontaneous consent from its citizens, this morale without which nations cannot survive" – as taking place "only when people sense their leaders to be people of capacity, sincerely devoted to the common good and possessed of the kind of character that compels respect."[14] Once this point has been reached, the society can be considered to be at the apex of its growth and prosperity.

"Wheel of Fortuna in Hortus Deliciarum of Herrad of Landsberg (after Straub and Keller)" From Kitzinger, page 351.

The society in question does not see itself as reaching its fullest potential – it is always trying to become a utopia while keeping itself from falling into dystopia. Vladimir Lenin presents a captivating definition for utopia as "a place which does not exist, a fantasy, invention or fairy-tale."[15] In regards to society and politics, it is a term used to define the perfect

---

[14] Smith, page 178.
[15] Lenin.

society and government – a sociopolitical structure where there is no crime, no suffering, everyone is happy, and everyone is equal. A dystopia is the opposite, described as an "imagined place or state in which everything is unpleasant or bad, typically a totalitarian or environmentally degraded one."[16] Thus, a society can be seen as resting on a scale between utopia and dystopia. It can never reach the two plateaus, for it goes against human nature to create a purely utopian society, and a truly dystopian society can never exist either, for the society would collapse in upon itself before this extreme is met. However, the society in question can move toward each extreme depending on the health of the society.

A society can be at its apex for an undefined amount of time – a couple of decades, centuries, possibly even some millennia. However, it will reach a point when it will start to decay, when the social structures will start to break down. This breakdown will cause the Wheel to turn to *regnavi*. The individual reasons for why the Wheel turns will differ depending on the circumstances surrounding the society in question. For Confucius, the most important aspect of the citizen-to-government relationship is very much in keeping with the views of many other philosophers. Huston Smith explains that "… popular trust is by far the most important, for [according to Confucius] 'if the people have no confidence in their government, it cannot stand.'"[17] When the people begin to lose faith or confidence in their government, the Wheel will turn, and the society will begin to decline. The length of this decline will differ from society to society, just as the apex. Eventually the sociopolitical environment will deteriorate to an unbearable point. Either the people will not be able to live in continued squalor, or the government will not have the ability to handle the internal and external pressures being exerted upon it. In Chinese philosophy, there is a concept that adequately defines this event. It is called the Mandate of Heaven. The Mandate of Heaven is broken down into four key principles that mirror the turning of the Wheel of Fortune. They are:

1. Heaven grants the emperor the right to rule,

---

[16] "Dystopia."
[17] Smith, page 178.

2.   Since there is only one Heaven, there can only be one emperor at any given time,

3.   The emperor's virtue determines his right to rule, and,

4.   No one dynasty has a permanent right to rule.[18]

The Mandate states that the people have the right to cast down their ruler when that ruler has lost his virtue. The emperor's virtue can be seen as how much trust the people have in his ability to rule. Once broken, the people can enact the Mandate of Heaven to remove the current ruler from power.

The last turn of the Wheel is known as *sum sine regno* (I have no kingdom). This is the state after the Mandate of Heaven has been issued, in which the social contract has been destroyed and the society has collapsed. It is an environment where there is no structure, production, or protection. After the collapse, total anarchy is achieved – anarchy being defined as "a situation of confusion and wild behavior in which the people in a country, group, organization, etc., are not controlled by rules or laws."[19] It is a state from which total freedom can be distilled, as there is no limit to the wants and excesses of the people. Total anarchy cannot exist as long as people are social animals, who will naturally repeat the cycle described earlier from basic pack structures to new governments and societies.

The transition between *regnavi* to *sum sine regno* is a cruel and bloody one. The idealistic portrayal of anarchism is described by anarchist Peter Kropotkin as:

> the name given to a principle or theory of life and conduct under which society is conceived without government – harmony in such a society being obtained, not by submission to law, or by obedience to any authority, but by free agreements concluded between the various groups, territorial and professional, freely constituted for the sake of production and consumption, as also for the satisfaction of the infinite variety of needs and aspirations of a civilized being.

Kropotkin continues:

> Moreover, such a society would represent nothing immutable. On the contrary – as is seen in organic life at large – harmony would (it is contended) result from an ever-changing adjustment and readjustment of equilibrium between the multitudes of forces and influences, and this

---

[18] Szczepanski.

[19] "Anarchy."

adjustment would be the easier to obtain as none of the forces would enjoy a special protection from the state.[20]

Many would say that the collapse of the government would be good, for it would allow political anarchy to do what has been described above. However, the notion of anarchism stems from an ultimately idealistic perspective. Typically when the Wheel turns and the social contract is destroyed, the results are horrendous. The newly found freedom would allow the more barbaric and morally bankrupt of society to further revel in acts like stealing, vandalism, murder, or rape. There is no organization or peaceful coexistence; there is only to take what one wants and leave nothing behind. Leaders eventually emerge out of the chaos of the collapsed society, but there is no equality to be found, nor peace. The societies that emerge are basic binary societies of leader and subject, which could be peaceful or completely barbaric, depending on the leadership.

A societal collapse is something that neither the government nor the people want. The government wants to continue to exist, and the people do not want to go through the above kinds of hardship if they can help it. However, as a society slips more into dystopia, its government will either loosen its hold over the populace or squeeze too tightly. Whatever the situation, the people turn to something else to try and keep the Wheel from turning. The super-hero can be thought of as a rebalancing agent, keeping the society from falling further toward dystopia – actually stopping the Wheel from turning. Take Batman's Gotham City, a society that can be seen as dystopian to the point where the city looks as though it is going to collapse in upon itself, or that the government will correct the city through force. However, through his work as the Batman, Bruce Wayne is able to create something that the people can believe and hope in. He also deals with the cancerous aspects of Gotham, removing the criminal and corrupt from play and inserting people who can be trusted to serve the common good. Through this good work and keeping the local economy healthy through Wayne Enterprises, Wayne keeps the local Wheel from turning to

---

[20] Kropotkin.

social collapse, thus sparing the people of Gotham from the pain and suffering that such a scenario would bring.

Even in *Watchmen* this principle can be seen. Ozymandias wants to unite the world and prevent a nuclear war. The way he does so is by inventing an alien creature to crash-land on Earth and wipe out New York City. It's an atrocious idea to be sure, but what is worse – the destruction of one major metropolis filled with millions of people, or the complete annihilation of all life on the planet? If both the U.S. and the U.S.S.R. in *Watchmen* declared war, nuclear war would have been all but guaranteed, eradicating the planet's biosphere for several millennia, and throughout the book, the reader can see the United States preparing for it. There is no doubt that Ozymandias's actions save humanity from itself. Ozymandias is never painted in a heroic way, but he nevertheless shares the same purpose and accomplishes the same effect.

Outside of fiction, where do these influential figures appear? Typically, they do not show up at all and people are forced to endure terrible hardships. Take the Roman Empire as an example. "The Roman Empire, at its height (c. 117 CE), was the most extensive political and social structure in western civilization."[21] The Empire is considered to be the backbone and the archetype of modern Western civilization, with whole governmental structures based on the original Roman template, and "lasting contributions to virtually every aspect of western culture."[22] But with all of its greatness, influence, and power, the Empire could not prevent itself from collapsing. How it collapsed is not known, but it is assumed that it was a combination of several internal and external factors, such as those described by the *Ancient History Encyclopedia*:

> Other influences which have been noted range from the corruption of the governing elite to the ungovernable vastness of the empire to the growing strength of the Germanic tribes and their constant incursions into Rome. The Roman military could no longer safeguard the borders as efficiently as

---

[21] Mark.

[22] Ibid.

they once had nor could the government as easily collect taxes in the provinces.[23]

Regardless, even this great empire, the archetype of all Western civilization, fell, and brought with it the period of chaos and strife that was the Middle Ages.

But Rome was not the only empire to fall in such a manner. Whether the Persian Empire, the Egyptian Empire, or several Chinese dynasties, countless civilizations have collapsed without anyone to save them. The means by which most cultures die can be rather diverse, but the aftermath is always the same. The best a society can hope for is to be absorbed by a stronger society, and at worst, to deal with a barbaric social landscape. As stated before, most people try to avoid this state of existence as much as possible. This is what leads to the creation of the hero. Since heroes seldom act as balancing agents in real life,[24] if people cannot experience such an event for themselves, they will use fiction to give them one. Through fiction, the people can experience what they have always wanted to happen, and as a byproduct, hope for something similar in reality.

The super-hero serves the exact same purpose as all other heroes who have come before in human literature, which is to serve as a beacon of hope to the suffering masses that the principles, laws, and the social identity of their society can be saved, fixed, and made better. Throughout human history the same kinds of characters can be found. In the legend of Robin Hood, Hood's modus operandi is that he steals from the rich to give to the poor, since the taxes in the region are too high, with the Sheriff and the King squeezing the populace too hard for their goods. This would have otherwise

---

[23] Ibid.

[24] Miyamoto Musashi is an intriguing example. He did not focus on a dying society or corrupt government, but wandered the Japanese countryside, improving the lives of the people he encountered from the toil or suffering they endured. He also improved his society's thinking through his work *The Book of Five Rings*, a source of philosophy that spans all walks of life beyond that of the martial arts. Fictional down-to-earth heroes in the western and crime genres can be seen to serve the same purpose. He was also, incidentally, the inspiration for Stan Sakai's Miyamoto Usagi of *Usagi Yojimbo*. For further reading on Miyamoto Musashi, see Wilson; and Yoshikawa.

In *Watchmen*, the traditional role of the super-hero is infamously fulfilled when Ozymandias stops the United States and Soviet Union from destroying each other by fabricating an alien invasion. Art by Dave Gibbons. © DC Comics.

led to a peasant rebellion if Hood hadn't started to ease the pressure off of the people. The legends of King Arthur do not seem to fit into this essay's theory, as he is building a complete utopia.[25] His story takes the formula and turns it on its head by not being concerned with keeping the Wheel balanced, but rather with tipping the scales completely toward a concrete utopian ideal.

Watchmen asks the question of "Who watches the watchmen?" What gives super-heroes the right to do what they do? The answer to that question is that we, the people, give them the right when we have no one else to turn to. We inherently want somebody to save us from ourselves, so that we can keep everything we have built, struggled through, and endured, and allow it to survive and be made better. The thought of losing everything we hold dear is one of the worst terrors that most can imagine. Thus, since we so rarely experience such heroes in reality, we dream of such people in our fictions, and in turn hope for something better.

Bibliography

"Anarchy." *Merriam-Webster.* Last updated 2015. http://www.merriam-webster.com/dictionary/anarchy.

Aristotle. *The Politics of Aristotle: A Treatise on Government,* trans. William Ellis (Auckland, New Zealand: The Floating Press, 2009). ProQuest ebrary e-book.

Darius, Julian. "58 Varieties: *Watchmen* and Revisionism" in *Minutes to Midnight: Twelve Essays on* Watchmen. Ed. Richard Bensam (Edwardsville, IL: Sequart Research & Literacy Organization, 2011). Kindle edition.

"Dystopia." *Oxford Dictionaries.* Last updated 2015. http://www.oxforddictionaries.com/us/definition/american_english/dystopia

Grossman, Lev. "All-*Time* 100 Novels: *Watchmen."* *Time.* 11 Jan 2010. http://entertainment.time.com/2005/10/16/all-time-100-novels/slide/watchmen-1986-by-alan-moore-dave-gibbons/.

Hume, David. "Part I, Essay V: Of the Origin of Government." *Essays, Moral, Political, and Literary.* Ed. Eugene F. Miller (Indianapolis: Liberty Fund, Inc., [1742] 1987). http://www.econlib.org/library/LFBooks/Hume/hmMPL5.html.

"The Iconography of Fortuna." *Decameron Web.* Last updated 12 Mar 2010. http://www.brown.edu/Departments/Italian_Studies/dweb/themes_motifs/fortune/iconography.php.

Immelmann, Klaus and Colin Beer. *A Dictionary of Ethology* (Cambridge: Harvard University Press, 1989).

---

[25] Malory.

Joseph, Nathan and Nicholas Alex. "The Uniform: A Sociological Perspective."
    American Journal of Sociology Vol. 77, No. 4 (Jan 1972). Pages 719-730.
    http://www.jstor.org/stable/2776756.
Khoury, George. *The Extraordinary Works of Alan Moore* (Raleigh: TwoMorrows
    Publishing, 2003).
Kitzinger, Ernst. *The Art of Byzantium and the Medieval West: Selected Studies.*
    Ed. W. Eugene Kleinbauer (Bloomington, IN: Indiana University Press, 1976).
Kropotkin, Peter. "'Anarchism,' from *The Encyclopædia Britannica*, 1910." *Anarchy
    Archives.* Accessed 25 Aug 2015.
    http://dwardmac.pitzer.edu/Anarchist_Archives/kropotkin/britanniaanarch
    y.html.
Lenin, Vladimir. "Two Utopias." *Marxists Internet Archive.* Originally written October
    1912. https://www.marxists.org/archive/lenin/works/1912/oct/00.htm.
Malory, Thomas. *Le Morte d'Arthur: Sir Thomas Malory's Book of King Arthur and
    of His Noble Knights of the Round Table* (Charlottesville, VA: University of
    Virginia Library, 1996).
Mark, Joshua J. "Roman Empire." *Ancient History Encyclopedia.* 28 Apr 2011.
    http://www.ancient.eu/Roman_Empire/.
"Primary Documents in American History: Declaration of Independence." *The
    Library of Congress.* Last updated 2 June 2015.
    http://www.loc.gov/rr/program/bib/ourdocs/DeclarInd.html.
Rousseau, Jean-Jacques. *The Social Contract & Discourses*, trans. George
    Douglas Howard Cole. Released by *Project Gutenberg* 19 July 2014.
    http://www.gutenberg.org/files/46333/46333-h/46333-h.htm.
Smith, Huston. *The World's Religions: Our Great Wisdom Traditions, The Revised
    & Updated Edition of the Religions of Man* (San Francisco: HarperOne, 1991).
Steinberg, Rebecca. "Social Animals." *Encyclopedia.com.* 2002.
    http://www.encyclopedia.com/doc/1G2-3400500306.html.
Szczepanski, Kallie. "What is the Mandate of Heaven?" *AboutEducation.* Last
    updated 2015. http://asianhistory.about.com/od/ancientchina/f/What-Is-
    The-Mandate-Of-Heaven.htm.
Watchmen #1-12. Alan Moore (writer), Dave Gibbons (penciler/inker/letterer),
    and John Higgins (colorist). Ed. Len Wein. DC Comics, Sept 1986-Oct 1987.
Wilson, William Scott. *The Lone Samurai: The Life of Miyamoto Musashi* (Boston:
    Shambhala Publications, Inc., 2013).
Yoshikawa, Eiji. *Musashi: An Epic Novel of the Samurai Era* (New York: Harper &
    Row/Kodansha International, 1981).

Turtles on Trial: The Double Standards that Mutate Society

by John Loyd

The Teenage Mutant Ninja Turtles need to be locked up and pay penance to society for multiple counts of murder, manslaughter, and excessive force. While they're at it, the cops should probably also round up Casey Jones and Splinter. Reptiles or not, these cold-blooded killers and friends all belong behind bars instead of sewer grates for taking the law into their own hands and slaying people en masse based on their own split-second judgments.

Many readers will likely consider this verdict pretty harsh. *The Turtles are the good guys.* They aren't *killers*, and if they did kill people, the victims probably deserved it as bad guys. And yet, the Teenage Mutant Ninja Turtles (TMNT) have killed ever since their first appearance in 1984.[1] Whether or not they should be tried and convicted provides us with an examination of their motives, and in so doing offers a handy focal point about our

---

[1] *Teenage Mutant Ninja Turtles* Vol. 1 #1.

understanding of super-hero characters in general, and our own justice system.

When the Evil Shredder Attacks...

Calling the TMNT killers will most likely raise more than a few eyebrows, particularly from aficionados raised on the 1990s films, Playmates toy line, and 1987-1996 cartoon show. In fact, TMNT licensing agent Mark Freedman – the man chiefly responsible for their translation into toys, cartoons, and film characters – has said, "A ninja is literally a hired assassin. How are you going to sell that to Toys'R'Us and Kay Bee? We needed to play up the humor and deemphasize the violence."[2] For the first television adaptation, the Turtles' primary opposition, ninja of the Foot Clan, were robot soldiers, allowing a convenient fix for children's viewing. However, even a quick reading of the TMNT source material will provide evidence that the accused have, in fact, largely operated far from the Playmates parameters, killing on myriad occasions, and have incontrovertibly killed the Shredder – twice.[3] On one occasion when the Shredder appears, the Turtles' mentor, Master Splinter, shouts "Claw him! Rend him! Kill him! My brave, honorable children... Crush him now! He is yours."[4] This is to say nothing of the countless criminals, Foot Ninja, and Triceratons who have been felled by the Green Machine – but this is not to say that the issue is black and white.

Taking a fine-tooth comb to the Turtle canon in search of their stance on killing is a bit like combing the mats out of a rat's fur – as we shall see, every time progress is made, another knot tangles up the argument of whether they are *killers* or not. Although Splinter orders the TMNT to rend and kill Shredder on the occasion mentioned above, in their first clash with Old Hob and his goons in the IDW series, Master Splinter tells the Turtles, "sons... none must die."[5] Even in the first volume of the original Mirage

---

[2] Farago, page 55.
[3] Yes, in the original issue, Oroku Saki died by detonating the thermal grenade he was holding. On the other hand, Leonardo had just offered him his katana to commit the ritual suicide of *seppuku*; either way, the TMNT ensured his death.
[4] *Teenage Mutant Ninja Turtles* Vol. 1 #35, pages 15-17.
[5] *Teenage Mutant Ninja Turtles* Vol. 1 #1 [IDW], page 4.

It is easy to forget that the signature weapons brandished on a daily basis by the TMNT are deadly – Leonardo fatally wounds the Shredder in the Turtles' very first issue, subsequently giving Oroku Saki the opportunity to commit *seppuku*. Art by Kevin Eastman and Peter Laird. © Mirage Studios / Nickelodeon.

comics, Splinter specifically stops Raphael from drowning a terrorist who is part of an extremist attempt to detonate an atomic bomb.[6]

None of the characters provide more poignant examples of the TMNT struggle with killing than Raphael. As early as his one-shot micro-series appearance – just three issues after they were making sure Oroku "Shredder" Saki was toast – Raphael intervenes in the vigilante efforts of Casey Jones. Although Raphael himself just thrashed several muggers for stealing a woman's bag and attempting to rape her at knifepoint,[7] Raph intercedes when he realizes Casey is "not letting up! He's not just stopping those punks – He's gonna *kill 'em!!"*[8] Very interestingly, in the same encounter, while claiming he just wants to take Casey's bats away, Raphael also shouts, "You started this – but I'll finish it!"[9] – lunging at Casey with the point of one of his *sai* forward, which could impale Jones. So Raphael stops a killer just to try to kill him? Slightly later in the original Mirage continuity, as Raphael holds the aforementioned atomic bomb terrorist underwater, he sports a crazed grin, and only stops because Splinter tells him not to kill the man.[10]

Raphael conveys a very different position on being a killer in *Tales of the TMNT* Vol. 2 #69. In the post-apocalyptic future, the adopted daughter of Casey Jones and April O'Neil is a ninja named Shadow. Having seen her deadly future,[11] Raphael is hesitant to train Shadow, despite Casey's begging. "With your martial arts know-how and my street smarts, we'll teach Shadow how to be one major ass-kickin' fighter! She's gonna be a real killer!" Casey beams. "Yeah…" Raphael replies, "that's what I'm afraid of."[12] Conversely, in *Bodycount*[13] – Kevin Eastman and Simon Bisley's ode to action movie director John Woo[14] – Raphael can be seen crashing through a

---

[6] *Teenage Mutant Ninja Turtles* Vol. 1 #12.
[7] Wouldn't see that in the cartoon, would you?
[8] *Raphael: Teenage Mutant Ninja Turtle* Vol. 1 #1, page 9.
[9] Ibid., page 10.
[10] *Teenage Mutant Ninja Turtles* Vol. 1 #12.
[11] Thanks to the help of Renet Tilley, the Timestress, in the same issue.
[12] *Tales of the TMNT* Vol. 2 #69, page 29.
[13] Eastman and Bisley.
[14] Ibid., on the first page of "The Bodycount Gallery: A Look Back."

skylight while firing a handgun, shouting, "Death from above, Johnny Woo Woo! Time to eat some hot lead!!"[15] Later in the publication, he also shoots at people, throws hand grenades, and shouts, *"Man*, I love this gun shit – *Chew bullets*, you *punks... Kill man kill* – It's what they *want*, dude..."[16] In a moment of clarity, however, he laments, *"Guns...* I've seen their beauty and their *ugliness, death!"*[17] Although *Bodycount* is rather set apart from the core TMNT continuity, as a character, Raphael remains idealistically erratic even when we examine him in one publication's story arc at a time. For example, even if we forget *Bodycount,* and only look at the *Teenage Mutant Ninja Turtles* issues from Image Comics, Raph is all over the place. In issue #7, Raphael tells the other Turtles that he has been "tagging along" on Foot Clan missions.[18] In a solo mission, Raphael is poised to complete a Foot Clan-commissioned assassination – but stops, thinking, "Murder, extortion, gambling, vice, drugs... killing him would be doing society a favor. But I can't do it. Because then I'd be just as rotten as him! Him and the entire Foot Clan. Leo was right! They *are* just criminals – and we're not. We've got to draw the line somewhere."[19]

In issue #12, the Foot Clan leaders are angry with Raph for backing out. "What help are *pretend* ninjas who are *afraid to kill*?" one leader demands. "*Afraid*?" Raphael retorts. "Step down here and say that to my face."[20] Is he implying he would skewer the leader on his *sai*, which are ready and drawn during his rebuttal? Ten issues later, Raphael is in a death match with Pimiko, a character Image Comics introduced as the likely daughter of Shredder. In this case, she fights Raphael for leadership of the Foot Clan in New York City, and had already demonstrated her eagerness to kill him. But when Raphael defeats her, he claims, "I play by my own rules. This fight is over. She's disabled and not a threat to me right now. She'd be dead if I wanted – and I *don't*! She isn't my enemy. There is much that I could learn

---

[15] Ibid., page 74.
[16] Ibid., page 76.
[17] Ibid., page 94.
[18] *Teenage Mutant Ninja Turtles* Vol. 3 #7, page 6.
[19] Ibid., page 17.
[20] *Teenage Mutant Ninja Turtles* Vol. 3 #12, page 18.

from her – and vice versa."[21] The Foot leaders tell him to kill her; Raph tells the "bloodthirsty clowns" to go back to Japan.[22]

It's worth noting that the post-apocalyptic Raphael introduced above who wishes to keep Shadow from being a killer is an aged veteran, which could explain a contrast in motives and perspectives thanks to natural character development. We see the same maturation in Leonardo in *Tales of the TMNT* Vol. 2 #6. Here, the Turtles' "great leader"[23] helps widower Cha Ocho, a police officer turned Foot Soldier hell-bent on finding the man who (accidentally) shot his wife and caused her to fall in front of a subway train. When they finally find the killer – now a remorseful bum – Leonardo is outraged to realize that Cha is completely intent on executing him. "There is no honor in killing, Cha," Leonardo says. "*None*. As a warrior who follows the code of *Bushido*, you should know that revenge has no place. There is only *honor*."[24] Cha indignantly asks, "What *the hell* are you talking about? This *is* about honor. Honor of the highest kind."[25]

After momentarily knocking Leonardo away, Cha cuts off the hand of his wife's begging, kneeling killer. When he proceeds to slice his head off, Leonardo seems stunned, and an emotional argument ensues:

> **LEONARDO:** I should have known better than to have helped you. You Foot are all alike. Killers to the core... Do you realize what you've just done? You've just *killed a man*! How does that make you feel?
>
> **CHA:** Pretty damn good actually. And I didn't just kill a man. I just killed the man *that killed my wife*. There's a world of difference. One that you'll never understand.
>
> **LEONARDO:** Perhaps not. But I do know that there is no honor in vengeance. No honor in killing.
>
> **CHA:** Honor? Vengeance? But you and your brothers killed *Oroku Saki* for the sake of your master's vengeance! You even killed him a second time! How can you deny me *my* vengeance?!

---

[21] *Teenage Mutant Ninja Turtles* Vol. 3 #22, page 15.

[22] Ibid.

[23] As Raphael sarcastically addresses him in the 1990 film.

[24] *Tales of the TMNT* Vol. 2 #6, page 17.

[25] Ibid.

LEONARDO: Because. Because I have learned that vengeance sows the seeds of future sorrow.[26]

Leonardo finishes by telling Cha how blind and "warped"[27] his anger has made him, and slashes a "mark of shame"[28] across the latter's eye from his forehead to his cheek.

There were years of publication between the two instances in which the Turtles killed Oroku Saki. Since they made the same choice on separate occasions with a considerable amount of time for reflection and development, we might assume the TMNT were consciously aware of the ramifications – a tangled situation, indeed. So, while it is clear that the four brothers have repeatedly killed, we are left wondering why exactly they do what they do, and why we as readers seem hesitant to label them for what they clearly are. In this case, a survey of the TMNT's historical context might provide a sort of introspection that could explain what we have expected from the Turtles culturally over time, in turn pointing us toward their characterized motivation.

Turtles in Time: The Ingredients of Ooze

A case study of the accused begins in the early 1980s, when TMNT creators Peter Laird and Kevin Eastman drew inspiration from icons of the very publishers that turned them down, such as the Ronin, Daredevil, and the X-Men.[29] While Eastman and Laird have widely noted the visual influence and inspiration[30] they took from comic artist Jack "King" Kirby,[31] to really understand and discuss why the TMNT do what they do, we need to examine the work of another comic book creator in the early 1980s – Frank Miller, often cited as a fundamental influence by Eastman and Laird. In particular, his work on *Daredevil, Ronin,* and *Wolverine* provide preeminent

---

[26] Ibid., pages 20-21.

[27] Ibid., page 21.

[28] Ibid., page 24.

[29] Murray.

[30] Ibid.

[31] Eastman (annotation), *Teenage Mutant Ninja Turtles: The Ultimate Collection, Vol. 3*, pages 42, 196; *Donatello: Teenage Mutant Ninja Turtle* Vol. 1 #1. See the "Turtle Tracks" introduction on the inside cover of the book.

archetypes for the Green Machine, so understanding where and how these eponymous characters touched the TMNT creators can provide clarity in seeking out the Turtles' general motives.

Kevin Eastman offers insights on Miler's influence directly within a commentary on *Teenage Mutant Ninja Turtles* Vol. 1 #17. In this story, Eric Talbot took the reins on a solo project depicting Michelangelo in feudal Japan, very similar in spirit to *Ronin*. Eastman writes:

> with this story, he [Talbot] really fully embraced all the "Ronin-isms" we [Eastman and Laird] both totally dug. To us, Frank Miller was not only one of the most awesome artists out there at the time, but he was also a fellow New Englander (raised in Vermont) so we claimed him as a brother. And, like the rest of the world, we devoured and were inspired by everything he did.[32]

Notably, even the covers of *Ronin* Vol. 1 #1 and *Teenage Mutant Ninja Turtles* Vol. 1 #1 sport uncanny resemblances in their layouts, dark tones, and fonts. And in *Ronin*, we see the tale of an ancient samurai turned ronin (masterless samurai), whose subsequent saga for vengeance across time readily translated into the TMNT stories.

Captured in time by the demon Agat's spell, the Ronin's consciousness manifests in the body of telekinetic Billy Challas. Throughout the six-issue miniseries, the Ronin's intent is to kill the undying demon to avenge his master,[33] a plot we are offered in various TMNT iterations. In the Turtles' first appearance, the Turtles are intent on killing Oroku Saki for murdering Master Splinter's owner (master) Hamato Yoshi,[34] and in the 1990 film, the story is basically the same.[35] Even in the IDW retelling decades later, Yoshi –

---

[32] Kevin Eastman (annotation), *Teenage Mutant Ninja Turtles: The Ultimate Collection, Vol. 3*, page 155.

[33] It's worth noting that the demon's character type appears across the board in the comics we're mentioning. In *Ronin*, the demon is nigh immortal. In Miller's *Daredevil* run we see Kirigi, the literally undying bane and slayer of ninja across centuries, whose apparent resurrections bear noticeable similarity to the various deaths and resurrections of Oroku Saki, the undying Ninja Turtle nemesis. See *Daredevil* Vol. 1 #174-176. And: *Teenage Mutant Ninja Turtles* Vol. 1 #21.

[34] *Teenage Mutant Ninja Turtles* Vol. 1 #1.

[35] In the original comic, Saki killed Yoshi to avenge his older brother, Oroku Nagi, who Yoshi had killed after Nagi attacked Yoshi's lover, Tang Shen.

and his love, Tang Shen – are killed by Saki, and the Turtles, in this version reincarnated from previous lives as the sons of Yoshi, are reborn in the hope of finding Saki.[36]

If the original Turtles were only a take-off on *Ronin*, their role as assassins (killers) would be unquestionable. And yet, where *Ronin* provides a transcendent origin, the way that the Turtles' plot plays out alludes more to Miller's celebrated run as writer and artist on *Daredevil* in the years preceding the initial TMNT appearance. In these issues, Daredevil is plagued by a ninja force called the Hand and trained by his aged mentor, Stick.[37] Miller's work in this volume is also foundational *Daredevil*, in that he is responsible for Stick's first appearance[38] – which is also the first real background readers saw of Daredevil's training – as well as establishing the backstory for Matt Murdock's lover turned ninja assassin, Elektra.[39]

In Daredevil and Elektra we have two very poignant, very different role models for the Turtles. Although Daredevil has ninja-like training, performs like a ninja, and fights off myriad Hand ninja, he is no assassin. Even in Japan, fighting opponents who might prefer a glorious death in battle, the Man Without Fear refuses to kill them, in a story written by Denny O'Neil after Miller's run.[40] Most revelatory is an incident in which Daredevil's murdering nemesis, Bullseye, is lying unconscious on subway tracks after a battle. Daredevil is tempted to leave Bullseye on the tracks as a train approaches. "He'll be killed…" Daredevil thinks. "You deserve to die Bullseye… you'd just kill again… I hate you."[41] When asked on the next page why he pulled him from the tracks, Daredevil explains, "I – I wanted him to die, Nick. I detest what he does… what he is. But I'm not God – I'm not the law – and I'm not a murderer."

After sparing Bullseye's life once, however, a dangling Daredevil lets go of Bullseye's hand in *Daredevil* Vol. 1 #181, allowing him to drop from a

---

[36] *Teenage Mutant Ninja Turtles* Vol. 1 #5 [IDW].
[37] "Teenage Mutant Ninja Turtles #1 First Print."
[38] *Daredevil* Vol. 1 #176.
[39] *Daredevil* Vol. 1 #168.
[40] *Daredevil* Vol. 1 #198.
[41] *Daredevil* Vol. 1 #169, page 21.

power line. While Bullseye is crippled at the issue's end, Daredevil says Bullseye will "kill no one – ever again," before letting him fall.[42] Whether he intended to cripple or kill Bullseye is unclear, but in this decision we see Miller's developing characterization of Daredevil. Perhaps Miller's own conception of the Daredevil character had changed between Matt Murdock's self-reflection that he is "not God" in issue #169[43] and the judicious Daredevil dropping Bullseye in issue #181. Either way, by having Murdock describe his mission as the betterment of society through protecting the law, then acting blatantly outside the law by dropping Bullseye, Miller forced Daredevil out of a static, hollow hero trope and into a dynamic, conflicted character as capable of change on each page as living people are from one moment to the next. Daredevil demonstrates this whimsy, in that while he is willing to sentence Bullseye to paralysis or death, the Devil of Hell's Kitchen continues to retain a deep sanctity for life, which we can see in the "Fog" story written by Denny O'Neil.[44] Here, Daredevil gets an urgent, late-night call for help from his ex-girlfriend, Heather Glenn. After rushing to her apartment, he leaves when he believes she is not in danger. When Heather is believed to have hanged herself following his departure, Daredevil is tormented by the guilt of culpability.

Contrarily, the Elektra character would not likely feel such qualms. In Miller's work, Elektra is an assassin for hire, even to the bidding of Daredevil's archenemy, the Kingpin. Although Elektra and Daredevil were formerly in love, she ensnares him in a trap and collapses a brick wall on him under the Kingpin's commission.[45] While the TMNT also function as assassins in their initial appearance, there is in fact little evidence to view them as such in an ongoing nature, as we shall see. Perhaps they are more like a blend of the two: ninja applying Elektra's methods to Daredevil's mission of bettering society. In this sense, they are also therefore more like

---

[42] Page 35.
[43] *Daredevil* Vol. 1 #169, page 21.
[44] *Daredevil* Vol. 1 #220.
[45] *Daredevil* Vol. 1 #179.

the Ronin – or Wolverine – who both uphold an honor code by killing without mercy or hesitation those deserving of death.

In Wolverine we have a character closer to the Turtles in both form and function than either Daredevil or Elektra. A member of the X-Men touting martial arts training, Wolverine was the star of a 1982 four-issue story by Miller and writer Chris Claremont.[46] "The setting for the story was Japan, where Wolverine was forced to judge himself and his actions against the samurai code of honor," explains comic history author Les Daniels in *Marvel: Five Fabulous Decades of the World's Greatest Comics*.[47] By citing the Bushido code of honor, Miller and Claremont invoked semiotics that had been creeping ubiquitously through Western culture for more than a decade. This particular Wolverine storyline – followed shortly by the birth of the TMNT – came in the middle of a martial arts frenzy erupting from the kung fu movies and television of the 1970s.[48] Eastman and Laird have themselves noted their influence from this very media,[49] and its salience is obvious on the covers of *Iron Fist*, which promised "Kung Fu Action in the Mighty Marvel Manner."[50] Throwing all of these martial arts influences under one umbrella makes it difficult to reconcile what it means to be a Teenage Mutant *Ninja* Turtle. On the one hand, we expect them to be killer assassins – on the other, we expect them to adhere to some sort of martial arts altruism laid out by Daniel-san in *The Karate Kid* (1984),[51] which hit theaters the same year the Turtles first appeared.

Looking at the TMNT as a mirror for Wolverine, however, we have a set of characters who are not normal people, have ninja training, and are forced to wade through a time period that is mismatched for their skill set. While Wolverine has been notoriously lethal throughout his career, Claremont and

---

[46] *Wolverine* Vol. 1 #1-4.
[47] Daniels, page 189.
[48] Carter.
[49] Eastman (annotation), *Teenage Mutant Ninja Turtles: The Ultimate Collection, Vol.1*, page 275.
[50] See for instance: *Iron Fist* Vol. 1 #7.
[51] Who Raphael jokingly alludes to in the short story "Complete Carnage an' Radical" in *Tales of the Teenage Mutant Ninja Turtles* Vol. 1 #5. Later, Casey also shows Raph how Chuck Norris throws a shuriken.

Miller attempted to dissect his psyche to develop him beyond being merely a "berserker."[52] When Wolverine – who often boasts that he *is the best at what he does* – savagely kills a handful of assassins in front of his love, Mariko, he feels humiliated for being so barbaric in front of her, and wrestles with his self-image throughout the rest of the story. Mariko later tells him he has acted with honor. Here, we see a mainstream hero whose lethal actions are justified by a code of honor.

You Dirty Rat...

Even in more recent TMNT issues, the Turtles struggle to reconcile the character and honor we expect from noble samurai into our own gritty, modern world where a ninja's ways seem more practical. The hodgepodge, *Karate Kid* martial arts idealist image persists, but in shades of grey. In one issue from 2010, Michelangelo and Donatello want to see a movie, but have no money. When Michelangelo excitedly finds a wallet with over $1000 in it – enough for the movie and more – he wants to play finders keepers.[53] Donatello rebukes him, saying, "We may have been raised to be assassins, but we weren't raised to be thieves. Give it back."[54] In the amalgamation of their martial arts roots, it seems the Turtles are assassins trying to live up to some code of honor that has no noticeable roots in their history.

Why can the Turtles kill people, but feel bad about taking a guy's wallet? Perhaps it is their very work as assassins that prompts them to in fact preserve life where possible. For instance, at the conclusion of *Teenage Mutant Ninja Turtles* Vol. 1 #12, April asks Donatello why he sounds sad despite having rendered the aforementioned atomic terrorist bomb, in Splinter's words, "relatively harmless."[55] The Turtles' token intellectual gloomily replies:

> Shouldn't I April? A man died yesterday – a sick, deluded, misguided man, yes – but still a living being. I could never agree with his logic or methods... but I *can* sympathize with his most basic aim! After all, in this world

---

[52] From Claremont's introduction to the collected edition of *Wolverine* Vol. 1 #1-4. Also see Daniels, page 189.

[53] *Tales of the TMNT* Vol. 2 #67.

[54] Ibid, page 8.

[55] Page 36.

plagued by terrorism and poised on the brink of nuclear Armageddon, who doesn't want to survive?[56]

Additionally, in stark contrast to what we might expect from hired or vendetta-driven killers, the Turtles in this issue do function more like super-heroes. Years later, the Turtles play cape-and-cowl again in their crossover with Image Comics super-hero Savage Dragon. An interesting counterpoint, Savage Dragon is the light to the TMNT shadow; where the Turtles strike from the darkness, Savage Dragon is an oversized man-dragon police officer operating within the parameters of the law and getting the limelight for his valor. And yet, when the super-powered police officer wants to fly back to Chicago, the Turtles insist that he cannot until they solve a case in which stone gargoyles are being brought to life.[57] This standalone crossover is just as vital to any conversation tracking down TMNT motive as any of their other stories – we cannot accept this more textbook super-hero "do-goodery" as part of their character and at the same time discount Raphael's bloodlust in *Bodycount*. Either both must be reconciled with the general TMNT characterization, or neither should be.

Interestingly, although the Turtles might run around and play super-cop with one of their own, they detest the notion of themselves being "reduced to the neighborhood watch."[58] To the casual shell-head, this detestation might seem confusing, since the Turtles seem to constantly be on patrol. To this the more well-read shell-head could reply that the Turtles don't articulate their actions as *patrols*, but as "training runs,"[59] which again grounds them in their identity as warriors, even if their war is a foggy one. What are they training for, anyway? If they are training to kill the Shredder, that vendetta has been realized. If they are training to take over the Foot Clan, that goal has been within Raphael's grasp.

---

[56] Ibid.
[57] *Savage Dragon/Teenage Mutant Ninja Turtles Crossover* Vol. 1 #1.
[58] *Teenage Mutant Ninja Turtles* Vol. 1 #51, page 24.
[59] *Teenage Mutant Ninja Turtles* Vol. 1 #55, page 12.

F*ck Michael Bay

Even with all of the TMNT reactants in mind – mutant warriors with samurai skills and ethics cast into a martial arts frenzy – readers nevertheless have a schema that provides expectations for what the Turtles fully are: *Teenage, Mutant, Ninja, Turtles*. Examining what this means to readers will focus our understanding of comics as a whole, and likely challenge views of culpability in the real-world justice system. Are there exceptions to this schema? Some readers might challenge the inclusion of *Bodycount* and *Teenage Mutant Ninja Turtles* Vol. 1 #35 (the story in which Splinter tells the TMNT to "rend" and "claw" Shredder) in this examination. These stories, one might argue, are sort of standalone tales created outside of the ongoing TMNT storyline and history, and so cannot be considered part of the normal TMNT canon and character development. While this might be true in terms of plotline, it presents two questions concerning character development: Do fictional characters have a transcendent motive? In other words, must they remain coherent and consistent to a general nature throughout their various permutations? Second, if characters do have a general modus operandi, how do we treat their first appearances? TMNT creators and fans alike seem to think their beloved heroes in a half shell do, in fact, have a general nature. In *Teenage Mutant Ninja Turtles: The Ultimate Visual History*, Peter Laird says, "Frankly... I don't think anyone really 'gets' the Turtles like Kevin and I do."[60] That there *is* something to *get* lends agreement to the notion of a general, transcendent character.

As with anything else, fans of the TMNT are profusely vocal when they feel that something is not true to the Turtles' character, as producer Michael Bay certainly discovered after announcing that the Turtles in his 2014 movie would be from "an alien race."[61] There was enough backlash across fan forums that Bay personally responded to say that the script would be in line with the Turtles *mythology*[62] – despite that some fans

---

[60] Farago, page 142.
[61] Snetiker.
[62] Child.

"pointed out (in the comics) the mutagen which was the catalyst [for the Turtles]... was created at the Techno Cosmic Research Institute (T.C.R.I.), a secret base of operations for an alien race known as the Utroms."[63] On one fan site, the news had fans responding with such comments as:

- TMNT should be mutant Turtles... not some alien species that resemble humanoid Turtles. It's just lame to me how people can't just stick to the source material if they think it's worthy of a film adaption.
- Changing dialogue is one thing... changing origins is another altogether. Bay didn't want to make TMNT, he wanted to make an alien film and TMNT is popular now...
- F*ck Michael Bay and his continual raping of my childhood memories.
- Michael Bay will never be happy until he destroys all of my cherished childhood heroes. This is simply a travesty.[64]

The Guardian wrote that the "furore among fans" led Bay to having "finally admitted defeat over plans to make the stars... 'lovable aliens.'"[65] The filmmakers ultimately pushed back the release date of the movie, though it is uncertain to what degree any script changes might have been to blame.

Most of us likely take it for granted that characters have a general nature to which they adhere. If they did not, what would be the point of Elseworlds style stories like Superman: Red Son, in which we reimagine the Man of Steel raised in the Soviet Union?[66] The details are changed, but the heart is the same, which indicates that tales like Bodycount do have relevance to a commentary on our understanding of TMNT character. Therefore, what role does initial appearance play in developing that character? If this appearance defines the parameters for a character's actions from that point forward, then we know for sure that killing is in the Turtles' nature as assassins. If, however, we decide that first appearances are more arbitrary than instructive, our understanding of the Turtles and our beloved characters in general will fall under completely different parameters.

---

[63] Schaefer. In addition, this source uses the term "mythos."
[64] Lesnick.
[65] Child.
[66] Superman: Red Son #1-3.

The question becomes one of a struggle for authority. Does the first issue – or any *one* issue – need to dictate the general nature of the characters, even if we later round them out with more details? If so, the Turtles are killers and assassins, and should be denounced and locked up as the introduction of this chapter presented. So should Batman by this thinking, since he was throwing people off of rooftops in 1939,[67] despite his reverence for life ever since, and his claims that "... the *real* Batman *never kills.*"[68] This ideal is rampant in mainstream super-hero comics, and certainly within the Batman Family, such as in one particular issue of *Robin* where, in a startling turn while pumped up on the Aramilla super-speed drug, Robin kills Lady Shiva to defend his friend, Dava. During the fight, Robin thinks, "Shiva's a *killer*. Everything she *touches* turns to death. She tried to make *me* a murderer like she is. She almost turned *Batman* into a killer. The anger comes out of me in a scream."[69] Standing in shock of killing her, the Boy Wonder is outraged that he broke his vow to never kill for any reason. We should note here that Robin – a character from within Batman's own universe – does not consider Batman to be a killer. In this sense, we see the canon providing elbow room for characterization over time, rather than a case law in which initial appearances set a precedent.

All Sons Care for Their Fathers

Of course, there are super-heroes for whom killing is part of their identity. The Punisher is a very A-list hero who routinely hands out corporal punishment like it's Halloween candy. Enter the power of semantics. Perhaps we, as readers, treat Frank Castle differently, since he is a sort of *soldier*. Even in the news, we many times condemn a police officer's hasty use of a firearm, but hardly bat an eye at the idea of members of our military doing the same. Yet, in one retelling of the Robin origin story, Batman tells young Dick Grayson to get, "On your *feet*, soldier. You've just

---

[67] *Detective Comics* Vol. 1 #27.
[68] *Batman* Vol. 1 #510, page 3.
[69] *Robin* Vol. 2 #51, page 18.

been *drafted*. Into a *war*."[70] So what is the difference between the *War on Terror* and the *War on Crime*?

Donatello comments quite directly on the matter in an argument with Raphael over the latter's involvement with the Foot Clan. Leonardo exclaims that the Foot are "hired killers." Raphael retorts that they themselves have all killed, and that all other ninja kill. "Yeah," Donatello replies, "in self-defense or in battle! Not for *money* and not in cold blood – ."[71] While Donatello's language casts the Turtles as soldiers (since they are in *battles*, not *fights*), we have to wonder if they are all fighting the same war. With four different Turtles come four personalities.

Where the divergent personalities of the heroes in a half shell might pull them apart, their roles as brothers – and, therefore, as sons – might anchor their paths. We could certainly make the case that as teenagers, the TMNT are Splinter's impressionable pawns. Noted as an X-Men parody, Splinter is nicely typecast as the Charles Xavier of the New York City sewer system. The likeness is particularly apparent in Eastman and Laird's "Pre-Teenage Mutant Ninja Turtles: The Passing."[72] Splinter, deep in meditation, comes into ethereal contact with the dying Gosei Hatsumi, who wishes Splinter's aid in passing on the spirit power of the Gosei samurai clan to his grandson in New York. The preadolescent Turtles then set out on a rescue mission without even being told why. To lead them, Splinter and Gosei Hatsumi pull a *Freaky Friday* (1976, 2003) mind swap. The Turtles are none the wiser, and in the end we see Splinter using his meditation in ways that Professor X would use his mental powers, with the Turtles blindly following Splinter's orders. Even in their debut issue, we see that the Turtles have been training without knowing why, as Splinter's monologue describes the history of Hamato Yoshi and Oroku Saki to both the reader and the Turtles for, apparently, the first time.

If one were trying to deny Turtle culpability on the basis of their being brainwashed to fight Splinter's battles, it certainly doesn't hurt to see how

---

[70] *All Star Batman & Robin, The Boy Wonder* Vol. 1 #1, pages 22-23.
[71] *Teenage Mutant Ninja Turtles* Vol. 3 #7, page 6.
[72] *Teenage Mutant Ninja Turtles* Vol. 1 #9.

lost they seem without their mentor in the "City at War" story arc. Separated from Splinter and hiding out in a water tower, the Turtles struggle to find their bearings in a conversation from *Teenage Mutant Ninja Turtles* Vol. 1 #54:

> **LEONARDO:** This confusion... this lack of clear purpose... it weighs on me... like the cold of the approaching winter, it seeks to paralyze me... and I can't seem to shake it –
>
> **DONATELLO:** Hey, loosen up, Leo... we can't have you quitting on us – !
>
> **LEONARDO:** Not quitting Don... accepting reality. Trying to come to grips with these two facts: We need to do something... and we don't know what the hell we're doing!
>
> **RAPHAEL:** Maybe... maybe if Splinter was here... he'd know...
>
> **LEONARDO:** Maybe... and maybe not. It's time for us to grow up, Raph... time to accept our limitations. And time to see the world for what it is... Time to accept our true place in it. Maybe... time to turn away from all this.
>
> **MICHELANGELO:** Leave? But... but... what about our duty? What about honor?
>
> **LEONARDO:** Honor? Heh... I'm beginning to think there's no place for honor in this world. Greed... hatred... violence... the lust for vengeance... these are the primary motivators.[73]

When asked what his motivation is, Leonardo replies that he doesn't "have a clue."[74]

Leonardo struggles with this lack of purpose again years later. In *Tales of Leonardo: Blind Sight,* a former Foot Ninja uses a toxin to vindictively blind Leo for the Foot Soldier's own loss of sight, accidentally taken by Leonardo in battle years before. Struggling with his situation, Leonardo asks Michelangelo if he ever wondered "... about us? About what our purpose is?" When Michelangelo says he isn't sure, but supposes they are "warriors," Leo agrees. "But what are we fighting against?" Leo asks, continuing, "And... if that's true, then what if I were to take off my swords and cast them off the edge of this roof? Then what would I be? Am I those swords? Am I simply a weapon?"[75]

---

[73] Page 14.
[74] Ibid., page 15.
[75] *Tales of Leonardo: Blind Sight* Vol. 1 #1, page 4.

Left alone after the conversation, Leonardo climbs to the top of a rooftop radio tower. He imagines himself throwing his swords down and falling to the street below. He dreams that his demise causes a chain reaction of events that lead to the police raiding the Turtles' lair and killing Raphael. Although Raphael's last words in the dream are, "Leo... if only you'd been here... this wouldn't have happened,"[76] Leo still releases his swords to fall when his vision ends.[77]

Even more apropos to our point at hand is that much of Leo's strife comes from the idea that he had accidentally killed a bystander after being blinded. As the inside cover introduction of *Tales of Leonardo: Blind Sight* Vol. 1 #2 says, "... left to face the awful knowledge that during their battle he had been tricked by the blind ninja into taking an innocent life, Leo withdrew into himself."[78]

When the other Turtles note, "Leo's whole thing is about control. This blind ninja guy took that away from him,"[79] Master Splinter leaves Leonardo alone in the woods without explaining why. Stumbling in his blindness, Leonardo encounters an unnamed forest creature who claims that he is "... the trees and the rocks. I am the wind and the rain. I am the sun in your face and the thorn in your toe."[80] The creature tells Leo that all creatures bow down to him, and attacks Leonardo, asking, "What are you fighting for, creature? ... I've already beaten you."[81] Leonardo appears transported back to the rooftop where he was blinded, his opponent transformed into the blind Foot Soldier. Telling Leonardo that he allowed himself to be poisoned, the shadow creature claims, "The real poison – that was inside you all along."[82]

In the storyline's conclusion, Leonardo is taken into yet another vision. This time, Leonardo realizes:

---

[76] Ibid, page 26.
[77] *Tales of Leonardo: Blind Sight* Vol. 1 #1.
[78] *Tales of Leonardo: Blind Sight* Vol. 1 #2.
[79] Ibid., page 1.
[80] Ibid., page 17.
[81] Ibid., pages 21-22.
[82] Ibid., page 25.

> I let the swords get to me. Their reason is clear – they take life. My fear
> was that that was my purpose as well. But now I see that although we are
> tied together, the swords are but only a part of me. They do not define
> who I am.[83]

Although this realization provides peace for Leonardo, it really only provides
us parameters for what the TMNT are not. This helps in narrowing down
their purpose, but it is hardly specific.

Bodacious Bad Guys?

In the end, tracking down a single, overriding motive for the TMNT is a
circular endeavor, not because there are four characters, but because they
are four very developed, rounded out, dynamic characters that have had
the richness to endure. As a situated text from the boon of martial arts
media, they are the eclectic product of a cultural misunderstanding, in
which we took all of the action and philosophies we liked best and rolled
them into one. Letting such a concoction ferment over the decades will
naturally lead to a mutation that is much more complicated than its parts.
What's left is to decide how we as readers and citizens think about the sort
of epistemology the Turtles present us with. Ultimately, the way that we
regard general character and how we treat the first appearance of a
character both offer sharp focal points for how we view our own justice
system.

It was suggested above that most people wouldn't like to think of the
Turtles as *killers*, even though they do kill. As we have seen, they do not see
themselves as assassins, though this goes against their nature as ninja. Nor
would we consider Batman a killer, though the first we heard of him, he
was, in fact, *killing bad guys*. Quite helpfully, the question of identity by
means of general tendency versus single action is broached in the "Shades
of Gray" story.[84] Casey Jones accidentally kills a young mugger who attacked
him, and a character named Nobody, personifying the stereotypical caped
hero, happens upon the scene. A police officer by day, Nobody tries to
arrest Casey, calling Casey a "Stone Killer." Michelangelo does not know

---

[83] *Tales of Leonardo: Blind Sight* Vol. 1 #4, page 17.
[84] *Teenage Mutant Ninja Turtles* Vol. 1 #48.

what to do, but Raphael recalls Nobody's own use of lethal force, and insists, "Casey is a lot of things... but, he's no killer."[85] Casey goes on to struggle with emotional turmoil throughout the rest of the story arc, trying to rectify his identity and his actions. Ultimately, Casey's "heavy drinking"[86] following the tragedy leads to a showdown with Donatello, and Jones leaving town.[87] While Raphael is right – Casey has not *murdered* anyone – his actions, and the ongoing tactics the Turtles employ, do bring up some interesting legal questions.

Why might a court look differently at a first-time offender than someone with a history of repeated offenses, while the general public does not seem to do the same? Does the Punisher deserve the death penalty? Is his idealism any less radical than those waging war domestically on innocent victims? Consider even those tried for acts of terrorism – why do we consider them to be killers based on a single act, and not our own beloved heroes? Surely the shocked families of the convicted could argue that they knew their loved ones' general nature just as well as we know a quartet of mutants. There is, of course, the distinction that people detonating explosives aim to kill blindly, while vigilantes at least do so on a case-by-case basis. But if we do base our verdict on the reasons, motives, and schemas for which someone kills, then is the Shredder really any different from the Turtles? To be clear, this is not to say that those guilty of such atrocities are heroic, but rather that our heroes are often crazily guilty.

Consider now a police officer who kills someone *in the heat of the moment*. Why are we so quick to link what might be a unique situation with a growing issue in real life, but tend not to do the same for our favorite super-heroes? What is so different about the Turtles cutting down Foot Soldiers en masse? As we have seen, over and over, single actions alone do not establish the true nature of an individual. Casey Jones killed a boy in a

---

[85] Ibid., pages 23-25.
[86] Kevin Eastman (annotation), *Teenage Mutant Ninja Turtles: The Ultimate Collection, Vol. 4*, page 60.
[87] The inebriation and showdown mentioned above are featured in *Teenage Mutant Ninja Turtles* Vol. 1 #49; Casey does not actually leave until: *Teenage Mutant Ninja Turtles* Vol. 1 #50.

park. How is that different from police using excessive force? Perhaps the element of anonymity and objectification encourages us to disregard the personal lives of the Turtles' victims. We never know the backstories of the people behind the Foot Soldier masks. This is to say nothing of otherworldly creatures like the Triceratons that the Turtles kill.

While this sort of negligence in our thoughts seems relaxing within the bounds of comic book reading, this same generalization has profound implications in real life. Take for instance the widespread killings of black people by police officers in the United States. Whether or not any of the police officers were justified in their actions, it is the perceived cultural *thought* behind those actions – in which black people are perceived as some sort of object or idea, and not as living, human beings first – that has led to rampant killings inciting not only peaceful protests championing the value of life, but also violence, riots, looting, and tweeting around the country. Social media communication in turn also represents a crucial and powerful element of our cultural discourse. Since media, social and otherwise, reinforce a social construction of reality, the proliferation of certain ideas and movements through codes like hashtags creates schemas that can be applied more and more quickly as the crowd sentiment toward a particular issue grows. Whether in real life or on social media, our understandings are based on the terms we use. Thus, how do we reconcile our values in real life, on social media, and within the TMNT?

This is not – in any way or form – meant to exonerate those guilty or vice versa, but to point out the double standards in our cultural psyche and the timelessness of the art at hand. The TMNT stories are worthy of our respect, not as children's fanfare, but as legitimate art that, conceived decades ago, still implores us to call into account our views on human character and nature, justice in society, and the sanctity of life.

Bibliography

All Star Batman & Robin, The Boy Wonder Vol. 1 #1. Frank Miller (writer), Jim Lee (penciler), Scott Williams (inker), Alex Sinclair (colorist), and Jared K. Fletcher (letterer). Eds. Brandon Montclare and Bob Schreck. DC Comics, Sept 2005.

Batman Vol. 1 #510. Doug Moench (writer), Mike Manley (penciler), Joe Rubinstein (inker), Adrienne Roy (colorist), and Ken Bruzenak (letterer). Eds. Jordan B. Gorfinkel and Denny O'Neil. DC Comics, Aug 1994.

Carter, Rebecca. "RZA of the Wu-Tang Clan on Kung Fu, Philosophy and *The Man with the Iron Fists*." *Black Belt*. 6 Apr 2015. http://www.blackbeltmag.com/daily/traditional-martial-arts-training/kung-fu/rza-of-the-wu-tang-clan-on-kung-fu-philosophy-and-the-man-with-the-iron-fists/. [This article was originally published in print form in *Black Belt* Vol. 51, No. 5 [August-September 2013].]

Child, Ben. "Teenage Mutant Ninja Turtles Will Not Be Aliens in New Movie, Says Michael Bay." *The Guardian*. 30 Apr 2013. http://www.theguardian.com/film/2013/apr/30/ninja-turtles-aliens-michael-bay.

Daniels, Les. *Marvel: Five Fabulous Decades of the World's Greatest Comics* [New York: Harry N. Abrams, Inc. Publishers, 1993].

Daredevil Vol. 1 #168. Frank Miller [writer/penciler], Klaus Janson [inker], Doc Martin [colorist], and Joe Rosen [letterer]. Eds. Denny O'Neil and Jim Shooter. Marvel Comics, Jan 1981.

Daredevil Vol. 1 #169. Frank Miller [writer/penciler], Klaus Janson [inker], Glynis Wein [colorist], and Joe Rosen [letterer]. Ed. Denny O'Neil. Marvel Comics, Mar 1981.

Daredevil Vol. 1 #174-176. Frank Miller [writer/penciler], Klaus Janson [inker/colorist], Glynis Wein [colorist], Christie Scheele [colorist], Bob Sharen [colorist], and Joe Rosen [letterer]. Eds. Denny O'Neil and Jim Shooter. Marvel Comics, Sept-Nov 1981.

Daredevil Vol. 1 #179. Frank Miller [writer/penciler], Klaus Janson [penciler/inker/colorist], and Joe Rosen [letterer]. Ed. Denny O'Neil. Marvel Comics, Feb 1982.

Daredevil Vol. 1 #181. Frank Miller [writer/penciler], Klaus Janson [penciler/inker/colorist], and Joe Rosen [letterer]. Ed. Denny O'Neil. Marvel Comics, Apr 1982.

Daredevil Vol. 1 #198. Denny O'Neil [writer], William Johnson [penciler], Danny Bulanadi [inker], Glynis Wein [colorist], and Joe Rosen [letterer]. Ed. Linda Grant. Marvel Comics, Sept 1983.

Daredevil Vol. 1 #220. Denny O'Neil [writer], David Mazzucchelli [penciler/inker], Christie Scheele [colorist], and Joe Rosen [letterer]. Ed. Ralph Macchio. Marvel Comics, July 1985.

Detective Comics Vol. 1 #27. Bill Finger [writer] and Bob Kane [penciler/inker]. Ed. Vincent Sullivan. DC Comics, May 1939.

Donatello: Teenage Mutant Ninja Turtle Vol. 1 #1. Eastman and Laird [writer/penciler/inker], and Steve Lavigne [letterer]. Mirage Studios, May 1986.

Eastman, Kevin [annotation]. *Teenage Mutant Ninja Turtles: The Ultimate Collection, Vol. 1* [San Diego: IDW Publishing, 2012]. Page 275.

Eastman, Kevin [annotation]. *Teenage Mutant Ninja Turtles: The Ultimate Collection, Vol. 3* [San Diego: IDW Publishing, 2012]. Pages 42, 155, 196.

Eastman, Kevin [annotation]. *Teenage Mutant Ninja Turtles: The Ultimate Collection, Vol. 4* [San Diego: IDW Publishing, 2013]. Page 60.

Eastman, Kevin and Simon Bisley. *Bodycount* [Rockville Centre, NY: Metal Mammoth, Inc.: 2008]. Originally published as *Bodycount* Vol. 1 #1-4. Kevin Eastman [writer/penciler], Simon Bisley [penciler/inker], Steve Lavigne [colorist/letterer], Arnold Craig Farley [colorist], and Altered Earth Arts [colorist]. Image Comics, Mar-May, July 1996.

Farago, Andrew. *Teenage Mutant Ninja Turtles: The Ultimate Visual History* [San Rafael, CA: Insight Editions, 2014].

Iron Fist Vol. 1 #7. Chris Claremont (writer), John Byrne (penciler), Frank
   Chiaramonte (inker), Bonnie Wilford (colorist), and Joe Rosen (letterer). Ed.
   Archie Goodwin. Marvel Comics, Sept 1976.

Lesnick, Silas. "Platinum Dunes' Teenage Mutant Ninja Turtles to Feature Alien
   Origin." *SuperHeroHype*. 18 Mar 2012.
   http://www.superherohype.com/news/articles/169903-platinum-dunes-
   teenage-mutant-ninja-Turtles-to-feature-alien-origin.

Murray, Will. *Starlog's 100 Years of Comics*. Ed. David McDonnell (New York:
   Starlog Group, Inc., 1999). ISBN-10: 0-934551-79-0.

Raphael: Teenage Mutant Ninja Turtle Vol. 1 #1. Eastman and Laird. Mirage
   Studios, Apr 1985.

Robin Vol. 2 #51. Chuck Dixon (writer), Staz Johnson (penciler), Stan Woch (inker),
   Adrienne Roy (colorist), and Tim Harkins (letterer). Eds. Jordan B. Gorfinkel
   and Denny O'Neil. DC Comics, Mar 1998.

Ronin Vol. 1 #1. Frank Miller (writer/penciler/inker/editor), Lynn Varley (colorist),
   and John Costanza (letterer). DC Comics, July 1983.

Savage Dragon/Teenage Mutant Ninja Turtles Crossover Vol. 1 #1. Michael
   Dooney (writer/penciler/editor), Erik Larsen (writer), Robert Jones (inker),
   Eric Vincent (colorist), and Mary Kelleher (letterer). Mirage Studios, Sept
   1993.

Schaefer, Sandy. "Michael Bay Responds to 'TMNT' Alien Controversy and Villain
   Rumors." *Screenrant*. 20 Mar 2012. http://screenrant.com/teenage-
   mutan-ninja-Turtles-aliens-michael-bay-sandy-160115/.

Snetiker, Marc. "Michael Bay Says 'Teenage Mutant Ninja Turtles' Are Aliens,
   Reinvents Origin Story." *Entertainment Weekly*. 19 Mar 2012.
   http://www.ew.com/article/2012/03/19/michael-bay-teenage-mutant-
   ninja-turtles-aliens?iid=sr-link4.

Superman: Red Son #1-3. Mark Millar (writer), Dave Johnson (penciler), Kilian
   Plunkett (penciler), Andrew Robinson (inker), Walden Wong (inker), Paul
   Mounts (colorist), and Ken Lopez (letterer). Eds. Mike McAvennie, Tom Palmer
   Jr., and Maureen McTigue. DC Comics, Aug-Oct 2003.

Tales of Leonardo: Blind Sight Vol. 1 #1-2, 4. Jim Lawson (writer/penciler) and
   Erik Swanson (letterer). Ed. Peter Laird. Mirage Studios, June-July, Sept 2006.

Tales of the Teenage Mutant Ninja Turtles Vol. 1 #5. Eastman and Laird (writer),
   Jim Lawson (penciler), Ryan Brown (inker), and Steve Lavigne (letterer).
   Mirage Studios, May 1988.

Tales of the TMNT Vol. 2 #6. Dean Clarrain (writer), Chris Allan (penciler/inker),
   and Eric Talbot (letterer). Eds. Peter Laird and Steve Murphy. Mirage Studios,
   Nov 2004.

Tales of the TMNT Vol. 2 #67. Dan Berger (writer), Dario Brizuela (penciler),
   Michael Dooney (penciler), Andres Ponce (inker), and Eric Talbot (letterer). Ed.
   Peter Laird. Mirage Studios, Feb 2010.

Tales of the TMNT Vol. 2 #69. Dan Berger (writer/penciler/inker) and Eric Talbot
   (letterer). Ed. Peter Laird. Mirage Studios, Apr 2010.

"Teenage Mutant Ninja Turtles #1 First Print." *Recalled Comics*. Accessed 9 Dec
   2013. http:www.recalledcomics.com/TeenageMutantNinjaTurtles1.php.

Teenage Mutant Ninja Turtles Vol. 1 #1. Kevin Eastman and Peter Laird. Mirage
   Studios, May 1984.

Teenage Mutant Ninja Turtles Vol. 1 #9. Eastman and Laird (writer/inker),
   Michael Dooney (penciler/inker), Ryan Brown (inker), Jim Lawson (inker), and
   Steve Lavigne (letterer). Mirage Studios, Sept 1986.

Teenage Mutant Ninja Turtles Vol. 1 #12. Peter Laird (writer/penciler/inker) and Steve Lavigne (letterer). Mirage Studios, Oct 1987.

Teenage Mutant Ninja Turtles Vol. 1 #21. Kevin Eastman (writer/penciler/inker), Peter Laird (writer/penciler), Jim Lawson (penciler), and Steve Lavigne (letterer). Mirage Studios, May 1989.

Teenage Mutant Ninja Turtles Vol. 1 #35. Michael Zulli (writer/penciler/inker) and Rob Caswell (letterer). Mirage Studios, Mar 1991.

Teenage Mutant Ninja Turtles Vol. 1 #48. Eastman and Laird (writer), Jim Lawson (writer/penciler), Keith Aiken (inker), and Mary Kelleher (letterer). Mirage Studios, June 1992.

Teenage Mutant Ninja Turtles Vol. 1 #49. Eastman and Laird (writer), Jim Lawson (writer/penciler), Keith Aiken (inker), Eric Talbot (inker), and Mary Kelleher (letterer). Mirage Studios, July 1992.

Teenage Mutant Ninja Turtles Vol. 1 #50. Eastman and Laird (writer/penciler/inker) and Mary Kelleher (letterer). Mirage Studios, Aug 1992.

Teenage Mutant Ninja Turtles Vol. 1 #51. Eastman and Laird (writer), Jim Lawson (writer/penciler), Keith Aiken (inker), and Mary Kelleher (letterer). Mirage Studios, Sept 1992.

Teenage Mutant Ninja Turtles Vol. 1 #54. Eastman and Laird (writer), Jim Lawson (writer/penciler), Keith Aiken (inker), Charles Yoakum (inker), and Mary Kelleher (letterer). Mirage Studios, Dec 1992.

Teenage Mutant Ninja Turtles Vol. 1 #55. Eastman and Laird (writer), Jim Lawson (writer/penciler), Keith Aiken (inker), Charles Yoakum (inker), and Mary Kelleher (letterer). Mirage Studios, Jan 1993.

Teenage Mutant Ninja Turtles Vol. 1 #1 [IDW]. Kevin Eastman (writer/penciler), Tom Waltz (writer), Dan Duncan (penciler/inker), Ronda Pattison (colorist), and Robbie Robbins (letterer). Eds. Bobby Curnow and Scott Dunbier. IDW Publishing, Aug 2011.

Teenage Mutant Ninja Turtles Vol. 1 #5 [IDW]. Kevin Eastman (writer/penciler), Tom Waltz (writer), Dan Duncan (penciler/inker), Mateus Santolouco (penciler/inker), Ronda Pattison (colorist), and Shawn Lee (letterer). IDW Publishing, Dec 2011.

Teenage Mutant Ninja Turtles Vol. 3 #7. Gary Carlson (writer), Frank Fosco (penciler), Andrew Pepoy (inker), and Chris Eliopoulos (letterer). Ed. Frik Larsen. Image Comics, Feb 1997.

Teenage Mutant Ninja Turtles Vol. 3 #12. Gary Carlson (writer), Frank Fosco (penciler), Mark Heike (inker), and Pat Brosseau (letterer). Ed. Erik Larsen. Image Comics, Dec 1997.

Teenage Mutant Ninja Turtles Vol. 3 #22. Gary Carlson (writer), Frank Fosco (penciler), Mark Heike (inker), and Pat Brosseau (letterer). Ed. Erik Larsen. Image Comics, Jul 1999.

Wolverine Vol. 1 #1-4. Chris Claremont (writer), Frank Miller (penciler), Joe Rubinstein (inker), Glynis Wein (colorist), Lynn Varley (colorist), and Tom Orzechowski (letterer). Eds. Louise Simonson and Jim Shooter. Marvel, Sept-Dec 1982.

Those Blessed and Those Not Blessed: The Moral Positions in Frank Miller's *The Dark Knight Returns*

by Jaime Infante Ramírez

"The knights of infinity are dancers and possess elevation."
— Kierkegaard, *Fear and Trembling*[1]

Long before he embarked in the ideological debacle of his later works in the field of comics and in an odd filmic career, Frank Miller was able to accomplish a number of truly worthy pieces that still stand as remarkable examples of what can be achieved with American super-hero comics. One such piece is *The Dark Knight Returns* (*TDKR*),[2] which usually ranks very high in the unavoidable lists of the best super-hero comic books ever created – and such lists can at least be taken as a measure of durability. It is surprising, though, in the case of this particular comic, because rereading it,

---

[1] Søren Kierkegaard. *Fear and Trembling* (Fig [Publisher], 2012). Kindle edition. Page 448.
[2] Originally published as *Batman: The Dark Knight* Vol. 1 #1-4.

it turns out to be as dated as a period piece. It deals with the rise of Reaganomics, the Cold War hostilities between Russia and the United States, and insecurity on the streets of New York City – disguised as Gotham City – during the late 1970s and early 1980s, which are rather specific references. But it also has the quality of the imperishable. In my opinion, we must look for this property in its inherent thematic structure. In *TDKR*, there is one theme in particular that is the most interesting for us, since the matter at hand is criminal law: the relationship each character keeps with the concept of justice. The positions the characters hold in relation to one another may provide a structure we can analyse. Who stands on what side of the law? And what law is depicted in this comic? These are the questions we must try to answer in this text.

In this comic there are at least six positions surrounding the concept of law, divided into two groups. The first group is comprised of Batman, Superman, and Commissioner Gordon, all of whom are associated in some way with the "good" side of the law. At the other end of the spectrum, we find the unavoidable villains of the piece: the gang of the Mutants, Harvey Dent – formerly known as Two-Face – and the Joker. But this is not a Manichean work, so we must examine what kind of relationship each individual position bears to the others. The famous alignment system of *Dungeons & Dragons*[3] can be extremely useful in this respect. It may seem an unscholarly way of exploring a cast of characters, but it can be useful as a structuralist method. In the alignment system we have a total of nine possible moral positions. In the upper line we have "lawful good," "neutral good," and "chaotic good"; in the middle line, "lawful neutral," "true neutral," and "chaotic neutral"; and in the bottom line, "lawful evil," "neutral evil," and "chaotic evil." We are not going to fill every box in the square, but it will prove useful to see how they fit each of the aforementioned characters from *TDKR*.

---

[3] The game's alignment system first appeared in the original 1974 boxed set published by TSR, Inc.

Lawful Good	Neutral Good	Chaotic Good
Lawful Neutral	True Neutral	Chaotic Neutral
Lawful Evil	Neutral Evil	Chaotic Evil

Representation of the *Dungeons & Dragons* alignment system.

Superman would without doubt stand with "lawful good." He is one of the "good guys," and acts according to the law – the state-sanctioned law. Commissioner Gordon is an example of "neutral good," as he is still on the "good" side of the moral spectrum, and is an agent of law enforcement, but sometimes can use the help of someone on a greyer position, such as Batman. Batman himself is an example of "chaotic good," since he is also, at least for himself and Commissioner Gordon, on the "good" side of the square, but he is not ruled by any state-sanctioned law. However, these positions can be altered depending on whose point of view we adopt. For Superman, Batman could be an example of "chaotic good," but he can also be an example of "true neutral," or even step within "lawful evil," since he guides himself by a code, even if it is the wrong one for Superman. For Batman, Superman is a clear example of "lawful evil," given that Superman is firmly conducted by state-sanctioned law, a law that in *TDKR* is evil for Batman. For Superman, Batman is a vigilante; for Batman, Superman is a fascist. Another super-hero, the one-armed, cranky leftist called Oliver Queen, formerly known as Green Arrow, also shares Batman's position.

On the other hand, if we look at the baddies, the boxes seem much easier to fill. Harvey Dent is an example of "lawful evil," since he has a strict moral code, which is part of his madness. The gang of the Mutants, and its leader – who has always struck me as a truly interesting character, in which *Mad Max* (1979) and *The Road Warrior*'s (1981) influences are patent – as the embodiment of what its members represent, is "neutral evil," since the gang both exhibits a hierarchical organization and topsy-turvy conduct. The Joker, not surprisingly, stands for "chaotic evil." The ease in the definitive filling of these containers should not be unforeseen since we, as readers, tend to take positions of the "good" characters – as appealing as the rogues may seem – because their moral alignments seem to be closer to the ones that we, law-abiding citizens, take in our lives, and otherness is always simpler to pinpoint.

I will now restrict my thoughts to Batman's and Superman's loci regarding the state-regulated system of law. Given the protean nature of super-hero comics, no other incarnations of these two characters should be analysed here. Further, the villains in *TDKR* may be useful to define the heroes' positions, as there are many that Batman must confront as the protagonist of the piece, but they are not the ultimate antagonists of Batman in *TDKR*. They are obstacles he must overcome, conflicts he must solve in order to be able to confront what this comic is truly about – the antinomy between the Caped Crusader and the Man of Tomorrow.

Almost every story has already been told in one way or another. But even if the content or the structure seems similar, what matters is the form in which it is presented each time. The conflict between Batman and Superman in *TDKR* echoes that of Antigone and Creon as depicted by Sophocles,[4] which should not be surprising at all, given Miller's well-known

---

[4] Sophocles.

love for ancient Greece's lore.[5] One, like Antigone, guides himself by his own individual drives, while the other, like Creon, stands side by side with the public rules. That is the basic structure of this dispute. But seeing two people in toga burst into a verbal quarrel is not, tragic as its outcome may be, the same thing as seeing a man in iron armour and an all but almighty alien beating each other to death. And while Sophocles was able to portray Antigone and Creon's conflict in such a way that both parts were relatable, is Miller's rendition similarly unbiased? Perhaps another Greek image can add some epic flavour to this comparison. In Book Four of *TDKR*, Batman and Superman are Achilles and Hector in Homer's *Iliad*,[6] two men who might have in other conditions been friends in arms but who now must fight. Batman is obsessed with death, while Superman only wants to preserve his way of life. Of course, things do not end the same way in Miller's tragic epic.

TDKR has its antecedents, but every story is different since, among other elements, its characters are different. How are the characters in *TDKR*? How do they interact? Incommunicability, or the lack of any proper communication between characters or different systems of belief, is very patent in the case of *TDKR*'s characters, as it is common to most of the works of its author, whose characters are seldom good listeners, but very vigorous – and, indeed, manly – soliloquists. Perhaps this offers some insight into why the systems held by Batman and Superman could never match or come to any agreement within the pages of the book. The most prominent characters are given the opportunity to express their thoughts to the reader, so that he or she is able to understand them, but very little is allocated for them to understand each other. This technique of the misunderstanding amid enclosed consciousnesses is Shakespearean in its nature, and in *TDKR* it reaches its greatest expression during the final clash between Superman and Batman, when each character gives the reader the

---

[5] Most notably in his famous work *300*, but also in other comics, like *Sin City: The Big Fat Kill*, or, prior to both of them, in the creation of his Daredevil character, Elektra.
[6] Homer.

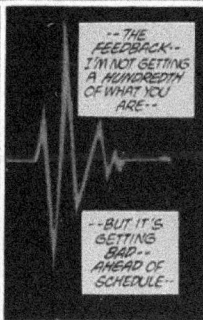

What do Batman and Superman actually hope to achieve in *The Dark Knight Returns*? Art by Frank Miller and Klaus Janson. © DC Comics.

motives of why he is fighting the other, but proves unable to communicate it to the other.

We most prominently read Bruce Wayne's thoughts, whose stream of consciousness leads the reader through the meanders of his mind as he journeys back to the role of Batman and beyond. It is also the case with Carrie Kelley, the new Robin, since her juvenile speech lets us know, during her first appearances, why she considers the life of a masked vigilante. But saying that Miller uses the structure of characters he sets in motion to justify his representation of Batman seems biased and reductionist: back in those days Miller was not the uncompromisingly monochrome author he tends to be nowadays, and he gave Superman some of the best lines, allowing the Last Son of Krypton to validate his position, if only just for the reader. Superman is also given some great internal monologues, as when he stops the flight of a Russian nuclear warhead and must absorb the vital strength of the planet Earth – to which he touchingly refers as "Mother"[7] – in order to live on.

Firstly, we must take a look at the central character of the oeuvre, so that we can understand his ways. Frank Miller in fact seems hardly neutral: he does in fact appear definitely on Batman's side. Greek tragic writers had one device through which they could convey the polis's opinion – authorial voice was an entirely different matter back in classical days, even if tragic writers were celebrities in Athens[8] – the chorus. In *TDKR* we can find something akin: the persistent panels depicting television shows, which represent the diverse views concerning what happens in the story. But can we find Miller's voice in them? Batman's critics are often portrayed as preposterous, but Miller is also able to expose Batman's supporters in the same way. So we must look somewhere else for his authorial position. I think it can be discerned in other characters, most prominently Carrie Kelley, who was created by Miller. Such a fresh character introduced by the author offers the reader a new pair of eyes from where he or she can see the already-established characters, and therefore the decisions Carrie

---

[7] *TDKR* Book Four, page 25.
[8] For more on ancient Greek tragedians, see Flower. See also Hanink.

makes during the story are not neutral. We are encouraged to admire what she admires, and to hate what she hates. With Carrie, we are induced to be afraid of characters like the Mutants or the Joker, but we are also aligned to Batman's side, which means that we are not with Superman. The fact that another, much-beloved character like Green Arrow also stands side by side with Batman similarly exposes that Miller is in no way being neutral – even if, in Green Arrow's case, it serves to deepen the piece, since the mad leftist characterization Miller gives him does not seem to fit with Miller's ideology either, adding to the rich *tableau vivant* of what the Caped Crusader stands against and for.

Let us take a detour so we can see what seems to be underlying Miller's political account of the world, as represented in *TDKR*. It is alarming the far-reaching influence that the Objectivist philosophy, developed and promulgated by the Russian American novelist Ayn Rand, has had upon the American super-hero comic book genre, the most prominent case being that of Steve Ditko, the graphic creator of Spider-Man, whose stern moral convictions seem to have permeated the field.[9] Miller does not seem to be exempt from this influence either. Alan Moore notoriously conceived his own rendition of Ditko's Objectivism, incarnating it in *Watchmen*'s Rorschach,[10] with whom he paid homage to the Question and Mr. A, both created by Ditko and epithets of the latter's ideology. But Moore was on the side of the critic, commenting on comic book history and lore, and thus compromised with no one, putting himself in a position from which he could criticise everyone. In *Watchmen*, Moore sets a distance between the characters and his own personal and authorial position. However, in *TDKR*, Miller does not, at least with Batman. Miller's rendition of Batman – although perhaps not necessarily representing the author wholeheartedly – seems certainly close to Rand's views, and the reader is meant to identify with him.

---

[9] In 2007 Jonathan Ross conducted an interesting television program for BBC Four in which other authors, including Alan Moore, talked about Ditko's Randian thought. See *In Search of Steve Ditko*, directed by Peter Boyd Maclean. BBC Four, 2007.
[10] *Watchmen* #1-12.

Rand believed in the need of "a code of values to guide man's choices and actions – the choices and actions that determine the purpose and the course of his life."[11] She upheld that the first thing to ask is not what should the code of values be, but, "Does man need values at all – and why?" to which she answered, "It is only the concept of 'Life' that makes the concept of 'Value' possible," and, "the fact that a living entity is, determines what it ought to do."[12] Thus, ignoring some centuries of criticism, say, by David Hume, she assumed that an ontology reveals a deontology. For her, the fact that a person *is* necessarily sets in motion all moral machinery. Rand's explanation of values presents the view that an individual's primary moral duty is to achieve his or her own wellbeing, to which his or her moral code is conditioned. This manner of ethical thought is typically called *ethical egoism*, and shares much of the ethics built around economic liberalism. Rand believed that *rational egoism* is the logical consequence of humans following evidence wherever it leads them – the only alternative being that they live without orientation to reality. And for her, of course, such orientation was a must.

As I said earlier, Miller seems to have less of an ironic detachment than Moore did. Politically speaking, in his own way, Miller turns not to the right nor to the left, but to a kind of individualistic anarchism that permeates his works, from *TDKR* to *Sin City*,[13] and from *Elektra: Assassin*[14] to *Martha Washington*.[15] It is even more evident in Miller's continuation of *TDKR*, entitled *The Dark Knight Strikes Again* (*TDKSA*),[16] which received mixed reviews. In that comic, television and the internet are as ubiquitous as the news and talk shows in *TDKR*, and once again evoke the chorus of the Greek tragedies. During one of the many talk shows represented in *TDKSA*, Oliver

---

[11] Rand, page 13.

[12] Ibid., page 18.

[13] A recent edition compiles the entire series: *The Big Damn Sin City* (Milwaukie, OR: Dark Horse Books, 2014).

[14] *Elektra: Assassin* Vol. 1 #1-8.

[15] This comic has had many limited series over the years, the first being *Give Me Liberty* Vol. 1 #1-4.

[16] Originally published as *Batman: The Dark Knight Strikes Again* #1-3.

Queen calls the Question "Mr. Atlas-Shrugged-Is-The-Word-Of-God," to which Question answers, hilariously, "I'm no *Ayn Rander*! She didn't go *nearly* far enough!"[17] This amusing disdain for both sides hints that Miller's ideology radicalized through the years – his own detachment from Rand's Objectivism not only turned into agreement, but went beyond her ideology. With *TDKSA*, one side of Miller's brain knows that Ayn Rand was irredeemably crazy, but the other side shrugs – so to speak – as if saying, "So what?" This anchoretic kind of thought confirms his individualistic anarchism: he does not approve of Ronald Reagan in *TDKR*, nor *Elektra: Assassin's* Democrat Ken Wind. Even further, in *TDKSA*, the President of the United States turns out to be a hologram created by Lex Luthor and Brainiac.

Therefore, in Miller's rendition of the character, Batman personifies Rand's creed, and since we have seen that Batman stands with Miller, we can with confidence assume that Rand's creed is also Miller's locus. Let us develop this point. In *TDKR*, Batman is against the official government, or against any kind of state, but he is not an outright individualist. First of all, he needs others, but others who stand under his command, fundamentalists drunk with the uproar of his personal vision of the world – or, at least, as unobtrusively helpful as Alfred Pennyworth. Secondly, what he does, he does for the people. Even if it is some sort of narcissistic need that encourages his actions, the fact is that he would willingly jeopardise himself to save other people. So here we have found his uniqueness: his vision, his mission, and his self-appointed fate can only be selfish, exclusive, and individual, but its outcome must be altruistic. Ultimately, he is acting as a source of deliverance for Gotham City's social stresses. In this way, he becomes a paradigm of Ayn Rand's idea – working toward his individual vision, he creates, as a collateral effect, an entirely better world. But does he?

The state portrayed in *TDKR* is a satire of 1980s politics. Declaring that Miller portrays the state as incompetent and corrupt may seem like criticism of his work, since it would justify Batman's attitude; also, it would make

---

[17] *TDKSA* #3, page 74.

Superman's position too simple, and, as said before, Miller gives Superman moments of complexity. But this portrayal of the state does not really tilt the scale toward one side or the other in the quality judgement of the book – corrupt states were almost a prerogative in the works produced during the 1980s. In Miller's previous celebrated run on *Daredevil*, he portrayed New York City's criminal underworld – and Wilson Fisk as its personification – as the tragic, true sovereign of the city, with no official state having any authority in its zone of influence, as in *Daredevil* Vol. 1 #170, when the Kingpin returns from his retirement in Japan and begins to reclaim his criminal empire. Alan Moore went for an Orwellian dystopia with *V for Vendetta*,[18] in which a totalitarian and crooked party rules England. But who could blame these authors for having such bleak visions of the future, with Reagan and Thatcher as the governors of their respective countries?

Batman's lack of esteem for the law sanctioned by a government that he considers unethical seems to fit with Rand's ethical considerations. Miller makes sure that the state is unmistakably corrupt – a state so incompetent that it has forsaken Gotham City to its own fate. The fact that the President decides to take action on Gotham's insecure situation only after Batman has already re-entered the scene amazes the reader. The mischief triggered by the gang of the Mutants seems to be acceptable by that society's moral standards, since we are given absolutely no hint of any punitive action on the government's side. But as soon as Batman starts setting things right according to his own, individual moral code and defeats the Mutants' leader, the state feels compelled to act, and thus Superman, as its herald, erupts onto the scene. However, he does not even fight the Mutants, and only deals with the first of their subsequent permutations, Bruno's Nazi-aesthetics-based gang, at the very beginning of Book Three, on his way to speak with Bruce. The people he rescues from the train – and indeed, themselves – on the way there are very much representatives of society as a

---

[18] *V for Vendetta* #1-10.

whole, and to Superman, an afterthought.[19]

The gang of the Mutants and its various permutations are unambiguously threats, but nonetheless acceptable ones that the state is able to define as its absolute otherness, by-products of spiteful youth – and reasonably profitable by-products, too, for a measure of urban insecurity has never shown to be bad for a state in need of some legitimacy. "They are immoral, we are moral," *TDKR*'s state appears to proclaim; the fact that the members of the Mutants are so utterly strangers to any moral code makes the official moral structure so much more appealing and, one could argue, unique. On the other hand, Batman proposes a different moral behaviour, one that seems to be incommunicable and individual, yet even more attractive. And eventually, what is the definitive incarnation of what began as the Mutants? In Book Four they become the Sons of the Batman.

Now we can address the source of Batman's morality. For, as it should be clear, he does have a strict moral code, even if it is not one sanctioned by any state, as Superman's is. As we have seen, Batman is a source of his own form of justice, as well as a criminal. The aforementioned incommunicability of his ways seems like a form of theodicy, or divine justice. He is a Knight of Faith,[20] in Kierkegaard's meaning, bound to his mission. But in his case, the provider of such an assignment is not an external God but his inner Bat. We see this get some attention in every chapter of *TDKR*.

In the first chapter of the book we see the Bat, Bruce Wayne's inner strength, his real source of morality, break through his chest when he feels his great love – Gotham City – under siege by the gang of the Mutants. But he keeps it inside for a while, even as the struggle intensifies. The last link of the chain keeping it confined is broken by the disappearance of Harvey Dent, who had seemingly reformed with the mutilated half of his face repaired with plastic surgery. Bruce Wayne needs to be sure Dent is the good person the former had always believed.

---

[19] Perhaps, after years of saving people from similar situations, it has become an automatism for Superman, a void gesture, lacking real weight or meaning for him. Thus his disdain for humans in *TDKSA*.

[20] Kierkegaard.

But is this Bruce's true impetus? It could also be that he is merely anxious to find an excuse to put on the cape and cowl again. His death drive is so strong – "This would be a *good* death... but not good *enough*"[21] – that he is truly in need of a pretext to be back on the streets, looking for a truly good ending, to die as a knight, to die as a sacrifice to the Bat. Any other death would show a lack of meaning that would be insulting to him. In Miller's version of the myth, Bruce Wayne simply could not die as a rich man, spending his capital during a respectable old age. The car race that opens Book One is one sign, and his recently acquired drinking habit is another; both methods to ease the aching of traumas never resolved. This incapability of fulfilling death is reminiscent of Richard Wagner's character Amfortas, from his opera *Parsifal*, of which Slavoj Žižek writes:

> Amfortas' problem is that as long as his wound bleeds he cannot die, *he cannot die*, he cannot find peace in death; his attendants insist that he must do his duty and perform the Grail's ritual, regardless of his suffering, while he is desperately asking them to have mercy on him and put an end to his suffering by simply killing him.[22]

Dressing and acting as Batman is Bruce's Grail ritual. Accepting the fact that he is just Bruce Wayne, a mortal man, means that he is neglecting something, and that something is placed, in this particular statement of the myth, inside of him, and is very blatant on the page: the massive, ominous Bat, which traces the lines between the real human being and the symbol. The significant part that is lacking, the hidden "truth," is a void embodied for Bruce Wayne by the figure of the Bat. This is the Bat speaking, in Book One:

> The time has *come*. You know it in your *soul*. For *I* am your soul... You cannot *escape* me... You are *puny*, you are *small* – you are *nothing* – a hollow *shell*, a rusty *trap* that *cannot* hold me – Smouldering, I *burn* you – burning you, I *flare*, hot and bright and fierce and *beautiful* – You cannot *stop* me – not with *wine* or *vows* or the weight of *age* – you cannot stop me but still you *try* – Still you *run* – You try to drown me out... But your voice is *weak*...[23]

---

[21] *TDKR* Book One, page 10.
[22] Žižek, page 76.
[23] *TDKR* Book One, pages 25-26.

As we see, what is concealed is even given a voice. If it talks, it can be reasoned with, but this voice, as it says, is stronger than Bruce's, so perhaps no negotiation is likely – much like the other select individualized voices in the book. But is this only a Bat, or is it the symptom of something else? It is an important question, since we are asking about the source of Batman's moral code, and thus, his position in the law system. It is significant to see how, at the very moment that something excruciating is about to hatch out of Bruce's mind, it is the Bat that surfaces, as if to save him from something worse. It is when the blocked memory of the murder of his parents is about to catch him that the figure of the Bat arises, and it does so even at Bruce's old age. Perhaps his death drive was both a fear of the fulfilment of his own ending and a flirtation with his true desire: being again innocent as a child, his eyes immaculate, and reunited with his parents. For this is his real categorical imperative: that no other child ever sees his or her parents murdered before his or her eyes. And that defines Bruce's whole idea of right and wrong, lawful and criminal.

But even if his position is legitimate, how could it possibly be communicable, and thus, made universal, or at least as widespread as any state law can be? If the Bat represents everything we have seen, how could this morality, so deeply based on a single man's struggle between life and death, be valid to any other person, or to a larger community? Assuming that Miller is using Batman as his speaker, what does this say of his position? Is he for this kind of individualistic ethic? In order to understand this, we must scrutinise his rendition of Superman.

Near the beginning of this text, I submitted that Sophocles's *Antigone* works as a structural blueprint for *TDKR*. Actually, that would be its *classic* ancestor, but it also has a *modern* one: John Milton's *Paradise Lost*.[24] According to this comparison, Batman would be the head of the rebel angels, while Superman would be God's enforcer. Milton's example may prove fructiferous, since Miller's support of Batman's revolt may seem as obvious as one might think of Milton's support of Satan in *Paradise Lost* if one were to read *Paradise Lost* out of any context. Milton, however,

---

[24] Milton.

although he prefigured the Romantics, was not at all on Satan's side – at least, not willingly. He was on God's side. What about Miller here? I think he is successful in making Superman an appealing and well-rounded character, with deep motifs we can empathise with. I think he loved the character so much that he needed to portray him as sympathetically as possible, but still needed the agonism between Batman and Superman in order for this comic to work. But this positioning makes things a lot greyer: is Superman truly against Batman's ideas? Are they categorically antagonists? I say this because, as if resenting what he did in *TDKR* by letting Superman be on the side of the corrupt state, Miller twisted things a little bit further in *TDKSA*: he made Superman one of the rebels in Batman's definitive revolt. But that's a whole other story.

Superman in *TDKR* is identified with the state-sanctioned law, the American – the Reagan – way and with life itself. This is the truly postmodern version of the Kryptonian's myth. He remains the ultimate immigrant, the definitive alien, overly identifying with the values and morals of his shelter world. The United States is a nation made by the hands of those who were originally strangers, and thus, Superman is one of its most well-rounded myths. Here he identifies so much with America that we can see him carrying an Eagle, the symbol of the state and of fate. Yet, he has his own ways of reaching the reader. As previously mentioned, Miller is very clever: he gives Superman some of the best lines. And yet, he is even cleverer than that: he makes Superman a powerfully ambivalent character.

In one of the best character-defining moments of the book, Superman reflects as he destroys some U.S.S.R. warplanes:

> The *rest* of us learned to *cope*. The *rest* of us recognized the *danger* – of the endless *envy* of those not *blessed*. *Diana* went back to her *people*. *Hal* went to the *stars*. And I have walked the *razor's edge* for so long... But you, Bruce – you, with your wild *obsession* – [25]

This is Miller at his best. Superman's line "the endless envy of those not blessed" is full of compassion, pride, self-knowledge, and superiority. It defines this character as what he is: a god being sympathetic with his people. He must identify with something like a state, as perhaps any god

---

[25] *TDKR* Book Three, page 15.

would, because otherwise he would become a megalomaniac totalitarian ruler. He tries to help the people not by avoiding the war – he could easily end it by killing all the soldiers and population of the U.S.S.R., but he does not – but by palliating some of its most destructive effects, like stopping nuclear warheads. He is the kind of mother who lets his son fall, but always keeps an eye on him, just in case. But why is he like this in this book?

In *TDKR*, he could do so much more than he does. But that is exactly the point of the character in Miller's hands; he is an all-too-human god. His inner struggle is represented while he fistfights Batman. He could kill Bruce and end the troublesome situation, but he does not. For him, Bruce and the rest of the population – "those not blessed" – are the same: "Bruce – this is *idiotic* – You're just *bone* and *meat* – like all the rest."[26] It is chilling that such a creature could ever exist, and his posture is neither comfortable nor hopeful: it is uneasy.

In this book, Superman is a state-man, but what kind of state does he stand for? His own motives for aligning with the state are, as we have seen, altruist: regardless of his misgivings, he is there for the people. We are uncertain of what he stands for, except life itself. We can say that he is with the state as far as the state works as a way of regulating human society, as a device oriented towards the preservation of human life and welfare. But we cannot address what kind of economical or societal organization he might stand for. He is neither communitarist, nor truly liberal; he could be a benign king, but he is too respectful of the value of the individual to discard democracy.

The whole thing ends, as has been mentioned many times in this text, with a brawl. Superman's position, although aligned with the state, is ambivalent and scary, while Batman's individualism is Randian and isolating. Yet Batman's actions lead to what perhaps defines best Miller's position, while Superman is left with only remorse. Batman inspires other people's spirit of self-sacrifice, their altruism, as seen when Gotham is blanketed with darkness and turmoil after the electromagnetic pulse. But that is exactly Rand's point: *individual* drives lead to *communal* wellbeing.

---

[26] *TDKR* Book Four, page 38.

And yet, in the last three pages of the book, neither Batman's nor Superman's position is the definitive. Bruce Wayne sneers from beyond the grave, while Clark Kent, overhearing his heartbeat and discovering his deception, winks at the reader. How does Miller reconcile with his view? I think the answer was provided with the *Paradise Lost* example: he is on the side of the rebels. He is with Batman, but he needs Superman. Near the beginning of this essay, I used the alignment system of *Dungeons & Dragons* to clarify *TDKR*'s moral topology. I argued that Batman's position can be correlative to Superman's position: Superman's square is clearly "lawful good," while Batman's can be either "chaotic good" or "lawful evil."

So, finally, who stands on either side of the law? What law is ultimately depicted in this comic? I think that what Miller does here – and this is something he deepens in *TDKSA* – is something quite remarkable: he turns Superman and Batman into real super-men, as in Nietzsche's famous notion of the *Übermensch*. I think this is true especially in Batman's case, since he is human. Both characters are *transvaluators*, destructors of what they find decadent, and builders of new moral values. But Batman's reappearance is the spark that sets the whole world on fire. Batman's exceptional individual moral code, based on his trauma and his self-appointed fate, is made universal. Batman and Superman are revolutionaries that turn over the moral structure of the world. They can make decisions that "those not blessed" – us – cannot, which is as paternalistic and elitist as any attitude can be. The moral law depicted in this comic is obsolete: the state can sanction the actions of puny human beings, but not those of the blessed. They stand as a parallel moral structure, one that intends to surpass humanity's laws. Superman only acquiesces with the state because it is a way of restricting himself from his own power, which is a position that Batman would consider rather decadent. What Batman seems to say to Superman is: "Embrace your power. Do not lower yourself to the poor people's level." This may be awe-inspiring, but it is also one of the most dangerous positions one can adopt. I am not sure if, while creating *TDKR*, Miller stood strictly with this idea or thought of it as possible for the real world, but I at least think this is the way his operatic vision works.

In the end, Batman fakes his death, as he surreptitiously plans a definitive clandestine revolution that would, perchance, obliterate the state, substituting it for… a kingdom of the blessed? An anarchist utopia? This is Miller trying to top Milton: his Satan does not end in tears and chagrin, but instead proudly preparing for his last and decisive assault on Heaven. Alas, the fulfilment of such an endeavour is perhaps a letdown, since *TDKSA* is not as good a book as its predecessor, but *TDKR* is nevertheless a worthy effort.

But let us confine ourselves to the ending of *TDKR*. As we bid goodbye to the characters of the book, we are left with a hesitant upbeat: the ending is as sombre as it is anticipative. Batman and Superman's quarrel in Miller's universe is endless. Their relationship, and their fluctuations between the systems of the law, are forever bound into an endless *agon*, perhaps even when aligned. And it is a merry, scary, hysterical one.

Bibliography

300 #1-5. Frank Miller (writer/penciler/inker/letterer) and Lynn Varley (colorist). Ed. Diana Schutz. Dark Horse Comics, May-Sept 1998.

Batman: The Dark Knight Vol. 1 #1-4. Frank Miller (writer/penciler/inker), Klaus Janson (inker), Lynn Varley (colorist), and John Costanza (letterer). Eds. Dick Giordano and Denny O'Neil. DC Comics, Mar-June 1986.

Batman: The Dark Knight Strikes Again #1-3. Frank Miller (writer/penciler/inker), Lynn Varley (colorist), and Todd Klein (letterer). Eds. Bob Schreck and Michael Wright. DC Comics, Dec, Jan, July 2001-2002.

Daredevil Vol. 1 #170. Frank Miller (writer/penciler), Klaus Janson (inker), Glynis Wein (colorist), and Joe Rosen (letterer). Ed. Denny O'Neil. Marvel Comics, May 1981.

Elektra: Assassin Vol. 1 #1-8. Frank Miller (writer), Bill Sienkiewicz (penciler/inker/colorist), James Novak (letterer), and Gaspar Saladino (letterer). Eds. Daniel "D. G." Chichester, Mary Jo Duffy, and Archie Goodwin. Marvel Comics, Aug 1986-Mar 1987.

Flower, Michael Attyah. *The Seer in Ancient Greece* (Berkeley: University of California Press, 2008).

Give Me Liberty Vol. 1 #1-4. Frank Miller (writer), Dave Gibbons (penciler/inker/letterer), and Robin Smith (colorist). Ed. Randy Stradley. Dark Horse Comics, 1990-1991.

Hanink, Johanna. *Lycurgan Athens and the Making of Classical Tragedy* (Cambridge: Cambridge University Press, 2014).

Homer. *The Iliad*, trans. Peter Jones (London: Penguin Classics, 2003).

Kierkegaard, Søren. *Fear and Trembling* (Fig [Publisher], 2012). Kindle edition.

Milton, John. *Paradise Lost* (London: Penguin Classics, 2009).

Rand, Ayn. *The Virtue of Selfishness* (New York: Signet, 1964). Page 13.

Sin City: The Big Fat Kill Vol. 1 #1-5. Frank Miller (writer/penciler/inker/letterer). Ed. Bob Schreck. Dark Horse Comics, Nov 1994-Mar 1995.

Sophocles. *The Three Theban Plays: Antigone; Oedipus the King; Oedipus at Colonus*, trans. Robert Fagles (London: Penguin Classics, 1984).

V for Vendetta #1-10. Alan Moore (writer), David Lloyd (penciler/inker/colorist), Siobhan Dodds (colorist), Steve Whitaker (colorist), Steve Craddock (letterer), Elitta Fell (letterer), and Jenny O'Connor (letterer). Eds. Karen Berger and Art Young. DC Comics, Sept 1988-May 1989.

Watchmen #1-12. Alan Moore (writer), Dave Gibbons (penciler/inker/letterer), and John Higgins (colorist). Ed. Len Wein. DC Comics, Sept 1986-Oct 1987.

Žižek, Slavoj. *The Sublime Object of Ideology* (London: Verso, 1989).

Defenders of the
Status Quo

by Paul Jaissle

Since the dawn of the genre, super-hero stories have focused on issues of crime and punishment. For example, the first appearance of Superman in *Action Comics* Vol. 1 #1 shows the character stopping the execution of a wrongly convicted inmate, rescuing a woman from her abusive husband, and helping expose the crimes of a corrupt politician. These early heroes and stories tapped into a Depression-era populist resentment against a seemingly unfair social structure,[1] and despite the changes in the genre, the intrinsic appeal of super-hero narratives is to see criminals – both small-time and cosmic in scope – held accountable for their actions. Even though super-heroes have evolved from being simple vigilantes fighting crime to grand, almost mythological figures, at their core they still seem to embody a desire for justice to be served, since that's something that rarely seems to

---

[1] "In reality, Superman is fighting the living conditions the Great Depression created. He is fighting the politicians that cannot or will not fix the situation. He is battling the bullies that prey on the weak because they can... In these early stories, Superman is the fictional embodiment of the New Deal spirit, and the Man of Steel fights to restructure society in a more fair and equitable manner." Johnson, page 16.

happen in the real world. However, despite their abilities, super-heroes never seem to stop crime as a whole or adequately address its root causes. Despite the growth of the genre and the characters, super-heroes are still reacting to the symptoms of injustice rather than using their physical or moral strength in a proactive way to enact social change. This raises an important question of just what super-heroes are fighting for: are they defending justice, or just preserving the status quo?

It is important to clearly define what "justice" means in super-hero stories. In these stories, there is a distinction between what is legal and what is "truly just." There is an obvious tension between super-heroes and the criminal justice system: costumed heroes are, despite their good intentions, breaking the law. The conceit, of course, is that super-heroes are operating alongside law enforcement and judicial systems and doing what is best, albeit using legally questionable methods. One reason for this is that in stories featuring super-villains and cosmic beings, the necessity of super-heroes is obvious since the police and military are unable to handle the enormity of the threats. This trope is parodied in the *Batman* television show of the 1960s, in which Commissioner Gordon and Chief O'Hara solemnly agree again and again that the Gotham police force is woefully ill-prepared to capture that week's villain before reluctantly dialing the red "Batphone." Even though they were condoning the work of a vigilante, Gordon and O'Hara recognized that Batman and Robin served the important function of protecting Gotham from the colorful criminals that plagued the city when the police force's best efforts could not. On the other hand, other Batman stories such as *Batman: Year One*[2] portray Gotham's police force as corrupt and vindictive, with Gotham's crime problem rooted in the city's political and social structure. In this case, Batman represents a purer or higher form of justice, one that contrasts the fragile and easily corruptible legal system.

The difference between these types of stories is subtle but important. The Batman of the television show is working alongside the police in order to preserve the established system, one that he implicitly trusts. Miller's

---

[2] Originally published as *Batman* Vol. 1 #404-407.

Batman – which has essentially become the default version of the character for the past 25 years – exists because the system in Gotham is flawed and cannot be trusted. In this case, Batman, along with James Gordon, who is the lone "good" cop in the story, fights against the Establishment in the name of a greater "justice," one that exists beyond the legal definition. Another, more obvious, example is in Miller's *The Dark Knight Returns*,[3] in which Superman is presented as a government stooge dutifully taking orders from the President. Batman in that story is a vigilante seeking to restore order to a chaotic Gotham City. Miller's implication is that law enforcement has been made ineffectual due to liberalism, and only a strong-willed libertarian like Batman can confront the chaos of modern crime. The penultimate confrontation between Batman and Superman drives that contract home with all the subtlety of a super-human fist to the face.

This notion of super-heroes representing a "deeper" conception of justice is an intrinsic part of their appeal. In the real world there are countless examples of guilty defendants avoiding conviction due to technicalities or loopholes in the legal system. Although these frustrating oversights are an unavoidable part of our legal system, criminals can always be held accountable in the realm of fiction. This is the central feature of Daredevil stories: as a lawyer, Matt Murdock understands the flaws of the legal system and works as a vigilante to "correct" them. The Murdock/Daredevil dichotomy serves as a shorthand for the difference between "legal" and "just," and the tension between the two makes the character more complex and interesting than a typical vigilante. For example, the early Daredevil stories were stereotypical super-hero stories that pitted the hero against uninspired gimmicky super-villains like Stilt-Man and Leap-Frog. By contrast, a character like Kingpin makes a much more fitting adversary, since he is a criminal operating with legal impunity. Although Murdock may not be able to convict Wilson Fisk in a court of law, Daredevil can confront Kingpin by circumventing the legal process. Again,

---

[3] Originally published as *Batman: The Dark Knight* Vol. 1 #1-4.

this contradiction is excused since Daredevil is operating in service of "justice" as opposed to mere legality.

Even Batman has tried to walk that narrow line between legal justice and vigilantism. In the 1969 story "One Bullet Too Many!" writer Frank Robbins introduced a "new era" for Batman, who briefly gave up his violent "war" on crime and founded the "Victims, Inc." charity as a way to help those whom the legal system had failed. Bruce Wayne's justification for giving up vigilantism is that the most powerful criminals are the gangsters hiding behind a veil of respectability. As he explains to Alfred, "Today this new breed of rat – uses the modern weapons of... 'phoney respectability' – 'big business fronts' – 'legal cover-ups' – and hides in the fortress towers of Gotham's metropolis!"[4] While Batman might strike fear into the hearts of superstitious, cowardly criminals, the heads of organized crime working behind the scenes go unpunished. However, in this story, Bruce Wayne realizes that he can use the wealth and reputation of the Wayne Foundation to hold those mob bosses accountable and get justice for their victims. Although the purpose of the Victims, Inc. program is to help the victims of gangsterism, the process of uncovering these gangsters and their crimes obviously requires the sort of "extra-legal" detective work in which Batman is trained.

In this story, Bruce Wayne tries to use his wealth and social influence to help people, but he still has to be Batman in order to do so, especially when it turns out that he is the next target of the criminal syndicate he is investigating. Rather than effecting any change in Gotham's social safety net, the program largely existed to provide a setup for a typical Batman story. In the end, the Victims, Inc. program was a short-lived idea that was sort of briefly revisited with Grant Morrison's Batman Inc. concept, which put a distinctively "super-hero" spin on the idea.[5] What the Victims, Inc. story does show is that Batman cannot really operate "above the board," so to speak – he exists to catch the criminals that slip through the net of the legal process.

---

[4] Batman Vol. 1 #217, page 5.
[5] See the series Batman Incorporated.

It seems that the flaws in the legal system necessitate the existence of super-heroes like Daredevil and Batman: if the courts and police force were truly effective, then there would be no need for vigilantism. However, the continuing stories of those characters indicate that their work is, in a sense, futile. Kingpin has the politicians and police in his pocket, and the Penguin will inevitably escape Blackgate prison. This perpetuating cycle is obviously a narrative necessity since there is a continuing demand for stories, but it does raise the question of the characters' effectiveness. No matter how entertaining or engaging the stories are, they seem to establish a status quo of their own that may undermine their conceit: the deeper sort of "justice" the characters are fighting for is elusive and impermanent, and their hard-fought victories are sadly short-lived. Although these stories may hint at the importance of true justice, the fact is that justice cannot be attained through fisticuffs any more than through normal legal means. Despite their best efforts, super-heroes are caught up in their own status quo, the endless battle, the – in the words of Grant Morrison – "unbearable inevitability of Batman and the Joker."[6] Establishing a truly just society or legal system would require breaking this cycle, which is something that super-heroes – despite their great power – seem unable to do. Of course, they may be able to address these issues in individual stories, but these victories are short-lived as the continuing narratives of serialized stories may not allow for effective, productive discourse. Instead, these characters seem to be fighting for order instead of justice: they target the symptoms of social and economic inequality rather than work to address or correct these problems.

This endless cyclical relationship between justice and super-heroes isn't one that creators usually address, although that may not be any fault of their own. It could in fact be part of the genre's conventions that prevent these issues from being adequately explored, since comics and super-hero stories are primarily written as entertainment and not political or social commentary. Although there certainly are examples of social commentary in super-hero stories, the primary focus of the genre is on action, not

---

[6] The title of Chapter 10 in *Batman* Vol. 1 #663, page 21.

discourse. For example, in an interview about his work on Batman, writer Grant Morrison addressed an intrinsic classism of the character:

> Watching a billionaire Batman disarm poorly-trained, poverty-stricken muggers effortlessly or beating up skinny junkies might be fun for a scene or two but does tend to raise thorny issues of class and privilege that the basic adventure hero concept is not necessarily equipped to deal with adequately.[7]

Rather than working to eradicate or address the root causes of crime, Batman is preserving the inequality that perpetuates the vicious cycle of poverty that causes crime: he's fighting for the status quo rather than changing it. Despite Morrison's interest in and concern for the issues of privilege, he points out that super-heroes exist primarily in the action genre, and these issues don't really lend themselves to exciting stories – it's much more entertaining to see Batman throw punches than explore the social and economic causes of crime, especially when doing so might reveal that Batman is as much of the problem as the small-time crooks he is fighting.

The focus on action and entertainment in the super-hero genre dictates how the characters operate in terms of social and political responsibility. Bruce Wayne obviously does donate part of his wealth to help eliminate poverty or boost the education system in Gotham through charities like the Wayne Foundation. However, this philanthropy is rarely the focus of Batman stories. Again, the super-hero genre does not lend itself to stories about community service or wealthy philanthropists, despite the fact that investing in Gotham's social safety net would certainly be more effective in fighting crime than dressing like a bat and punching random criminals in the face. The idea of a billionaire using his wealth to beat up the desperate and less fortunate is indeed incredibly cruel, and the fact that Bruce Wayne is a part of Gotham's elite does make for some uncomfortable subtext. The image of a billionaire beating up pickpockets or drug addicts is troubling, since small crimes such as those are often motivated by poverty and desperation. All of the gadgets and wealth at Batman's disposal are useless

---

[7] "Grant Morrison Tells All About Batman and Robin."

Introduced in *Detective Comics* Vol. 1 #457, Leslie Thompkins actually goes about her crusade against crime far more effectively than Batman. Art by Dick Giordano. © DC Comics.

against the root causes of crime: poverty, disenfranchisement, and systemic discrimination.[8]

Morrison's point is that this inconvenient truth about Batman shows the necessity for the character's "rogues gallery," and the need for entertaining stories is why super-villains have become an integral part of the genre. Seeing Batman take on muggers and drug dealers over and over again would obviously make for some dull comics, which is why even "grittier" stories like Batman: Year One or Batman Begins (2005) focus on larger crime syndicates rather than individual petty criminals. Christopher Nolan's Dark Knight films address this sort of "escalation," as Batman moves from taking on street level crime to fighting bigger, more dangerous foes. Super-villains are not only more interesting than petty criminals, they are also on the same level as Batman: instead of "punching down," Batman can confront these characters as an equal without raising any of the tricky social issues of class or privilege. Super-villains allow Batman to "fight crime" without disrupting the social order of Gotham, and as long as that social order remains, crime will continue.

The discrepancies between Batman's war on the symptoms of crime and its root causes have not gone completely ignored in Batman stories. In the 1970s, Denny O'Neil introduced the character Leslie Thompkins,[9] a renowned surgeon who tends to the impoverished and neglected in Gotham, offering refuge and treatment for drug addicts and victims of violence. Thompkins – who helped raise Bruce Wayne after his parents' murder and knows that he is Batman – categorically disapproves of Batman's methods, and her clinic has a "no violence" policy. Of course, Thompkins cannot dissuade Bruce from his mission, and her presence in the stories seems to be to serve as a conscience of sorts for Batman and the readers: violence may seem inevitable or necessary in Batman's war on crime, but that doesn't mean it is right or even effective. As a doctor, Thompkins offers an alternative to Batman, a way of addressing Gotham's social problems through more compassionate, healing means rather than

---

[8] See this anthology's introduction.
[9] Detective Comics Vol. 1 #457.

simply treating its symptoms. Like all super-heroes, Batman is simply reacting to crime rather than trying to correct its systemic causes. Leslie Thompkins is an example of how to fight crime proactively – by helping treat drug addicts, providing shelter and aid to the impoverished, and stressing nonviolent conflict resolution. However, since there are no comics or movies devoted to Thompkins, it is clear that this type of crime prevention does not make for exciting stories. It also shows that there are no easy fixes to crime. It is far more tempting to believe that a few skilled individuals can use their powers and fists to solve society's ills rather than accepting the shared responsibilities required to curb crime. Perhaps this is why there are so few examples of proactive heroes: they are unglamorous, unexciting reminders of our responsibility – and our failure – to help others.

The concept of a proactive super-hero is interesting since super-hero stories are based on fighting, rather than preventing, crime. Of course, as seen above, the main purpose of super-heroes is to entertain rather than instruct, so seeing comics or movies that explore the concepts of community policing or the systemic causes of crime is unlikely. As mentioned earlier, super-heroes also offer a form of catharsis: we know that the legal system is not always just or fair, and we long to see the truly guilty held accountable. Seeing criminals – especially those who evaded the legal system's punishments – get their comeuppance seems to be far more gratifying and interesting than watching social workers or counselors at work. That does not mean that super-hero comics cannot explore these themes of proactive policing or crime prevention, and there are examples of characters that try to use their powers in proactive ways – to prevent crime by changing society for the better. Of course, these stories are usually critiques of this idea, as well as the super-hero genre itself. It is easy to see why these stories are critical, since they confront the contradiction at the heart of super-hero stories: if super-heroes are so powerful, why don't they use their abilities to make the world a better place? These critiques essentially ask how super-heroes would act if they existed in our real world, where their actions would have tangible consequences, and their very presence would radically upset the current political power structure and social status quo.

One example of this sort of critique is obviously *Watchmen*[10] by Alan Moore and Dave Gibbons. The only super-powered character in that story, Dr. Manhattan, is a super-human with godlike powers – he is virtually invulnerable, able to observe all of time, and has complete control over atoms and subatomic particles – that he tries to use to better humanity. The story implies that Dr. Manhattan initially used his abilities to spur scientific and technological advancement, as well as reduce the casualties in military conflicts: his powers led to the development of alternative energy and electric cars, and his intervention in Vietnam ended the conflict much sooner than in "real life." Despite these positive contributions, Manhattan becomes disillusioned with his place in society and as a part of the political power structure. He functions, for the most part, as a tool of the United States government without any true autonomy. Dr. Manhattan is effectively neutered by the military-industrial complex, which implies that the political structure is more powerful than a godlike super-human. On one hand, the relationship between Dr. Manhattan and the government is based on fear: Manhattan's powers represent a profound threat that needs to be contained and applied in ways that preserve the political status quo. Interestingly, Dr. Manhattan does not really represent a threat to the power structure at all since he shows no interest in challenging it. In the end, his power does not corrupt him, but instead pulls his focus toward the foundations of reality, which make human struggles seem trivial in comparison. Jon Osterman remains a curious scientist devoted to research rather than changing society.

Moore's is obviously a cynical take on the role of super-heroes, even ones as powerful as Dr. Manhattan. The other characters in *Watchmen* are even less effective in changing society for the better since they are caught up in their own personal relationships and neuroses. The obvious exception is Ozymandias, who actually does make a concerted effort to effect change, albeit through morally reprehensible means. In the book's penultimate scene, Ozymandias attempts to force a sort of world peace – or at least a sort of détente – by staging a fake alien invasion. In the process, however,

---

[10] Originally published as *Watchmen* #1-12.

millions of people in New York City are killed. His argument, of course, is that the ends justify the means. However, it is hard to accept that justification, and the ending of the book is unclear about how effective the plan is or how permanent any change might be. Whether or not it is an acceptable trade-off is largely left up to the reader to decide – although the other characters of the book hardly agree with his actions. Ozymandias's choice to sacrifice innocent lives for a supposed greater good is an example of the theme of moral ambiguity that permeates *Watchmen*, since it challenges the established mores of both ethics and super-hero stories. In the end, however, Ozymandias's actions, regardless of their intent, seem to be categorically unacceptable to both the other characters in the book and to the book's readers. Even if he achieves his goal of a peaceful lull in the Cold War and a more compassionate society, he will still be seen as a villain of sorts due to the consequences of his actions. Ozymandias's decision presents a sort of double bind: the ability to effect a shift in the status quo, but murdering thousands of innocent people as a result. It seems to be an unacceptable choice, suggesting that not challenging the status quo might be the only option – or as the film *War Games* (1983) puts it, "The only winning move is not to play."

With *Watchmen*, Moore is obviously critiquing the usefulness of super-heroes by demonstrating that any sort of radical change to the status quo is either impossible or demands too high a cost. In terms of super-heroes and their ability to effect social change, Ozymandias and Dr. Manhattan represent two sides of the coin, so to speak. On one side, Dr. Manhattan is capable of effecting a lasting change for humanity's betterment, but is uninterested in doing so – he possesses the means, but not the vision or desire. Ozymandias, by contrast, is a mortal – albeit very intelligent and rich – human who strives to make the world a more peaceful and just place, but can only achieve that by compromising or breaking established social mores. Interestingly, Alan Moore's take on Marvelman (or Miracleman, as the book was retitled in the United States) is an example of a supremely powerful super-hero who uses his abilities to establish a "utopia" of sorts. Of course, as the old adage about absolute power goes, the utopia he creates is instead a totalitarian society shaped by Marvelman's personal vision rather than a just and egalitarian one. His attempt to create order is corrupted by his own egoism since he is viewed as a god, detached from the moral obligations or expectations of humanity. Even though Marvelman does in fact instigate a massive shift in the status quo to create a more orderly society, his attempt is ultimately flawed and futile. He is wracked with guilt and questions whether or not he has done the right thing. In the end, it is another example of how limited super-heroes are in their ability to effect actual, lasting positive change.[11]

Like Dr. Manhattan and Ozymandias in *Watchmen*, Moore uses Marvelman to critique the super-hero genre, specifically the ineffectiveness of the characters when faced with real-world moral dilemmas. Moreover, these books point out the static nature of the genre itself: super-heroes can never really change, because the genre and the marketplace is rooted in nostalgia. Despite the limitless possibilities of super-heroes and the comic book medium, the same stories seem to be told over and over again, offering only the illusion of change instead of any actual shift in their status quo. That is not to suggest that creators cannot tell interesting or engaging stories, but any radical change in the characters or their motivations can be reversed and rewritten: such is the nature of an ongoing serialized fictional narrative. That said, the fact that these are fictional characters means that they can be adapted to a variety of different stories. More importantly, creators can use the genre's conventions to explore these themes of justice, morality, and power – and while comics have, over the decades, explored these questions, they remain largely unasked in the pop culture adaptations. Even though super-hero stories are now seen as a viable film and television genre, it's somewhat surprising that the meanings of these characters seem to be unaddressed in these new media.

The most obvious example of how a live action film adaptation of a comic book story can miss – or even change – the themes of the original material is Zack Snyder's 2009 version of *Watchmen*. While Alan Moore and Dave Gibbons's original comic is invested in exploring how super-heroes would approach, handle, and even change the seeming moral ambiguity of

---

[11] *Miracleman* Vol. 1 #16.

the real world, Snyder's film merely glosses over these ideas. Instead, the film is more concerned with recreating the look of the comic rather than its tone or subtext. Although capturing the look of Gibbons's art — especially the powers of Dr. Manhattan — is an impressive technical achievement, there is far more to the comic than its visual style. The ominous dread of the Cold War, which served as a backdrop for the interpersonal relationships of the characters, is nowhere to be seen or felt in the big-budget effects of the film. Instead, the film simply presents the events of the story, devoid of any deeper meaning or context. By focusing on the details and events of the story, the larger themes of *Watchmen* are at best ignored, and at worst radically changed. For example, the film's version of the penultimate scene with Ozymandias revealing his plot plays out without any of the moral ambiguity implied in the original text. As portrayed by actor Matthew Goode, Ozymandias is not a character driven by complex, if at times misguided, intentions. Instead, he is presented as a much more generic "super-villain" crafting a vengeful scheme. Part of that is due to the fact that the comic book medium relies much more on a creative engagement with the reader — the dialogue can be interpreted by the way it is read — than films, in which the actors and director have greater control over the way the audience engages with the story. There are also other constraints of the medium: a limited running time meant that large portions of *Watchmen* had to be condensed or cut altogether. The film also had to compete with the expectations of its audience, most of which was presumably unfamiliar with the original story. However, this difference of medium could have been acknowledged and overcome if Snyder had wanted. Instead, the film ends up falling into the sort of stale story Moore's book seems to be critiquing: the characters are simply playing out their traditional hero/villain roles without offering any meaningful change to the status quo. Whereas the book attempts to raise questions for the readers, the film only hints at them, offering the illusion of subtext and little else.

While its failures as an adaptation are obvious, it is also indicative of the problems with super-hero films in general, namely their focus on presenting familiar versions of characters and adapting popular stories rather than exploring some of their underlying complexities. Even when super-hero films attempt to explore more complex themes, they usually do so fleetingly in order to make room for visual action sequences. The most recent example of a super-hero film that flirts with larger ethical and social themes at the time of this writing is *Avengers: Age of Ultron* (2015), the main plot point of which centers around differing theories of peace. In the film, Tony Stark explains his vision for a peaceful, protected society – "I see a suit of armor around the world," he tells Bruce Banner. This may sound like the sort of proactive peacekeeping usually unseen in super-hero stories, but his main focus is obviously to stop the sort of interplanetary invasions the Avengers dealt with in the first film. Of course, a safe society is not necessarily a just or fair one, and peace does not simply mean security, but also equality.

In his attempt to establish this sort of shield, Stark inadvertently creates the film's antagonist Ultron, an artificial intelligence bent on "rebooting" humanity through a cataclysmic event. Whereas Stark sees security and peace as being the same, Ultron believes peace can only be achieved by wiping humanity out and starting with a "clean slate," so to speak. What both views miss, as usual, are the people caught in between these ideological – and physical – battles: the poor and disenfranchised, whose homes are frequently destroyed during the film's epic fight sequences. On one hand, the film does make an effort to show the Avengers protecting and saving people as their cities become rubble, which feels like a rebuttal of similar scenes in *Man of Steel* (2013). However, these people and their fate become little more than a plot point. For example, the film's climactic showdown takes place in the fictional Eastern European country of Sokovia, which has been decimated by years of conflict between more powerful countries. It's a marginal place, whose citizens are essentially powerless and forgotten, including Wanda and Pietro Maximoff, the Scarlet Witch and Quicksilver. Those characters initially join Ultron's cause due to their resentment of Tony Stark, as their parents were killed by weapons bearing the Stark Industries logo. This raises some interesting questions about the nature of international business and conflict, especially regarding those people and places considered "collateral damage." However, once they realize Ultron's plan will lead to extinction, the Maximoffs quickly begin helping the Avengers. Their sudden switch of allegiance is a narrative necessity, but it's also an example how the film glosses over its social and political themes.

In the film's climactic confrontation, Ultron seizes the city of Novi Grad and turns it into a doomsday device by elevating it above the Earth with the intention of smashing it into the surface like an asteroid. Sokovia, which for decades was trapped between ideological adversaries, is once again used like a piece on a chessboard, a pawn in a much larger game. While the Avengers are able to save the citizens of the city, it's hard not to see a deeper sociopolitical problem at play here, when the homes of innocent people are weaponized, used against them, and eventually destroyed. Even if the Avengers save the lives of the citizens, Sokovia itself is still seen as disposable, and its destruction is justified since it helps save the rest of humanity. As in real-world conflicts, the less fortunate are expected to sacrifice in order to preserve order, which is usually conflated with peace and security. In the end, *Avengers: Age of Ultron* may hint at these issues, but as always, the heroes of the film don't actually address the underlying political themes; they simply wait and train for their next major conflict.

By and large, Marvel's films portray large-scale, usually cosmic threats that are beyond the usual scope of legal or ethical justice. However, even films that supposedly feature more "realistic" takes on their characters, such as Christopher Nolan's Dark Knight Trilogy, regularly fall into the same genre conventions without offering much of a critique of the tropes on display. The most obvious example of this within the Dark Knight Trilogy is its conclusion, *The Dark Knight Rises* (2012), which hints at the implicit class issues of Batman, but never really engages with them in a meaningful way. The film, which roughly adapts a number of Batman stories, namely *The Dark Knight Returns*, *Knightfall*,[12] and *No Man's Land*,[13] centers around Bane's attempt to destroy Gotham by bankrupting its wealthy citizens and immobilizing its police force. Bane is presented as a militant revolutionary

---

[12] Originally published across several Batman titles, beginning with a prelude in *Batman* Vol. 1 #491.

[13] Originally told across all Batman titles from late 1998 to early 2000.

who calls for the impoverished and disenfranchised to overthrow the political and economic power structure of the city, represented by Batman/Bruce Wayne. Initially, much of Bane's revolutionary populist rhetoric echoes the concerns and demands of recent grassroots populist movements like Occupy Wall Street: he implores the citizens of Gotham to "take back their city" from those who economically exploit them. In fact, bankrupting Wayne Enterprises is a central part of Bane's plot, both to limit Batman's arsenal and make a political point. Even Selina Kyle recognizes the inequality in Gotham, telling Bruce, "There's a storm coming, Mr. Wayne. You and your friends better batten down the hatches, 'cause when it hits, you're all gonna wonder how you ever thought you could live so large and leave so little for the rest of us." Despite his appeals to economic and social equality, Bane is essentially a terrorist who holds the city captive with the threat of an armed nuclear device, simply following a predictable "super-villain" plot dressed in the guise of a social revolutionary. Batman, on the other hand, is presented as a hero sacrificing himself to save the city, despite the fact that Bruce Wayne is obviously part of the economic elite. In the end, of course, Batman is victorious and Bane's plot to destroy the city is averted. More importantly, order is restored, and the political structure of the city is intact – even if the physical infrastructure has been destroyed.

For a film that incorporates the language of economic liberation and revolution, *The Dark Knight Rises* is largely paying lip service to the issues, avoiding any salient political statements. In an essay about the film, Marxist philosopher Slavoj Žižek points out the film's underlying subtext, especially the contrasting economic ideologies of Batman and Bane. Žižek points out that, "Although viewers know Wayne is mega-rich, they often forget where his wealth comes from: arms manufacturing plus stock-market speculation... Arms dealer and speculator – this is the secret beneath the Batman mask."[14] Batman, in some sense then, is indebted to the military-industrial complex and exploitative capitalism. Even if his war on crime – along with the Wayne Foundation's support for orphans – helps keep order in Gotham, it does not change the overriding power structure. Bane, for all of his revolutionary

---

[14] Žižek.

talk, also reinforces an unjust and oppressive system by enforcing his own using fear and violence.

Although Žižek claims that Bane's actions are born out of a liberating love for the oppressed, the film essentially equates Bane's populist appeals with the totalitarian violence of other so-called "people's revolutions." In the face of this threat to the system, Žižek points out that, "For all the characters, Batman included, morality is relativised and becomes a matter of convenience, something determined by circumstances. It's open class warfare – everything is permitted in defence of the system when we are dealing not just with mad gangsters, but with a popular uprising." This moral relativity allows the filmmakers to sidestep the more politically charged themes of the film. Whatever issues regarding income inequality, military contracts, or exploitative capitalism that the film may hint at are ignored in favor of the familiar super-hero action plot points. In the end, the good guys win and order is preserved. The plights of poverty and social inequality may continue unabated, but they are of no concern to the film's heroes or audience. Instead, they are subsumed into Bruce Wayne's personal story arc. Even the film's conclusion, which hints at the young police officer John Blake taking on the Batman persona, functions as part of Wayne's personal agenda: Bruce has – presumably – left Gotham to find inner peace, while a new Batman is left to deal with the city's problems. Wayne may have left Gotham in capable hands, but the fundamental issues of crime and poverty are left unresolved. Despite its ending, the film only offers the illusion of change, and the status quo remains.

In the end, while the comic books that inspire the films have at least hinted at issues of social and political justice, expecting a nuanced examination of social issues or the nature of justice from big-budget super-hero films may be asking too much. The films' singular focus on action leaves even less room for introspection or debate than in comics. That said, as works of narrative fiction, these films are able to address anything the creators desire, much like the comics on which they are based. Like super-heroes themselves, these stories are capable of anything, even if audience expectations and narrative conventions of the genre seem to suggest otherwise. Using these stories as a way to bring up these important issues is one way to not only create more compelling super-hero stories, but to perhaps also actually lead to some real-world enlightenment and engagement on a wider scale. Even if super-heroes cannot change the status quo, it doesn't mean we shouldn't.

Bibliography

Action Comics Vol. 1 #1. Jerry Siegel (writer) and Joe Shuster (penciler/inker). Ed. Vincent Sullivan. DC Comics, Jun 1938.

Batman Vol. 1 #217. Frank Robbins (writer), Irving Novick (penciler), and Dick Giordano (inker). Ed. Julius Schwartz. DC Comics, Dec 1969.

Batman Vol. 1 #404-407. Frank Miller (writer), David Mazzucchelli (penciler/inker), Richmond Lewis (colorist), and Todd Klein (letterer). Eds. Denny O'Neil and Dick Giordano. DC Comics, Feb-May 1987.

Batman Vol. 1 #491. Doug Moench (writer), Jim Aparo (penciler/inker), Adrienne Roy (colorist), and Richard Starkings (letterer). Eds. Denny O'Neil and Scott Peterson. DC Comics, Apr 1993.

Batman Vol. 1 #663. Grant Morrison (writer), John Van Fleet (penciler/inker/colorist), and Todd Klein (letterer). Eds. Elisabeth V. Gehrlein and Peter J. Tomasi. DC Comics, Apr 2007.

Batman: The Dark Knight Vol. 1 #1-4. Frank Miller (writer/penciler/inker), Klaus Janson (inker), Lynn Varley (colorist), and John Costanza (letterer). Eds. Dick Giordano and Denny O'Neil. DC Comics, Mar-June 1986.

Detective Comics Vol. 1 #457. Denny O'Neil (writer) and Dick Giordano (penciler/inker). Ed. Julius Schwartz. DC Comics, Mar 1976.

"Grant Morrison Tells All About Batman and Robin." Interview by Graeme McMillan. *io9*. 1 July 2009. http://io9.com/5301435/grant-morrison-tells-all-about-batman-and-robin.

Johnson, Jeffrey K. *Super-History: Comic Book Superheroes and American Society, 1938 to the Present* (Jefferson, NC: McFarland & Company, Inc., 2012).

Miracleman Vol. 1 #16. Alan Moore (writer), John T. Totleben (penciler/inker), Thomas Yeates (penciler), Sam Parsons (colorist), and Wayne Truman (letterer). Ed. Letitia Glozer. Eclipse Comics, Dec 1989.

Watchmen #1-12. Alan Moore (writer), Dave Gibbons (penciler/inker/letterer), and John Higgins (colorist). Ed. Len Wein. DC Comics, Sept 1986-Oct 1987.

Žižek, Slavoj. "The Politics of Batman." *New Statesman*. 23 Aug 2012. http://www.newstatesman.com/culture/culture/2012/08/slavoj-%C5%BEi%C5%BEek-politics-batman.

Super-Heroes: Threat or Menace? Why Super-Hero Justice Only Exists in Fiction

by Ross May

You may recognise this article's title from Spider-Man comics. Editor J. Jonah Jameson splashes the headline "Spider-Man: Threat or Menace?" across the banner of *The Daily Bugle*. It is funny and makes Jameson's prejudice clear. Spider-Man must be some kind of danger to the public. The idea that Spider-Man is stopping crimes and saving people as he swings around New York never enters Jameson's mind, or into print in the *Bugle*.

Super-heroes are an appealing fantasy. Imagine filling the boots of Wonder Woman, the tights of Spider-Man, or the rocket pants of Iron Man. Granted super-powers, you could right all the injustices in the world, without politics or bothersome rules getting in the way. Being a wise and good person, you would use your powers responsibly and not abuse your position as a crime-fighter. You are probably already thinking ahead of me, understanding that this chapter will make a case against fascist super-heroes. I want to be clear that I love super-heroes, and do not agree with the principle that they are an inherently fascist notion. Superman protects

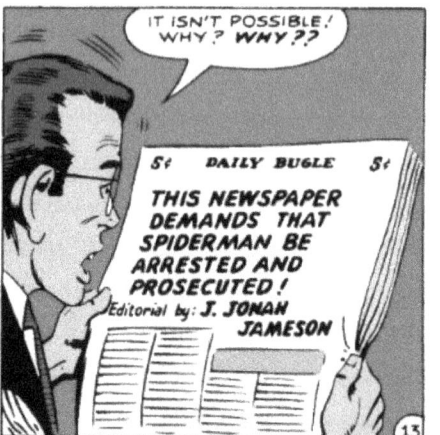

The classic Spider-Man experience would be commonplace among super-heroes in real life. From *The Amazing Spider-Man* Vol. 1 #1 [Mar 1963]. Art by Steve Ditko. © Marvel Comics.

people first and foremost, and apart from some outside canon stories in which he takes that role too far (*Kingdom Come,*[1] *Superman: Red Son*[2]), he is not an oppressive figure. The real case I intend to make is that while super-heroes are a great fictional concept, they cannot exist in the real world. If it were possible to transplant a super-hero out of a comic book or movie and into reality, you would no longer have a super-hero.

Let's Get Real About Batman

Batman is a good starting point in this discussion. Fans have said time and again at comic shops and on the internet, "Batman is a super-hero who *could* exist." This is technically true, but this statement needs to be explored further. We are all familiar with the fact that Batman has no supernatural powers, but roughly speaking, his impressive abilities that still enable him to qualify as a super-hero are:

1. A genius mind with an education in everything related to solving crimes.
2. A body at the peak of human athletic perfection coupled with a mastery of all martial arts.
3. Incredible wealth, granting access to the world's best technology.

Could a person fitting these descriptions exist in the real world? Certainly! I am more unsure if immortal ninja cult leaders and criminals needing refrigerated suits could exist, but we will set Batman's rogues aside for now. When someone says Batman "could" exist, that person means the conditions described above are all possible. What a lot of people do not consider is that Batman *does* have a super-power. It is not unique to him, because it is in fact very common among fictional heroes. Batman is *always right about things that matter*. This is not the same thing as infallibility, which would make his adventures uninteresting very quickly.

Consider how often he prowls the streets of Gotham attacking villains. Have readers ever seen Batman grievously assault someone who did not deserve it? He stops muggings in back alleys, but what if he misinterpreted a situation and it was really just some teenagers joking around with each other? Or when a huge drug shipment is taking place and Batman swoops in

---

[1] *Kingdom Come* #1-4.
[2] *Superman: Red Son* #1-3.

to apprehend gang members, after the dust settles you never see that some of the gang members were undercover federal agents and Batman just derailed plans to bring down mob bosses. And when Batman is playing detective, often with confiscated police evidence, you never see him hand the wrong person over to police. He might be unsure of the culprit for a time – showing his fallibility – but by the end of the story he has correctly surmised the true perpetrator of a crime.

I am not arguing for Batman to make huge, realistic mistakes in his comics. I love a good Batman story, and know it would be unsatisfying to see him bumble his way through a case. But this gets back to Batman being, like almost all super-hero fiction, a power fantasy. In our world the police make mistakes. Even setting aside corrupt, prejudiced, or power-mad cops, good officers will still sometimes arrest the wrong people, or misjudge a situation and use force when none is warranted. Police officers do not live in fictional Gotham City, and do not have the supernatural ability to be right every time it counts.

Yes, Batman could exist in reality, but this "could" is narrowly defined. Batman could successfully fight crime in New York City the same way a person could play the lottery each week – without cheating or having some special insight – and win every time for 50 years straight. You can argue that both are technically possible, but these are both fantastical daydreams, and are not going to happen. They *could* happen, but they *won't*.

Authority

This leads into the other major difference between Batman and real-life defenders of justice. In our world the police are to be held accountable to the public they serve. Other professionals defending life and justice are required to be held accountable as well, including lawyers and judges – not to mention people frequently involved in crises such as firefighters, doctors, and so on. Because society recognises the importance in what these people do, and that it might mean life or death, society insists that they need to be trained and qualified to do their job. Fair enough for Batman, who has spent years of training to become a ninja detective. But police officers can be charged with misconduct for a host of reasons, including excessive force, corruption, or giving false evidence or testimony. Doctors and nurses can be charged with malpractice for gross medical errors. Lawyers can be charged with legal malpractice by not acting in their clients' best interests.

For all of these professions, accountability requires the public knowing their identities. We will set aside the issue of undercover cops and secret agents, as in theory they are held accountable by superiors, who in turn are held accountable by the public. We will also set aside the issue of police who remove their badges to hide their identities, often in violent situations in order not to be charged later. The point of this chapter is not to explore how some people fail to live up to their roles. We know there are good and bad cops, good and bad lawyers, and so on. We also know Batman is a paragon of virtue in fictional Gotham City, so saying he is better than a real dirty cop only proves Batman is a great character to read about.

Take Batman out of Gotham City. If there were a costumed man running around, punching people out, is that the sort of person you would want defending justice? As readers, we know Batman is always right about things that matter. But there is the crux: *we know as readers*. We are real people looking into a fictional world. We give Batman licence to act because we know who Bruce Wayne is, what his training his, and how noble he is. We can even peer into his mind through thought bubbles and narration boxes. A reader can know Batman in a way John Q. Public could never know an actual mysterious masked vigilante.

Many stories have tried to find pretexts validating Bruce Wayne dressing up as Batman. These pretexts are as follows:

1. Gotham's legal system is corrupt

Fixing Gotham's police department and courts is an excellent argument. The notion of having an incognito vigilante be somehow able to repair the law in Gotham is a fantasy in keeping with Batman never making a mistake. Yes, society should not have to be plagued by an unjust system. Even so, that does not mean it is right for someone outside the law to try hammering it back into place. In reality, when cities have become corrupt, citizens band together and demand action. They work in their communities while also appealing to higher levels of government. Though it has been highly fictionalised, consider the task force in Chicago nicknamed "the Untouchables" formed in 1929. President Herbert Hoover knew Chicago had a corruption problem leading back to Al Capone, so U.S. federal agents were charged with stopping his criminal empire and cleaning up the city.

You might be saying, "But what if the Untouchables' leader, Eliot Ness, was also corrupt? Then we would need a Batman!" This is going down a rabbit hole. Yes, there is always the danger of anyone in society, and everyone in any position of power, being corrupt. History is littered with such examples, and taken to the extreme we can point to warlords and dictators who still exist in the world today. But trusting a masked vigilante is not going to be a better option than a known member of the public who is subject to oversight, checks, and balances. Remember that we actually know Batman and his motives, so we put our trust in him as readers and fans.

In real life, any person could be corrupt. Batman, we happen to know, is not. But if Batman started working in New York City, how would we know that he is sincere in his fight against crime, or that he is effective, or that he is as good or better than any New York police officer? The answer is that New Yorkers would not know. The public would not know him, not give him authority, and have no means to arrest or sue him if he assaulted an innocent person. Suppose Batman attacked you one night while you were leaving a bar. Can you charge him with assault? You can try, but the police do not know who he is and cannot bring him in for questioning.

In certain stories, Batman and Robin, while still maintaining secret identities, are held in high esteem by the people of Gotham thanks to their continued good works. Think of the 1966 *Batman* television series. But what happens if other people dressed as the dynamic duo? You could never really trust people dressed as Batman and Robin, because you could never be sure they were the genuine articles. Hopefully you are starting to see problems in Bruce Wayne's whole "masked crime-fighter" idea. The public would have no recourse against a man in a mask, and we could not even trust Batman's track record! Anyone could dress up as Batman, making it impossible to know what good or bad deeds Batman has actually done. There would be multiple problems resulting from Batman's anonymity. Copycat Batmen and Batwomen might bumble around Gotham, getting themselves and others into trouble. Villains could dress as Batman, smearing whatever good reputation the real Batman had built up for himself. Finally, if Batman ever made any sort of mistake himself, he would have an easy method of deniability by claiming it was committed by an inept copycat or a villain. If the real Batman attacked you by accident, he could later argue it was someone simply dressed as himself, because we all know the *real* Batman would never do such a thing. Giving any licence to masked crime-fighting would simply not work.

To get back to the very root of this point, that Gotham is corrupt, consider this – does Batman ever actually fix the broken system of Gotham in any of those stories? You might think Christopher Nolan's Dark Knight movies show Batman cleaning up a corrupt Gotham, but rewatch those movies or, better yet, read a summary of their plots. Batman does not actually clean up the corruption in Gotham! He frightens criminals and inspires the public in *Batman Begins* (2005), but does not solve the corruption problems. It is all very well and good if Batman inspires Gotham's public, but pay attention to how corruption is actually stamped out in the second and third movies. Batman foils some plots, and plays into others in *The Dark Knight* (2008), but actually does nothing to aid the state of Gotham's politics or police department. Jim Gordon is promoted to police commissioner, ostensibly for being a hero in events. The movies actually do away with Gotham's corruption off-screen before *The Dark Knight Rises* (2012) begins. The late Harvey Dent is idolised as a hero, with the public mistakenly believing he died for justice and that Batman is his killer. The police and prosecutors are given new powers that skirt the line of being unconstitutional. These laws might be effective, but not everyone is comfortable with them, including Commissioner Jim Gordon. Meanwhile, a reclusive Bruce Wayne is sad for losing the love of his life, but can be satisfied in knowing that he changed Gotham City for the better. But Batman did not bring about those changes! How could he have known what laws would be enacted based on his actions? Besides, the "Dent Act," which is never fully explained as to what it encompasses, apparently eradicates organised crime, but is meant to honour Dent's sacrifice against the actions of Batman. But Batman is not a member of organised crime, and the Dent Act does nothing to address his presence anyway. This is bordering on a critique of the movies, but the point here is that the films act as if Batman improved the state of Gotham City. All those improvements happen between installments, and thanks to forces Batman has no control over!

In the comic book story *Batman: Year One*,[3] Batman fights street crime and scares the corrupt people in power, but never gains any evidence that can be used in court. In fact, Batman would not be able to make use of evidence for the purposes of gaining convictions, as anything he turns over to police and prosecutors could be argued as being tampered or fraudulent, coming from some guy's bat cave rather than the scene of a crime. Instead, Batman threatens people, who turn over and give testimony against those higher up. In *Year One* a criminal named Skeevers testifies against the corrupt Detective Flass, and Flass later testifies against Commissioner Loeb. Ultimately, any corruption Batman uprooted was through brute force and intimidation, and not through any particular cunning. One can argue he was effective, but he could just as easily have not been. What if these men had been more afraid of their bosses than Batman, or actually had some sense of loyalty? Batman had no real leverage to use against them other than proving he could break into homes and harass people anytime he wanted to.

In the real world, enough guards *would* stop Batman from breaking in, and growling and punching at "a superstitious cowardly lot"[4] might not always get things to go Batman's way. If it did, police who use intimidation and force to get confessions from people – many of whom might be innocent – would always be a good thing, when we know from real life it is neither moral nor routinely effective. A famous American case was the 1989 assault and rape of Trisha Meili in New York's Central Park. Five black and Hispanic teenagers aged 14 to 16 were coerced by police into pleading guilty. They were innocent, and DNA evidence later proved it. The police investigators' actions based on their faulty assumptions and prejudices ruined five young lives, allowed the real perpetrator to go free, and cost

---

[3] Originally published as *Batman* Vol. 1 #404-407.
[4] *Batman* Vol. 1 #1.

taxpayers $41 million in eventual settlements.[5] Batman has never made such a mistake because he is always right when it matters, but real people do not have this power. Threatening people into "telling the truth" frequently does not lead to justice.

The Batman stories I have mentioned are excellent, but they are super-hero stories and power fantasies. They might try to place super-heroes into a "realistic" setting, and attempt to justify Batman's existence, but the ways in which Batman improves Gotham City are still fantastical and beyond his control. Like any good Batman story, he is proven right because he is the protagonist, but when applied to reality, his actions do not justify the existence of unknown vigilantes. What Bruce Wayne should be doing is trying to improve things from within systems themselves, higher up the chain of command such as in elected government, or being a public advocate for social change. In real life Batman would be harming the law, not helping it, and any suggestion of him inspiring the public would probably be in the direction of them becoming vigilantes themselves. After all, he is not directly inspiring anyone to be open and accountable.

2. Batman and his allies are deputies of the Gotham City Police

This idea has been employed to various degrees over the years. On the 1966 *Batman* television show, Batman and Robin are full deputies, a source of good humour for how square they are. In the comic series *Gotham Central*, which tries to keep Batman more mysterious, it is pointed out that the police force's relationship with Batman is murky because they claim to not condone his actions, yet everyone in Gotham has seen the light from the Bat-Signal shining from police headquarters.[6]

Having Batman authorised to act from a law enforcement agency fixes some of the issues being raised. The police are meant to serve the public, so Batman is thus fighting crime at the will of the people. It does, however, again bring up the question of why Batman does not reveal his identity. As covered already, it is very important that members of law enforcement be held accountable, and that requires letting their identities be known. More

---

[5] Nesterak.
[6] As explored in *Gotham Central* Vol. 1 #25.

than one story has involved someone else impersonating Batman, so if you were to charge Batman with assault, he would be able to say, "That was someone else dressed up as me. Or Clayface. I'm pretty sure it was Clayface."

What Batman should do is reveal his identity to Commissioner Gordon, thus allowing himself to be vetted by superiors. He should also remove his mask permanently and make himself known to the public he serves. You might recognise this as "being a police officer."

3. Only Batman can handle the threats Batman faces

Otherwise known as the comic-booky answer. Fine, so the Joker is threatening to poison the entire city, or Ra's al Ghul is set to kill off most of humanity on Earth. We do not really want to refuse help from the one person able to save us, right? On the surface, absolutely agreed. But as always for this chapter, we must take Batman out of Gotham and consider him within our world. Being an exceptional person is not the same thing as being the *only* person capable of stopping super-villains, and in our world there is no single, special person able to stop threats that others cannot. If a bomb is going to go off in a city, who is more likely to stop it: a man working with some kids, a cool car, and an admittedly fancy computer, or a team of hundreds or thousands of people poring over data, interviewing suspects, and sweeping entire city blocks? By sheer force of numbers, police and federal agents can comb over data, people, and ground faster than Batman's small operation could.

Could bureaucracy and oppressive rules from a large organisation hamper the pursuit of justice? Yes. Sometimes guilty parties still walk away from courtrooms as free men and women, found not responsible due to lack of evidence or legal technicalities. It may sound trite, but we must remember that those legal rules exist for a reason, to try to prevent innocent people from receiving punishment from a vengeful public. As for the scenario of Batman trying to stop a super-villainous plot – what we might refer to as a terrorist plot – it is only conceivable as a matter of chance that Batman could succeed where others fail. Bureaucracy is not going to get in the way of the FBI following every lead and covering as much ground as possible looking for a bomb. The only thing they will hopefully not do that Batman routinely does would be to attack and torture suspects until answers are given. This might seem to be the one decent argument for the case of Batman, or any vigilante, working outside the law, but in reality it is rarely effective. Accurate evidence can stop terrorist plots, but torture only compels people, either guilty or innocent, to say anything to make the torture stop. In 2001, Fouad al-Rabiah, father of four, Kuwaiti national, and airline executive, was in Afghanistan doing humanitarian work for refugees. He was arrested by the U.S. military, accused of being a terrorist, and shipped to the Guantanamo Bay detention camp where he was later tortured. His American captors presumably hoped to learn secrets about Al Qaeda's inner workings and plots, so he was isolated, exposed to intense heat and cold, shackled into painful positions, forced into nudity, exposed to loud noise, sexually humiliated, as well as endured emotional torture including having his religion, Islam, ridiculed. Under all this physical and emotional pain, he eventually caved in and falsely admitted to being a terrorist. But Fouad al-Rabiah had a long and public history of working as a humanitarian with no ties to terrorist groups, so his innocence could be easily proven. In 2009 he was finally released.[7]

When Batman dangles people from rooftops, growls at them, or punches them into submission, this is another comic book fantasy. The readers know that Batman has always swooped up a guilty party. But imagine if Batman grabbed an innocent father and threatened to drop him from a four-storey building if he did not tell the Caped Crusader where the Joker toxin was hidden. If *you* were suddenly four storeys up and about to fall, how would you respond? You would profess your Innocence, but what happens if Batman does not like your answer? What do you do or say when Batman will simply *not accept that you are innocent*? Fortunately, Batman never makes such a mistake, but real police, prosecutors, soldiers, and intelligence agents do. Batman's methods of shaking out information is really a very bad example.

And finally, apologies for being repetitive, but if Bruce Wayne really is the world's greatest crime-fighter and preventer of disasters, why does he need to work primarily on his own? What would stop him from joining a

---

[7] Worthington.

branch of the police, military, intelligence agency, or government? And if any of those branches are corrupt (see Pretext 1), why not try to clean it up from either inside, or at a higher branch of oversight? In the real world, Bruce Wayne would be using his talents and resources in the least effective way possible by operating within a small, private group that has no accountability to the public.

Powers and Abilities Far Beyond Those of Mortal Men

Let us move away from Batman, because he invites comparison to real enforcers of the law. Does having super-powers or technology only one person possesses change the situation at all? Superman is the prime example. He is as morally just as Batman, but has super-powers. Superman is classified as a super-hero – the whole concept is named after him, after all – but he functions in several capacities:

1. Disaster Preventer and Rescuer

A bridge is collapsing after an earthquake, so Superman supports it underneath until cars and people are safely off. A flood threatens a small town, so Superman helps evacuate it. One cannot argue against these good deeds, and Superman should absolutely be encouraged to help in disaster situations, whether he does so as unknown protector Superman or super-powered civilian Clark Kent.

There is no issue in this category of what Superman should or should not be allowed to do, but there is the question of whether he is using his powers as effectively as possible. Imagine the small town he is evacuating due to flooding. Nobody will argue against him helping at all, but what if he were always actively working with a disaster relief agency? Instead of evacuating the town, Superman might be advised that the best use of his powers would be to quickly build a dam to slow down flooding, which would give all the residents even more time to evacuate. By working with other agencies, Superman might achieve a better result, and even be able to stop some disasters entirely. For instance, an agency might spot potential for flooding and ask for Superman's assistance *before* a flood bears down on the town. Yes, Superman has helped with infrastructure in his stories, but by working regularly with others, he could maximize his time and efforts.

"But Superman does work with others!" you say. Yes he does, and a story always reaches a satisfactory result when he confers with the Metropolis Police or S.T.A.R. Labs (we will discuss the merits of the Justice League shortly). But Superman still works as a super-hero, showing up when he thinks he is needed and working with others in an ad hoc capacity. What if he worked more closely with some agency and knew when he would be needed? If we go back to the "But what if X agency is corrupt?" argument when discussing Batman, then fine, maybe Superman does not want to work with some high branch of the United States military that he does not trust. But who says he needs to work with a group he does not agree with? What if Superman worked with UNICEF, or Doctors Without Borders, and made a concerted, coordinated effort to improve the lives of people around the world? Superman operates the way he does in fiction because it makes for good drama. In real life, if Superman were to use his "powers and abilities far beyond those of mortal men,"[8] he would be most effective by working with others in a more official capacity.

2. Crime-Fighter

This category is just as problematic as it is for Batman. Suppose Superman finds evidence to a murder, and he hands it to police. That evidence cannot be used in court because Superman is not a police officer. His identity is not even known! Alternatively, in some stories the public believes he has no civilian identity, but he is still then a mysterious person not accountable to the public. Similarly to Batman, consider Superman foiling a robbery. Unless there are other witnesses or camera footage, Superman has no proof he caught people in the act of committing a crime. And if that were to go to trial, the fact that Superman either hides his identity or does not participate as a regular citizen would certainly be brought up, giving the criminals even more leverage to be declared not guilty. Remember the scene in the 1978 film *Superman* where he apprehends a jewel thief dressed in black on the side of a skyscraper? In all likelihood that thief would go free! Superman has no proof of what

---

[8] As the *Adventures of Superman* radio and television programs of the 1940s and 1950s put it.

happened, and the thief can claim that any jewels on him were planted there by Superman.

If Clark Kent, FBI agent or Clark Kent, super-cop were on the scene, there would be no problem, but having Superman operate the way he does, he would likely never get any convictions. Superman is limiting his effectiveness as a crime-fighter by hiding his identity and not actually being a member of a law enforcement agency. Clark Kent does a great amount of good as an ace reporter, but this has only a limited connection to him apprehending criminals. Real-life reporters do not make arrests.

3. Rampage Stopper

Like Category 1, functioning in this capacity is actually fine for Superman. If some monster like Doomsday or Titano is stomping around a city, then certainly Superman should be given licence to stop it. Hopefully he tries to take the battle out of populated areas. It would be pretty terrible if he did not care about collateral damage while battling, say, Zod, right?

Unlike the argument for Batman being the only one capable of stopping certain threats, this could conceivably be true for Superman, assuming giant monsters or comparably powerful villains also existed. Even so, it would always be preferable if there were some regular means of communicating between Superman and public officials. A monster might rise up from the ocean and stomp on a city while Superman is taking a nap at the North Pole. In the same way that emergency services can be called, it would be nice to be able to ask Superman for help when needed beyond his pal Jimmy Olsen owning a special watch. And just like when advising him during a flash flood, it might be helpful if experts could advise Superman in a regular capacity on all of the different kinds of threats he faces, such as how he could take fights out of populated areas.

Nevertheless, while having super-powers increases the number of things a person can physically do, when it comes to issues of morality and justice, nothing much changes. If a person is drowning, and you happen to be a good swimmer, then one hopes you will go and rescue that person. The same goes for Batman, Superman, or any super-hero. Protecting your identity or having super-powers does not change the moral aspect of that situation. But when it comes to issues of justice, of proving someone's guilt and preventing them from doing more harm, a super-hero would be incredibly ineffective. In fact, he or she would often be unwanted, and obstruct justice rather than aid it.

As promised, let us touch on Superman being in the Justice League. Certainly this could increase Superman's effectiveness by coordinating with Wonder Woman, the Flash, and other "super friends." One hero could help with disaster relief in one country while another could fight a monster somewhere else. But would it address Category 2 at all, and help stop criminals? No, because most members of the Justice League also shield their identities from the public. And if it is the Justice League of America, or Justice League International, and has some official ties to either the United States of America or the United Nations, then recall all the problems brought up by having Batman deputised by the Gotham City Police. A Justice League might be helpful in stopping monsters and saving people from earthquakes, but in stopping crimes, in actually seeking justice, a Justice League would be ironically ineffective. Nobody wants to turn away emergency help from people with incredible powers and abilities, but having a group of super-people together does not make it right for them to remain unaccountable to the public.

With Great Power Comes Great Responsibility

Batman and Superman are used extensively in this chapter because they are great examples of two super-heroes with and without powers. Touching on a few more briefly:

The Punisher

What is interesting about the Punisher is that he might be an even more realistic possibility than Batman. Batman needs to work very hard to solve crimes and fight off criminals while not killing them, while all Frank Castle really needs to accomplish his goals are guns and bullets. I bring up the Punisher to further illustrate that super-heroes are a fiction, and the higher authority that gives the Punisher licence to dispense justice is actually us as readers. Punisher stories are structured so that we see villains doing terrible deeds including murder and abuse. When the Punisher inevitably kills these scumbags, readers are satisfied that a brutal form of justice has been served. We almost never see the Punisher shoot a thief who accidentally killed someone after a robbery went bad. The Punisher never kills someone repentant, or about to turn themselves into police. Like Batman, the Punisher also never consistently attacks the wrong people, such as a civilian who just shares the same name as some homicidal maniac, or an innocent person running away from a crime scene in search of police and assistance.

I am not going to argue about the merits of what the Punisher does. There indeed is something appealing about the Punisher blowing away the worst and most violent offenders in society. Philosophical papers have been written on the merits of vigilante justice and revenge. I want to point out that he is power fantasy character much like Batman, only even more violent and brutal. The fictional Punisher always kills people who deserve to die. In real life, there are no such guarantees. The main argument against the death penalty is that occasionally innocent people are going to be found guilty and executed. As appealing as it might be to have one "righteous" man ignore all the rules and kill anybody who he thinks deserves it, what would actually happen is that innocent people would be murdered. The problem of innocent people dying in an effort to weed out the guilty would be compounded by it being through the perceptions and actions of one man. He might frequently rely on partners and informants to assist in his judgement, but it is still his imperfect judgement that is used to kill people. In his first appearance, Punisher tries to kill Spider-Man for mistakenly believing the Web-Slinger is a murderer![9] We already have Punishers living in the real world. The difference is that taken out of fiction, or removed from the fantasies in these people's own minds, they are not any sort of heroes at all. They are just murderers, and not achieving any form of justice.

Iron Man

As I have gone over with Batman and Superman, secret identities stand in the way of fighting crime and gaining convictions. So we will assume here we are dealing with an Iron Man who has let the world know that he is Tony Stark. Much of Iron Man fiction is concerned with Stark's interactions with the military. Should he let his most advanced weapons be used by the United States military, which is charged with protecting the American people? The military has a general mandate from the masses, and is meant

---

[9] *The Amazing Spider-Man* Vol. 1 #129.

to protect them. But it is often criticised by the American and global populace when it comes to specific actions. Consider the Vietnam War, which early Iron Man comics addressed. Superman's morality is simpler, because he never has to consider whether he should share his awesome powers with others. Superman's powers are innate to him. Tony Stark, however, could do all the good he is doing on his own, share it with trusted friends like James Rhodes and Pepper Potts, or share it with the military.

There is no simple answer here. A military, an organisation charged with defending a country's people, should be the one best armed to protect them. But we have seen, both in Iron Man fiction and in real life, that no military cannot be trusted absolutely. The United States has tested biological weapons on its own people, including two pathogens in 1950 over San Francisco that killed at least one man and infected many more.[10] Military dictatorships exist in the world. It is clear that organisations are not always to be trusted, but then again, neither should one person be trusted absolutely. Even if we granted the argument that the military should possess Stark's technology, what right do they have to it if Stark does not want to give it up? Tony Stark says as much at the start of the movie *Iron Man 2* (2010) – his dangerous technology is his property, and by what right should any person or body take it from him?

The *Iron Man* movies explore these themes quite well. The first *Iron Man* (2008) shows Stark living the super-hero power fantasy by single-handedly acting out what we wish the real military would do. He goes into war zones and stops bad guys without any hesitation, argument, or diplomacy. He saves children held at gunpoint, clearly showing who the good and bad guys are. *Iron Man 2* is rather bold because it reevaluates the first movie's theme, and the theme of super-heroes in general. Taking cues from the comic book storyline "Demon in a Bottle,"[11] we are reminded that Stark is human and fallible. He, and we as the audience, might have thought that Iron Man could do things better and achieve a greater peace and justice than the U.S. military could have. But just as the military is made up

---

[10] Crockett.
[11] Originally published as *Iron Man* Vol. 1 #120-128.

of human beings who may be good or bad, right or wrong, Stark is a human who does not understand all situations, who might generally mean well but might also get drunk, and might be in over his head in this super-hero and saving-the-world business. He needs someone else, in this case Lieutenant Colonel James Rhodes, both as a sounding board and another pilot in an armoured suit. *Iron Man 3* (2013) explores, among other things, the United States military's use of drones, and society's increasing use of digital presences instead of physical ones – in essence avatars, which the villains also make use of. Tony Stark is the creator of the Iron Man technology, but is he now really necessary? This still being a super-hero movie, the answer is ultimately that he is. Stark helps save the President, after all. And while there is no great solution to the issue of who should hold power and control, for a super-hero fiction the *Iron Man* movies come to a reasonably mature conclusion that society is made up of people, and people can do good or bad things. Iron Man might be a super-hero and fulfill that fantasy, but to be effective, he needs to work with others, including the military, which is designed to protect the people with checks and balances that Stark is usually not hampered by.

X-Men

The X-Men possess a lot of the traits I have been pointing out that interfere with justice. They have secret identities and, except for a few times working with S.H.I.E.L.D., do not work with law enforcement agencies. What sets them apart from other super-hero teams like the Justice League or the Avengers is that their number one goal as a group is the survival and advancement of mutantkind, and peaceful coexistence with *Homo sapiens*.

If we are talking about the X-Men actively trying to stop crimes like bank robberies or assaults that are not directed towards them, they are going about it the wrong way. If their current mission is in destroying a Sentinel robot factory, or in freeing enslaved mutants, then certainly they are aiding in justice. Unlike other super-hero teams who use their incredible abilities to maintain a peaceful status quo, the X-Men are a revolutionary group. The X-Men invite comparisons to real-world civil rights activists, albeit taken to the super-human extremes and glorified action of comic books. The X-Men are fighting against prejudices and an unjust society. Just as Gandhi and Martin Luther King, Jr. broke laws in unjust societies, the X-Men are less concerned with laws than they are with achieving rights for all mutants. In the graphic novel *X-Men: God Loves, Man Kills*,[12] William Stryker leads the Purifiers, a fanatical hate group that aims to exterminate all mutants. The X-Men seek to expose and stop Stryker and the Purifiers. The X-Men are not sanctioned by the people or the government, and that is partly the point. Stryker is trying to convince the world that mutants deserve to be exterminated, just as Nazis said it was acceptable to exterminate Jews, Romani, homosexuals, and other groups. Ideally, a law enforcement agency should handle the Purifiers' murders of mutant children, but more to the point, in an ideal world injustices such as murders should never happen at all. The story drives home the point that the X-Men are fighting for their basic rights, including the right to live. Dr. Martin Luther King, Jr. and thousands of African Americans had to advocate for their democratic rights through civil disobedience, and in *God Loves, Man Kills*, the X-Men need to demonstrate their rights by rescuing Charles Xavier and exposing Stryker. Sometimes societies are unjust, and action must be taken against society to achieve a better justice. If the X-Men really existed, I am certain there would be things they would do that could be argued against. Their core reason for fighting, however, is something that actually seeks justice, which is more than can be said for many other super-hero groups.

Spider-Man

I started this chapter writing about Spider-Man, so I want to touch on him again. Everything that applies to Superman applies to Spidey as well. If he were swinging around saving people from falling off of buildings in the real world, great! It is when he would try to stop criminals that he would be doing things the wrong way. Spider-Man stories are very smart because there is a realisation of the problems in the ways super-heroes function, giving Peter Parker more and more complications. But because he is a popular character in an ongoing series, ultimately those arguments against super-heroics are thrown away in order to ensure that Spidey keeps having adventures.

---

[12] *Marvel Graphic Novel #5 - X-Men: God Loves, Man Kills.*

In *The Amazing Spider-Man* Vol. 1 #4,[13] we see exactly what I said would happen in real life if a super-hero were to try to make an arrest. Three men are sneaking outside a store, and Spidey webs them up just before they break in. The would-be criminals turn the tables when they start shouting for a police officer, and accuse Spider-Man of assault! Spidey muses that he should have waited until after they broke in, but even if he had, I do not think things would have gone in his favour. Making a citizen's arrest would turn into a matter of credibility, and Spider-Man would not be able to establish any without revealing his identity.

J. Jonah Jameson is wrong about Spider-Man. Old Web-Head really is out to do good. But Jameson's reaction is one we would actually have in the real world. If a masked person were trussing up people around New York, we would all be wondering why the heck he is wearing a mask! Like Batman and Superman, Spider-Man should be working with the police. And like Iron Man, there is a question that perhaps he could also achieve a greater good by sharing his web-shooter technology.

A World Without Super-Heroes

Benjamin Fodor of Seattle, Washington has dressed up in a costume and mask and called himself Phoenix Jones, claiming to be a super-hero. Detective Mark Jamieson of the Seattle Police Department has said, speaking of Phoenix Jones and other would-be super-heroes, "They don't have the training. They don't have the authority."[14] Giving him the benefit of the doubt, I believe Fodor was trying to help people, and multiple reported incidents seem to suggest that. On October 9th, 2011, he was arrested, accused of pepper spraying innocent people.[15] It is one thing for a person to go about his or her daily life and, if seeing someone in distress, to make a judgement about the dangers present and assist others. But Fodor was continually endangering himself, possibly exacerbating some situations, and possibly assaulting other people. He wanted to live up to a fantasy. One can admire his intentions, but if he truly wanted to serve the public, and

---

[13] *The Amazing Spider-Man* Vol. 1 #4.
[14] Ng.
[15] Ibid.

justice, he should have become a police officer. Police officers are trained, can radio for assistance, can acquire evidence and help gain convictions, and are meant to be held to high standards. A "super-hero" is not. And even if a police officer fails in meeting those high standards, as history has often shown, a vigilante, not bound by any standards at all, is not the solution.

Super-heroes are a fictional idea. If a person, super-powered or not, did all the things a fictional super-hero did in our world, they would be a colourful individual, but still not a super-hero. The fiction itself says these characters are super-heroes and justified in what they are doing, while in our world no such higher justification exists. Super-heroes can only serve the cause of justice in their comic, cartoon, and movie worlds. We might feel cheated in our world when justice is not served, when rules and court systems fail victims, but the answer to this problem will never be found in the pages of comic books, as appealing as they might seem.

Bibliography

The Amazing Spider-Man Vol. 1 #4. Stan Lee (writer), Steve Ditko (penciler/inker), and Sam Rosen (letterer). Ed. Stan Lee. Marvel Comics, Sept 1963.

The Amazing Spider-Man Vol. 1 #129. Gerry Conway (writer), Ross Andru (penciler), Frank Giacoia (inker), Dave Hunt (inker/colorist), and John Costanza (letterer). Ed. Roy Thomas. Marvel Comics, Feb 1974.

Batman Vol. 1 #1. Bill Finger (writer), Bob Kane (penciler), and Sheldon Moldoff (inker/letterer). Ed. Whitney Ellsworth. DC Comics, Spring 1940. Page 2.

Batman Vol. 1 #404-407. Frank Miller (writer), David Mazzucchelli (penciler/inker), Richmond Lewis (colorist), and Todd Klein (letterer). Eds. Denny O'Neil and Dick Giordano. DC Comics, Feb-May 1987.

Crockett, Zachary. "How the U.S. Government Tested Biological Warfare on America." *Priceonomics*. Last updated 30 October 2014. http://priceonomics.com/how-the-us-government-tested-biological-warfare-on/.

Gotham Central Vol. 1 #25. Greg Rucka (writer), Michael Lark (penciler), Stefano Gaudiano (inker), Lee Loughridge (colorist), and Clem Robins (letterer). Eds. Nachie Castro and Matt Idelson. DC Comics, Jan 2005.

Iron Man Vol. 1 #120-128. Bob Layton (writer/inker), David Michelinie (writer), Jim Shooter (writer), John Romita Jr. (penciler), Carmine Infantino (penciler), Ben Sean (colorist), Carl Gafford (colorist), Bob Sharen (colorist), John Costanza (letterer), Irving Watanabe (letterer), James Novak (letterer), and Joe Rosen (letterer). Eds. Roger Stern and Jim Shooter. Marvel Comics, Mar-Nov 1979.

Kingdom Come #1-4. Mark Waid (writer), Alex Ross (penciler/inker/colorist), and Todd Klein (letterer). Eds. Bob Kahan, Mike Carlin, Dan Raspler, and Peter J. Tomasi. DC Comics, May-Aug 1996.

Marvel Graphic Novel #5 - X-Men: God Loves, Man Kills. Chris Claremont (writer), Brent Anderson (penciler/inker), Steve Oliff (colorist), and Tom Orzechowski [letterer]. Eds. Danny Fingeroth, Louise Simonson, and Jim Shooter. Marvel Comics, 1982.

Nesterak, Evan. "Coerced to Confess: The Psychology of False Confessions." *The Psych Report.* Last updated 21 Oct 2014. http://thepsychreport.com/conversations/coerced-to-confess-the-psychology-of-false-confessions/.

Ng, Christina. "Citizen Superhero 'Phoenix Jones' Arrested in Seattle." *ABC News.* Last updated 10 Oct 2011. http://abcnews.go.com/US/citizen-superhero-phoenix-jones-arrested-seattle/story?id=14704985&singlePage=true.

Superman: Red Son #1-3. Mark Millar (writer), Dave Johnson (penciler), Kilian Plunkett (penciler), Andrew Robinson (inker), Walden Wong (inker), Paul Mounts (colorist), and Ken Lopez (letterer). Eds. Mike McAvennie, Tom Palmer Jr., and Maureen McTigue. DC Comics, Aug-Oct 2003.

Worthington, Andy. "Judge Confirms Detainee Tortured to Make False Confessions." *Truthout.* Last updated 14 Oct 2009. http://truth-out.org/archive/component/k2/item/86449:judge-confirms-detainee-tortured-to-make-false-confessions.

Four Things You Always Wanted to Know about the Joker (but were too Afraid to Ask)

by Michal Siromski

When Batman made his debut in *Detective Comics* Vol. 1 #27 in May 1939, he immediately won the hearts of readers, and in 1940, a magazine dedicated solely to the Dark Knight followed suit.[1] The creators decided to prepare something special for the premiere issue, and it must be admitted that they succeeded, for its opening story was also the debut of one of the most fascinating comic book super-villains of all time – the Joker. We are now 75 years from that moment, and the Joker's popularity has not only gone unabated, but has actually intensified. The Clown Prince of Crime still raises strong emotions and controversy,[2] and also hides many mysteries concerning his identity, his past, and his motives. Fortunately, some of these

---

[1] *Batman* Vol. 1 #1.

[2] As I write these words, the internet is boiling after the publication of the Joker's first image for the Suicide Squad movie.

puzzles can be contemplated using psychological and criminological theories and knowledge.

Many scholars argue that we can learn a lot about history and social changes from comic books.[3] I would go one step further and say that some quintessential characters like the Joker can also tell us a lot about different psychological phenomena. Psychology can be a very useful tool in the analysis of comic book characters and vice versa. This text is such an attempt to look at the Joker through the prism of psychology and is constructed around four essential questions about him. As I reflect upon each question, I rely on both the content of the comic books in which the Joker is present, and my knowledge of psychology.

1. Is the Joker a Madman?

"Madness" is a colloquial term and does not occur in psychology and psychiatry. Therefore, before we start looking for the answer, we have to transform the question as follows: "Is the Joker mentally ill?"

The answer is seemingly obvious – after all, the Joker laughs hysterically all the time, behaving bizarrely and killing people without any scruples. How *can he not* be mentally ill? However, if we want to use the clinical categories, it turns out that this case is not so simple. The Joker occurs in many comic books, but in none of them, despite all of his time spent in Arkham Asylum, do we find his psychiatric or psychological[4] diagnosis. Of course, this can be justified by the fact that comic book creators are not specialists in the field of psychiatric or psychological diagnosis, but I see a more important reason: we cannot diagnose the Joker with any mental illness, because his profile does not fit into any existing disease.

The only exception where we find a psychological diagnosis is the Grant Morrison and Dave McKean graphic novel *Batman: Arkham Asylum*, in which Dr. Ruth Adams says of the Joker that he "seems to have no control over the sensory information he's receiving from the outside world. He can

---

[3] Witek.

[4] Psychological diagnosis focuses on personality traits and psychological mechanisms of functioning of a diagnosed person, while psychiatric diagnosis focuses on disorders.

only cope with that chaotic barrage of input by going with the flow. *That's why some days he's a mischievous clown, others a psychopathic killer. He has no real personality. He creates himself each day."* She calls this state even "super-sanity" and "a brilliant new modification of human perception."[5]

Morrison's idea of the Joker's "super-sanity" is very exciting and refreshing,[6] but has no confirmation in psychology or in other comics. If Morrison is right and the Joker does not have a permanent personality but instead creates one anew every day, it would mean that it would be impossible to identify any constant personality traits of the Joker. But that is not the case – despite the multiplicity of the Joker's interpretations, we can distinguish five traits present in the vast majority of the Clown Prince of Crime's stories, which I will introduce shortly.

Note that the essence of mental illness is a disorganization of behavior and impaired mental function, which results in the inability to correctly assess reality.[7] The Joker has demonstrated many times a remarkable perspicacity of mind, intelligence, long-term planning, and the ability to manipulate other people and accurately predict their reactions. In other words, if he were mentally ill, he would not be able to prepare and execute any of his deadly plans.

My theory is that the Joker only pretends "madness." In several comic books, at least, we can find evidence supporting this thesis. For example, in the story "Going Sane,"[8] the Joker believes that he has finally managed to kill Batman. Almost at the same moment when this awareness reaches him, the Joker becomes a normal and fully healthy man. He leads a perfectly ordinary life, finds work, and even falls in love and gets married. His murderous instincts suddenly return when the Joker discovers that he made a mistake and Batman is alive.

We must emphasize that spontaneous recovery from mental illness is not possible. Even if we agreed that the episode presented in "Going Sane"

---

[5] *Arkham Asylum: A Serious House on Serious Earth*, page 27.
[6] For further reading on Morrison's concept, see Garneau.
[7] Shahrokh and Hales.
[8] *Batman: Legends of the Dark Knight* Vol. 1 #65-68.

In *Batman: Legends of the Dark Knight* Vol. 1 #68, after struggling for months to live as a normal person named "Joseph," the Joker returns to the surface when he realizes that Batman is still alive. This is not representative of mental illness. Art by Joe Staton and Steve Mitchell. © DC Comics.

is not recovery, but only a remission of disease (the period of chronic disease in which symptoms fade away for a time), it seems unrealistic without proper treatment.[9] The Joker actually has no symptoms here; nightmares cannot be counted, because they would be a perfectly natural reaction to the experiences of the Clown Prince of Crime's "previous life." His spontaneous disappearance of symptoms proves that they never really existed. Further evidence can be found in *Batman: The Killing Joke*. In a remarkable, ambiguous final sequence, the Joker tells Batman a joke about two madmen escaping from an asylum. When one of the "lunatics" is afraid to jump from one roof to another, the second proposes that he turn on his flashlight so that the first can walk safely across the beam. "'Wh-what do you think I *am*?'" the Joker narrates, hardly able to contain his laughter, "'*Crazy*? You'd turn it *off* when I was half way *across*!'"[10]

This joke by the Harlequin of Hate can be interpreted in many different ways, but no matter which one we choose, it is clear that the two madmen represent two great antagonists, and the Joker is well aware that the spinning spiral of confrontation leads nowhere. Would a mentally ill criminal be aware of that? No, it is impossible – one of the characteristics of mental illness is a completely unrealistic perception of reality and the consequent conviction of the patient that he or she is completely healthy while others want to be harmful by telling the patient that he or she is sick.[11] For me, the final scene of *The Killing Joke* is extraordinary, in which, for a moment, the Joker's mask of "madness" falls and we discover that behind it hides a keenly intelligent mind aware of its actions. Does this mean that the Joker is completely normal? Of course not. Let's imagine mental health as a straight line. At one end of the line there are people with perfect mental health; they have a satisfying life and cope well with the problems they encounter. On the opposite end of the line are people with mental illness; they are unable to function independently and are not responsible for their actions

---

[9] Shahrokh and Hales.

[10] *Batman: The Killing Joke*, page 45.

[11] Shahrokh and Hales.

because their perception, thinking, and actions are completely disorganized.[12] Without specialized treatment, only suffering awaits them.

However, it is worth recognizing that between these two extremes there are many intermediate stages. One of them, situated at the center of the line, is a psychological disorder. Such individuals are characterized by certain behavior deviations and problems in internal (emotions) and external (relations with others) functioning. Sometimes we call these people "weird" or "crazy," but in a psychiatric sense they are not sick; their thinking and actions are consistent, and they are fully aware of their actions. Many of them can lead normal lives even without specialized psychological help, but often with mental suffering and feelings of unhappiness.[13] The Joker suffers from such a mental disorder, but the question is which one? If I had to name the most important of the Joker's personality traits, I would point to five: cruelty, high intelligence, the ability to manipulate people, a lack of fear, and narcissism. For psychologists, the diagnosis would be simple: we are dealing with a classic case of psychopathy. Psychopathy is a persistent personality disorder characterized by two elements: an inability to establish deep relationships with others and a deficit of fear.[14]

Wait a minute, you might say. Is not psychopathy a mental illness? In truth, the word itself creates confusion ("psyche" and "pathos" both come from Greek, for the soul or mind, and suffering, respectively). However, psychopaths are not mentally ill, because they do not lose touch with reality. Rather, their behavior is consistent, planned, and calculating. A psychopath, in contrast to a person with a mental illness, knows exactly what he or she is doing, which is why psychopathic murderers end up in prison or executed and not in a psychiatric hospital,[15] and in common usage, the term "psychopath" is often synonymous with insane criminals – murderers characterized by "madness." But psychopathy is also not synonymous with murderous deeds. Only a small percentage of psychopaths commit crimes, and only a small percentage of murderers

---

[12] Ibid.
[13] Meyer.
[14] Pospiszyl.
[15] Hare.

suffer from psychopathy.[16] A classic psychopath pattern matches the figure of the Joker 100 percent. Psychopaths have glibness and superficial charm. They are often funny, eloquent, and persuasive. Many serial killers lure their future victims not by force, but by coquetry and personal charm.[17]

Psychopaths suffer from emotional poverty – that is, they cannot feel stronger emotions or higher arousal states. They are unnaturally calm and cold, as if they are deprived of a nervous system (which in many cases, helps to commit crimes). Many of them do not know fear. Therefore they need strong incentives: they are looking for extreme sensations. They want to live "on the edge" and at the center of the action.[18] Often, committing crimes is for them is a form of seeking thrills. Psychopaths are deprived of a sense of guilt and they do not at all regret suffering they cause, likely due to a complete lack of empathy[19] (the ability to read human emotions and compassion). Normal people do not seek out the torture of others, because they can imagine the pain they would cause. Psychopaths do not have this problem. Doing harm to the victim not only causes them no mental suffering, but can also be enjoyable. For a long time it was believed that psychopaths could not read human emotions as a result of cognitive defect. Recent studies show that it is actually the contrary – they actually do not pay attention to the emotions of others, unless it can help them to manipulate.[20] A propensity to lies, cheating, and manipulation is typical of a psychopath. What is interesting is that for psychopaths, lies do not serve only to manipulate; many psychopaths lie for the sheer joy of unpunished cheating.[21]

The behavior of psychopaths is characterized by high reactivity, weak control, and impulsiveness. They can execute violent acts suddenly, without any notice or warning, only to gain instant pleasure or relief.[22] Psychopaths are also characterized by a complete lack of responsibility. Their promises

---

[16] Ibid.
[17] Czerwiński and Gradoń.
[18] Hare, page 61.
[19] Hare.
[20] Dutton.
[21] Hare.
[22] Ibid.

mean nothing and they do not fulfill commitments. They act recklessly, inconsistently and – incidentally – "without rules,"[23] recklessly endangering themselves and others. Psychopaths are very egocentric and have overstated self-esteem. They are confident, arrogant, and insolent. They believe that the world around them exists only to satisfy their needs. Wolman writes that a psychopath treats the whole world as an oil field designed for constant exploitation.[24]

So my final answer is that the Joker is not a "madman." Even if we were to use such a colloquial term, he instead uses a madman's mask to increase the terror of his victims. He is, however, a classic aggressive psychopath.

2. Is the Joker's "One Bad Day" Theory True?

Batman: The Killing Joke is one of the most important comics about the Joker. It is not only an original history of the Joker, but it also in a unique and rare style shows the villain's way of seeing and interpreting the world around him. It is here that he presents the concept that every person can be a potential lunatic murderer and needs only "one bad day" for madness to reign over his or her life. It is worth considering the Joker's theory, because it has several important implications. From a psychological point of view, the most interesting of course is the conclusion – that if Joker's theory were true, it would mean that every one of us at any moment could change into a maniacal killer: we would simply need an adequately strong personal tragedy. In *The Killing Joke*, the Joker attempts to prove his theory – mentally and physically torturing James Gordon to break him and change him into another Joker. The experiment is interrupted by the intervention of Batman, so the comic book does not definitively answer whether the Joker was right. Fortunately, psychological expertise can step in to help. Let us consider whether each of us can, due to personal trauma, turn into a Joker.

The etiology of killing behavior is very complex and consists of many factors. If we look at the problem from a psychological point of view, then we find that to be a psychopathic killer you need to have specific personality traits, such as hyperactivity, aggression, emotional immaturity, inadequate

---

[23] To quote Heath Ledger's Joker in *The Dark Knight* (2008).
[24] Pospiszyl.

self-esteem, and narcissism.[25] From the psychoanalytic perspective, narcissism plays a key role in the development of psychopathy, and a crucial factor is the first year of life. According to Sigmund Freud and his daughter Anna, we are all born narcissists, focusing only on ourselves, but then we direct our attention to our mother as an external object. If our mother does not show significant interest in us, we do not learn that there are other people in the world outside of ourselves, and our attention returns to ourselves, the power of our libido returning to us and forming a secondary narcissism – the root of psychopathic personality.[26] It is no coincidence that almost all biographies of serial killers include topics of maternal deprivation, emotional negligence, and even physical abuse in childhood. Psychoanalytically, a child's early contact with his or her mother determines the beginning of the socialization process. If the mother does not respond to the child's needs or hold its interest, the child never learns the proper control over impulses (especially sexual and aggressive) in establishing relationships, and would manifest insensibility typical for psychopaths.[27]

In contrast, cognitive behavioral theory puts emphasis on deficits of fear that prevent the assimilation of social rules.[28] From childhood we are taught to react with fear when we break norms. This conditioning takes place through penalties immediately following committing a prohibited act. The reflex of fear makes us learn to avoid these acts in the future. But psychopaths do not feel fear, so such conditioning does not work for them. We can also look at the killing phenomenon from a sociological point of view. Brought to the foreground are environmental factors (negative influence of the family, peer environment), social factors (pressure to achieve the appropriate level of consumption, social norms permissive to violence, ideologies), and situational factors (strong frustration, sudden sense of danger). We must also not forget about the biomedical aspect, taking into consideration issues of neurological dysfunctions or genetic predispositions. It is no accident that children separated shortly after birth

---

[25] Ibid.
[26] Freud.
[27] Pospiszyl.
[28] Ibid.

from biological parents are four times more likely to commit crimes when biological parents were criminals themselves.[29]

We can argue which of these perspectives best explains the phenomenon of killing, but none of them support the view that a strong trauma can completely change a healthy human into a maniacal killer. In fact, all studies indicate that the formation of murderous inclinations is a long-term process, and murder itself is merely the final stage of this process. Analysis of serial killers' cases shows that murderous tendencies never show up immediately in adulthood without symptoms during earlier periods. According to the Macdonald triad, there are three behaviors exhibited by almost all serial killers in childhood: involuntary urination (as a sign of rebellion against parents), orchestrating fires, and cruelty to animals. When these acts are not punished, more and more extreme fantasies are stimulated and gradually embedded into the person's life. Not every child exhibiting the Macdonald triad will certainly be a serial killer, but in the biography of every serial killer we find such behaviors.[30]

As for the Joker, very little is known about his past, particularly about the period before his criminal career. However, based on what is known about psychopaths, we can try to recreate his past with some certainty. Let's play a criminal profiler and speculate a little. It is likely that the Joker's father was a psychopath himself. This could manifest as strict brutal rules, emotional coldness, and the use of violence. From a psychoanalytic perspective, much more important in the development of the Joker's psychopathy would have been the mother figure. There would be no doubt that she could not reciprocate the attention of her son (let's call him Joseph, after the "Going Sane" story) and could not satisfy his emotional needs. The reasons could have been various, for example mental illness, serious emotional problems (depression), or addiction. It is also possible that Joseph grew up completely without a mother or even without both parents. At any rate, the lack of interest of the people closest to him in early childhood led him to focus on himself and his unmet needs, which

---

[29] Czerwiński and Gradoń.
[30] Ibid.

consequently contributed to the development of narcissism and self-centeredness. At school, Joseph probably often fell into conflicts with his peers and teachers, because of his impulsivity, tendency to aggression, and rebellious attitude. This resulted in a sense of rejection and alienation, and also created an image of the world as a hostile, unfriendly place. At the same time, Joseph had high intelligence and ease of learning, so his academic performance was good, and his teachers considered him a talented student.

It can be assumed that Joseph's situation turned around. Thanks to great intelligence, an amazing ease of manipulating people, and magnetic charisma, Joseph as a teenager could have been a social star, attracting especially members of the opposite sex. The result could have been numerous, although very short-lived, romantic relationships. At this time Joseph probably was also engaged in his first criminal or para-criminal behaviors (e.g. animal abuse, truancy, cheating, vandalism, beatings, sexual aggression), but thanks to his skills in manipulating and deceiving others, he was able to hide it well and get out of any trouble. It is difficult to ascertain how Joseph's early adulthood would have looked. Perhaps he was engaged in minor crime, but he could have led a completely normal professional life. As to the second case, I would predict a profession associated with acting (comedian?), because of the Joker's tendency for theatrical behaviors and the need to focus others' attention on himself.

It seems unlikely that Joseph was able to establish a happy marriage, which is what *The Killing Joke* suggests. Psychopaths are rarely able to show deeper emotions and rather tend toward shallow, labile emotions, a non-integrated sexual life, frequent betrayals, and domestic violence.[31] However, it is possible that the great and unconditional love of Joseph's wife worked as the best therapy, anesthetizing his internal demons for a while, making him want to become a better person, and making him believe in a normal, happy life. Unfortunately, his wife's tragic death and the disastrous course of the Ace Chemicals robbery as related in *The Killing Joke* would have made his psychopathic instincts come back with twice the

---

[31] Pospiszyl.

power. The illusion of a normal life would have fallen into ruin, with only an insatiable anger, lust for killing, and need for revenge on the world remaining. Joseph would have transformed into a super-villain – the seductive, brilliant, but unpredictable and deadly Joker.

Why would the Joker choose a clown figure as his image? Perhaps the reason is the multiplicity of meanings hidden behind the clown figure (carefree fun, laughter, childhood, but also hidden sadness or demonic qualities). Maybe this is, as *The Killing Joke* muses, an ironic reflection of his former profession. However, crucial is the jester archetype, whose role is set outside social norms. The jester is not concerned with any policies and has a right to do what he wants, even to ridicule the king. He is above all, as the Joker beats all the cards in the deck. With his narcissism, the Joker really sees himself as a super-being and truly believes that there are no rules that apply to him. He perfectly fits the words of one of the psychopaths studied by the famous researcher Robert Hare: "It's not that I don't follow the law… I follow my own laws."[32]

Therefore, "one bad day" cannot change a normally functioning human into the Joker; it can only be a trigger that would launch murderous predispositions present in the person already.

3. Is the Joker right when he says that madness is the only rational response to the modern world?

In *Batman: The Killing Joke*, the Clown Prince of Crime reveals his vision of reality to Jim Gordon. "Faced with the inescapable *fact* that *human existence* is *mad*, *random* and *pointless*, one in *eight* of them [people] *crack up* and go *stark slavering buggo!* Who can *blame* them? In a world as *psychotic* as this… any *other* response would be *crazy!*"[33] So to the Joker, not only is "madness" a natural reaction to the reality of the modern world, but even keeping mental health should be considered – in the Joker's opinion – a sign of madness.

---

[32] Hare, page 38.
[33] *The Killing Joke*, page 33.

Research shows indeed that today we experience mental problems much more often than in the past.[34] On the one hand, it is of course an effect of progress in psychiatric diagnosis; a lot of mental illnesses were once regarded as other things. But on the other hand, there is no doubt that the growing pressure, the daily influx of information, and the number and types of stressors cause more exhausting daily lives, and the consequence is an increasing number of mental and emotional disorders. In this context, we might indeed say that mental illness is the answer to a "psychotic world" ("*Madness* is the *emergency exit*," Joker says to Gordon as the latter enters the "Ghost Train" carnival ride[35]), but the answer is only in a statistical sense, not a functional sense: mental illness does not help to deal with life's difficulties. On the contrary – it affects thinking and action, and prevents rational problem solving.

But I think that the Joker speaking of madness as an adequate response was referring to his own "madness" – psychopathy. And that completely changes things. Although initially the concept of psychopathy was applied only to cold-blooded killers, it was quickly discovered that there are a whole lot of psychopaths who do not break the law. Lange-Eichbaum divided psychopaths into three groups: aggressive (cold-blooded killers), inadequate (eccentric misfits), and creative.[36] The last group have the typical psychopathic characteristics of charisma, clout, creativity, lack of guilt, and lack of empathy, but are at the same time without aggressive tendencies and often achieve huge success. In fact, if we look at the public sphere – politicians, actors, artists, athletes, and journalists – we find there are a whole lot of psychopaths able to draw crowds.

Kevin Dutton, in his provocatively-titled book *The Wisdom of Psychopaths*, says that we should all learn from psychopaths to deal with the modern world. Dutton evokes an interesting analogy between psychopathic characteristics and music mixing:

> If you push all [dials and sliders] to max, you'll have a sound track that's no use to anyone. But if the sound track is graded and some controls are

---

[34] Walton.
[35] *The Killing Joke*, page 21.
[36] Pospiszyl.

turned up higher than others – such as fearlessness, focus, lack of empathy, and mental toughness, for example – you may well have a surgeon who's a cut above the rest.[37]

Dutton also defines what he calls the Seven Deadly Wins: ruthlessness, charm, focus, mental toughness, fearlessness, mindfulness, and action.[38] He argues that we should develop these seven psychopathic traits in ourselves to lead a life full of success. Alan Harrington goes even further; in his famous book *Psychopaths*, he argues that psychopaths are actually the next stage of human evolution, and as a result of mutations, all humans will someday gain a new, *psychopathic nervous system*, which will allow us to survive the increasingly difficult psychological conditions of life.[39]

It is worth considering why so many psychopaths reach so much success. Two reasons are related to psychopathy itself. First, psychopaths embody many qualities that many of us dream of: confidence, strength, no doubts, and a lack of fear. Because many people do not have these qualities, they naturally admire them in others. Second, narcissism makes psychopaths spend a lot of time and effort earning recognition and popularity, promoting themselves and their achievements, while at the same time thwarting potential competitors. They also are often eccentric and variegated, so naturally attract attention. However, we must note that the modern world "promotes" psychopathic behaviors. The Protestant heritage of most of the Western world is manifested in strong individualism and an unrestrained desire for achievements. The famous "American Dream," or the belief in a career from rags to riches, is in fact a psychopathic myth, promoting a strong belief that independence, overcoming rivals, not giving up in the face of adversity, and relying only on ourselves are the most important values of life. No one will better meet the pursuit of the American Dream than a psychopath.

Erich Fromm singled out a new kind of personality that has evolved in response to the modern world – *personality for sale*.[40] Numerous people

---

[37] Dutton, page 11.
[38] Dutton.
[39] Harrington.
[40] Fromm.

nowadays do not think in internal self-development categories, but in the categories of external benefits that they can potentially accomplish. There are many studies proving beyond doubt that the people of the Western world (especially in America) are taught from an early age to think about how they present themselves and to maintain a positive reputation, which transitions into self-promotion and creating a brand – in school, in peer groups, in the labor market, in society, and in the media. Again, who can cope with such realities better than a fearless, confident, ruthless psychopath?

Another aspect which favors psychopaths is a crisis of human relationships, which manifests in shallow feelings, low emotional maturity, low durability of marriages, and the tendency to focus on your needs and not those of your partner. In a world where strength, superficial charm, and intense but short relationships are valued, the psychopath – social predator – feels like a fish in water. The loosening of relationships also results in the collapse of parental authority and significant reduction of elder prestige, which makes breaking social norms easier.

A major role in the "psychopathization" of life is also played by the mass media and the internet. Mass media – preferring cheap sensation over competent content – are real hatcheries for psychopaths: just watch any TV program like a reality show or talent show to see it. The internet works similarly, especially social networks like Facebook. Users write about every little thing they do, upload photos, and wait in suspense for comments – this is narcissism in its purest form. This "psychopathization" process is a fact. We can only discuss whether these trends can be reversed.

Thus, as to whether madness is the only rational response to the modern world and only a madman would feel good in it, if the Joker has in mind a mental illness, he is wrong; a mentally ill person without professional help is unable to effectively function in any reality. But if the Joker is referring to his "madness" (psychopathy), then he is right. Psychopaths are simply created to shine in our world, and we can find the same characteristics (only in a different intensity) in many serial killers, TV celebrities, successful scientists, charismatic politicians, and executives.

4. Are there real criminals like the Joker?

According to Holmes' typology,[41] serial killers can be divided into six groups:

1. Visionaries – they hear voices or have visions ordering them to kill. Voices can represent a divine force, the devil, or other forces that legitimize violence.
2. Missionaries – they lead a mission intended to eliminate a particular group (e.g. prostitutes) or to establish a specific world order.
3. Hedonists seeking gain – they kill mainly for a form of profit.
4. Hedonists seeking to satisfy lust – they bind killing with sexual pleasure. Often their killings are accompanied by various sexual activities.
5. Hedonists seeking thrills – they feel strong nonsexual pleasure and excitement during the act of killing and victims dying.
6. Power/Control – they feel pleasure from domination and total power over the victim.

With complete confidence we can classify the Joker to the fifth group, hedonists seeking thrills. An act of killing is for him a kind of exciting extreme sport. He avoids routine, and tries to be creative and unpredictable; at times he plans complicated crimes long in advance, while at others he kills chaotically and at random. Sometimes he gets more fun out of outwitting the police and Batman than killing the victim. He is often marked by unnecessary cruelty, torturing his victims using different items and weapons.

I have researched more than 60 cases of hedonistic serial killers, and have not found anyone precisely like the Joker. Of course, some real killers have exhibited similar characteristics. One of the most famous American serial killers, Richard Ramirez (the media gave him the nickname "the Night Stalker") was distinguished by great creativity and frequently changing methods. He could be completely unpredictable: he was convicted of 13 counts of murder, but spared many victims' lives. He emphasized his Satanism, but it seems that his main motivation was contempt for social norms and the belief that these norms are pure fiction.[42] After being sentenced to death, part of Ramirez's response was as follows:

---

[41] Holmes and Holmes.
[42] Czerwiński and Gradoń.

> You don't understand me. You are not expected to. You are not capable of it. I am beyond your experience. I am beyond good and evil... I don't believe in the hypocritical, moralistic dogma of this so-called civilized society... You maggots make me sick! Hypocrites one and all.[43]

These words are almost like a mirror image of the Joker's statement from *The Dark Knight*: "You see, their morals, their 'code' – it's a bad joke. Dropped at the first sign of trouble. They're only as good as the world allows them to be. I'll show you. When the chips are down, these... 'civilized' people, they'll eat each other."

On the other hand, John Wayne Gacy became famous for incredible intelligence and cunning. He brilliantly manipulated people, so he was very respected in his community, and was considered a lovable and friendly man. He led a successful construction company and in his spare time he performed at children's charity parties in the disguise of – a clown. However, privately he dealt with children in a different way: he was found to have murdered 33 young boys and men, and received the nickname the "Killer Clown."[44] Like the Joker, he had high intelligence and creativity, the ability to manipulate people, and strong narcissism manifested by high self-esteem and boldness. Similarities can also be found in the famous "Son of Sam," David Berkovitz. The nature of his crimes was different from the Joker's. Berkovitz attacked mainly young attractive girls and young couples kissing in cars. However, in his actions we can see a lot of similarities: Berkowitz was characterized by incredible audacity and arrogance. Although several times he was arrested by the police, each time he avoided trouble thanks to bravado and composure. When he finally fell into police hands, according to the officers' testimony, he smiled the whole time, "as if it was all child's play."[45] It is also worth drawing attention to Berkovitz's lyrics and poems, which were full of chaotic thoughts, pseudopoetic gibberish, and unrealistic metaphors. In this way it was extremely reminiscent of many of the Joker's tirades. Here is a small example: "I'm a demon from the pit without bottom, which here on earth is spread confusion and fear. I'm war,

---

[43] Bonn.
[44] Czerwiński and Gradoń.
[45] Translated from Ibid., page 238.

I'm death, I'm doom!"[46] We could put similar words in the Joker's mouth in almost every comic book in which he appears.

Berkovitz is connected with the Joker by one other thing. After his arrest, the murderer considerably expanded his own demonology. He claimed that he was the son of "Sam," a powerful demon who appeared to him in different forms and told him to kill. Berkovitz behaved as if he was completely insane, and his stories were very complex and consistent. However, after a year in prison Berkovitz suddenly called a press conference and declared that the whole story about Sam and demons was invented by him.[47] This behavior is very similar to the Joker's, who also behaves like a complete lunatic, but in fact plays a well-thought and sneaky game.

Thus, certain elements of the Joker's modus operandi can be found in existing criminals. However, none of them are an exact reflection of the Clown Prince of Crime. Moreover, I believe we will never see a killer exactly like the Joker. First, the Joker is no ordinary psychopathic killer. He is a kind of super-psychopath. If we recall Kevin Dutton's music mixing metaphor of psychopathic personality, then we realize that in the Joker's case all sliders are indeed set to maximum value. To prove this, let's call again five key Joker personality traits: cruelty, high intelligence, the ability to manipulate people, lack of fear, and narcissism. The Joker's cruelty jumps off the scale in sadism alone. Mental and physical torture not only give him visible joy, but are also an important element of his sense of absolute power over the victim, who is forced to bear the pain and humiliation without any opportunity to defend himself or herself (such as Barbara Gordon in *The Killing Joke*). High intelligence makes the Joker a true criminal mastermind. He can outsmart even the Batman (as in *Batman: The Man Who Laughs*[48]), and also shows incredible creativity and imagination (as with the "laughing fish" of *Detective Comics* Vol. 1 #475). The Joker's ability to manipulate people has reached such a level that he has almost magnetic charisma and can with great ease entice other criminals or even convert people from the opposite side, as in the case of Harley Quinn, who was supposed to be the

---

[46] Translated from Ibid., page 233.
[47] Czerwiński and Gradoń.
[48] *Batman: The Man Who Laughs.*

Joker's therapist. A lack of anxiety has grown so strong in the Joker's case that he actually lacks a self-preservation instinct. Many stories show that he doesn't feel any pain – he can laugh even when he is beaten or shot – and is not afraid to die. His behavior is not risky or reckless; he simply does not care whether he perishes or not. The intensity of the Joker's narcissism also exceeds all scales of theatricality. The Joker really seems to believe that all eyes are turned to him, and that he plays the most important role of all time. The whole world is a theater, other people are props, and Batman is the most important (or actually, the only important) audience. The literal confirmation of this fact can be found in the "Going Sane" story. When the Joker is confident about Batman's death, he says of his previous criminal activity, "No, it's not me. Not me at all. It's a role I've been playing, to keep the audience amused. But the audience is gone now. The theater's empty. And I don't have to play anymore."[49]

The second argument why there will be no real-life Joker results from the logic of the super-hero's myth. For there to be a super-villain, first there must be a super-hero. There is no Joker without Batman. Thus, until the real Batman appears in the real world (and this is rather impossible), there will be no archenemy. The third argument concerns the flow of information in the modern world. The Joker's greatest strength is his indeterminacy and unpredictability. We do not know anything about who he really is, who he was before, what drives him, and what shaped him to become as he is. This lack of identity is very important for him, because it transfers him from a real to symbolic sphere. Much like Batman, as a symbol he has great strength; he is indestructible and invincible. The discovery of his secrets will turn him back into a normal, weak man. In the real world, such anonymity is not possible. Note that we know almost everything about each modern murderer. It is no coincidence that after each famous crime case, when the police determine the perpetrator, the next day the media know everything about him or her: where he or she lived, his or her family, his or her grades in school, what he or she was interested in, and what mental problems or criminal record he or she had. This is possible because each of us leaves vast

---

[49] *Legends of the Dark Knight* Vol. 1 #65, page 24.

traces of information on the internet. On this basis anyone can restore the most relevant information about our lives and preferences. So if there really were a Joker, we could instantly learn all about him. Of course we can assume that the real Joker would not use any social networks, never use a blog or Twitter, and would not have a *YouTube* channel. But if we recall the Joker's extreme narcissism and egocentrism, then we realize that for him, refraining from the use of social media would be simply impossible.

And finally the fourth argument against the appearance of a real Joker – although the motives of serial killers are sometimes unpredictable, and while there are copycat criminals, it is very unlikely that anyone will take the Joker as an example and reproduce his crimes. The reason is that the Joker character is so rich in meanings that go far beyond a simple symbol of evil. On the basis of my experience with comics fans, I can say that the Joker's figure fascinates mainly intelligent, friendly, progressive, open-minded people, not the twisted and psychopathic. Many fans are not interested in him as a symbol of evil, but as a symbol of unstoppable force, charisma, independence, and anarchic freedom. Especially after Christopher Nolan's *The Dark Knight*, the Joker's image went far beyond the bounds of the comics and pop culture environment and became a commonly recognized symbol. Therefore I think that the Joker will sooner become the logo of some group or social movement than inspire a serial killer. Actually, it is happening already. In 2008, fans of the Polish football club Lech Poznań presented a huge flag with the Joker's image during the UEFA Cup qualifier game.[50] But they did not use it to glorify the comics super-villain. Rather, they emphasized their strength, vitality, lack of humility, and lack of fear in a celebratory way.

It is interesting that while the vast majority of inmates in prisons are utterly not like the Joker, many writers and readers still see him as a general representation of insanity and criminality. Some could consider this as a sign of ignorance on the parts of both the creators and the audience, but I see three different conclusions. First, iconic comics characters are somewhat overdrawn and exaggerated interpretations of real characters. They do not

---

[50] "Grasshoppers Zurych - Lech Poznań (28.08.2008) III."

occur in the same form in real life, and in spite of that – or because of it – much like a magnifying glass, they can tell us much about real phenomena. Secondly, the pop cultural existence of some characters like the Joker develops and exceeds the intentions of its creators. Thirdly, in spite of 75 years of exploitation, the Joker character still has a large untapped potential for fresh approaches.

Thus, despite some surface similarities, there are no real criminals exactly like the Joker, and it is also unlikely that the Clown Prince of Crime will inspire any murderers in the future. On the contrary, he becomes a symbol rich in meanings – which ironically inspires a lot of healthy people and social groups – and will be so for a long time in the future.

Bibliography

Arkham Asylum: A Serious House on Serious Earth. Grant Morrison (writer), Dave McKean (penciler/inker/colorist), and Gaspar Saladino (letterer). Eds. Karen Berger, Anton Kawasaki, and Art Young. DC Comics, 1989.

Batman Vol. 1 #1. Bill Finger (writer), Bob Kane (penciler), and Sheldon Moldoff (inker/letterer). Ed. Whitney Ellsworth. DC Comics, Spring 1940.

Batman: The Killing Joke. Alan Moore (writer), Brian Bolland (penciler/inker), John Higgins (colorist), and Richard Starkings (letterer). Eds. Dennis O'Neil, Mark Chiarello, and Dan Raspler. DC Comics, May 1988.

Batman: Legends of the Dark Knight Vol. 1 #65-68. J. M. DeMatteis (writer), Joe Staton (penciler), Steve Mitchell (inker), Digital Chameleon (colorist), Willie Schubert (letterer). Eds. Archie Goodwin and Jim Spivey. DC Comics, Nov 1994-Feb 1995.

Batman: The Man Who Laughs. Ed Brubaker (writer), Doug Mahnke (penciler/inker), David Baron (colorist), and Rob Leigh (letterer). Eds. Michael Carlin and Michael Michael Siglain. DC Comics, 2005.

Bonn, Scott. *Why We Love Serial Killers: The Curious Appeal of the World's Most Savage Murderers* (New York: Skyhorse Publishing, 2014). Kindle edition.

Czerwiński, Arkadiusz and Kacper Gradoń. *Seryjni mordercy* (Warsaw: Muza SA, 2001).

Detective Comics Vol. 1 #27 Bill Finger (writer) and Bob Kane (penciler/inker). Ed. Vincent Sullivan. DC Comics, May 1939.

Detective Comics Vol. 1 #475. Steve Englehart (writer), Marshall Rogers (penciler), Terry Austin (inker), Jerry Serpe (colorist), and Ben Oda (letterer). Ed. Julius Schwartz. DC Comics, Feb 1978.

Dutton, Kevin. *The Wisdom of Psychopaths: What Saints, Spies, and Serial Killers Can Teach Us About Success* (New York: Farrar, Straus, and Giroux, 2013).

Freud, Sigmund. *On Narcissism: An Introduction* (White Press, 2014).

Fromm, Erich. *The Sane Society* (New York: Henry Holt and Company, 1990).

Garneau, Eric. "Lady Haha: Performativity, Super-Sanity, and the Mutability of Identity" in *The Joker. A Serious Study of the Clown Prince of Crime.* Eds. Robert Moses Peaslee and Robert G. Weiner (Jackson, MS: University Press of Mississippi, 2015).

"Grasshoppers Zurych - Lech Poznań (28.08.2008) III." *YouTube* video, 9:46. Posted by Bulgarska on 30 Aug 2008. https://www.youtube.com/watch?time_continue=1&v=KoA9UNpF1xk.

Hare, Robert. *Without Conscience: The Disturbing World of the Psychopaths Among Us* (New York: The Guilford Press, 1993).

Harrington, Alan. *Psychopaths* (New York: Simon & Schuster, 1973).

Holmes, Ronald M. and Stephen T. Holmes. *Profiling Violent Crimes: An Investigative Tool*, 4th ed. (Thousand Oaks, CA: SAGE Publications, Inc., 2009).

Meyer, Robert G. *Case Studies in Abnormal Behavior*, 4th ed. (New York: Pearson Education Company, 1999).

Pospiszyl, Kazimierz. *Psychopatia* (Warsaw: Zak Wydawnictwo Akademickie, 2000).

Shahrokh, Narriman C. and Robert E. Hales. *American Psychiatric Glossary*, 8th ed. (Arlington, VA: American Psychiatric Publishing, Inc., 2003).

Walton, Alice G. "Why More Americans Suffer from Mental Disorders Than Anyone Else." *The Atlantic*. 4 October 2011. http://www.theatlantic.com/health/archive/2011/10/why-more-americans-suffer-from-mental-disorders-than-anyone-else/246035.

Witek, Joseph. *Comic Books as History: The Narrative Art of Jack Jackson, Art Spiegelman, and Harvey Pekar* (Jackson, MS: University Press of Mississippi, 1989).

Is the Truth Good Enough? Christopher Nolan's Dark Knight Trilogy and the Noble Lie in Justice and Politics

by Daniel N. Gullotta

Lies and deception have always featured prominently within the literature of heroes. Within Homer's classic, *The Odyssey*,[1] Odysseus lies constantly (particularly about his identity) and yet is held up as the ideal hero within the narrative. When he first arrives at Scheria, he claims to be a merchant from Crete; later he pretends to be a beggar, and in one of the epic's climactic moments, Odysseus conceals his identity to his wife, Penelope, as a means to test her faithfulness. Additionally, many of the supporting protagonists deceive the people around them. Athena continually disguises herself when in human company, Penelope repeatedly hoodwinks her suitors as a means to keep their advances at bay, and

---

[1] Homer, *The Odyssey*.

Telemachus lies to his mother about his trip to find his father. According to Homer, gods and heroes do not necessarily hold to the idea that honesty is the best policy.[2]

On a literary level, a hero's secrecy creates suspense within the narrative. After all, if Odysseus's foes should uncover his true identity, they would surely attempt to kill him. Moreover, this concealment also creates irony for the readers involved. While the people who encounter Odysseus continually ask for his name and origin, the reader knows full well who Odysseus really is. As classicist Bernard Fenik explains, "[I]rony demands that the audience know something the fictional characters do not; we can see, but they are blind."[3] However, given the value of truth within justice systems in general, and as gods and heroes are often seen as embodiments of justice, one might well ask: why do heroes constantly deceive those around them? How can deception be virtuous and heroic?

One of the main reasons that gods and heroes mask their true identities from others is as a means of testing others' virtue and intentions. This is done because gods and heroes are generally understood to be the guardians of the universe's moral code, and there is no better test of principles than how one treats a complete stranger.[4] Homer explains in *The Odyssey*, "Doomed man that thou art, what if haply he be some god come down from heaven! Aye, and the gods in the guise of strangers from afar put on all manner of shapes, and visit the cities, beholding the violence and the righteousness of men."[5] Simply stated, the gods bless those who honor strangers and punish those who do not. When Athena visits the home of Odysseus under the disguise of Mentes, the suitors treat her poorly and ignore their duties to her as a guest. Telemachus, on the other hand, provides her a meal and seeks to make her comfortable. Due to the poor behavior of the suitors, their bad manners towards a god will cost them their lives, but Telemachus's stewardship will be rewarded with the return of his father, Odysseus, and the restoration of their house. These deceptive

---

[2] Montiglio.

[3] Fenik, page 46.

[4] See Segal.

[5] Homer, *The Odyssey*, 17.484-487.

tests are also administered by the heroes whom the gods favor. After Odysseus tests the handmaidens and other servants, and witnesses firsthand the corruption of his house by the suitors under a false identity, the revelation of his true identity leads to the suitors' downfall. Through the use of falsehoods, great injustices can be answered. These themes of heroic deception can also be found within the legends of Heracles, Gilgamesh, King David, Beowulf, Jesus, and many other notable examples.[6]

In examining modern-day super-hero literature, many of these ancient themes of suspense, irony, and virtuous deception have carried across. The majority of super-hero characters lie to their friends and family about their alter egos or super-powers, and they deceive the masses by pretending to be mild-mannered and clumsy when in reality they are anything but. This practice of misinformation carries over into everyday language and dialogue, in which characters continually make excuses and invent stories to explain their strange behaviors and late appearances in order to maintain their secret identities. Physically, deception manifests in the masks that super-heroes wear. Masks are employed, not so much to protect super-heroes' faces in combat, but rather to conceal their true identities and project their alter egos. To put it another away, it is the mask that allows Bruce Wayne to deceive his allies and enemies that he is not Bruce Wayne, but in fact "the Batman."

In examining these deceptive acts and untruthful behaviors, we can see how the concept of the super-hero distorts reality and truth. After all, these acts and behaviors are generally used to protect super-heroes' loved ones from danger or in service of "the greater good," but nonetheless; they are not *true* representations of *reality*. Thus, it can be concluded that modern super-hero literature and cinema purposefully construct an *untrue*, or deceptive, narrative and character identity, and this untruth stands in stark contrast to the public perception of super-heroes as the embodiments of "truth, justice, and the American way." Despite being held up as paragons of truth, super-heroes are, in reality, liars. The perceived need for super-heroes to lie and deceive reaches new depths within Christopher Nolan's

---

[6] For a detailed study of lies, deception, and trickery within heroic tales, see Scheub.

Batman trilogy, but particularly within *The Dark Knight* (2008) and *The Dark Knight Rises* (2012). At their core, these Batman films discuss and deconstruct ideas of power, justice, and law within their storytelling, especially in conjunction with the films' use of lies. In fact, one of the key subjects within this saga is "the noble lie" and its use and abuse within society.

In *The Republic*,[7] ancient Greek philosopher Plato argues that a society believing in a "noble lie" would be "more inclined to care for the state and one another."[8] Plato describes the noble lie as "a contrivance for one of those falsehoods that come into being in case of need, of which we were just now talking, some noble one."[9] In sum, it is a falsehood created by the elite and taught to the lower classes in hope of maintaining a peaceful and lawful society. In this worldview, false propaganda, ideals, and beliefs for the sake of public welfare are completely acceptable. This falsehood could take various forms, such as a religious belief, political myth, or an exemplary figure. Regardless of how this falsehood is presented, the core idea is that deception becomes valuable when used for "the greater good." Therefore, on the basis of this noble lie, citizens can have faith in their governing body and in the established justice system.

In relation to super-heroes and the "noble lie," comic book readers will be familiar with this motif from the climax of Alan Moore and Dave Gibbons's *Watchmen*.[10] Adrian Veidt (Ozymandias) stages an interdimensional alien attack on New York, which frightens the United States and the U.S.S.R. into uniting against a common enemy, thus ushering an age of global peace. Knowing that the ongoing conflict between the United States and the U.S.S.R. would eventually lead to their mutual annihilation, Veidt constructs this plot in pursuit of peace. Despite their initial attempts to stop Veidt and their disgust at his actions, upon seeing the world's ceasefire and peacemaking plans, Dan Dreiberg (Nite Owl) and Laurie Juspeczyk (Silk Spectre) agree to remain silent in favor of the world

---

[7] Plato.
[8] Plato, 3.414.
[9] Plato, 3.415.
[10] Originally published as *Watchmen* #1-12.

living peacefully. However, Rorschach dies refusing to accept this so-called noble lie. Utopia is achieved in *Watchmen*, but only through deception.[11]

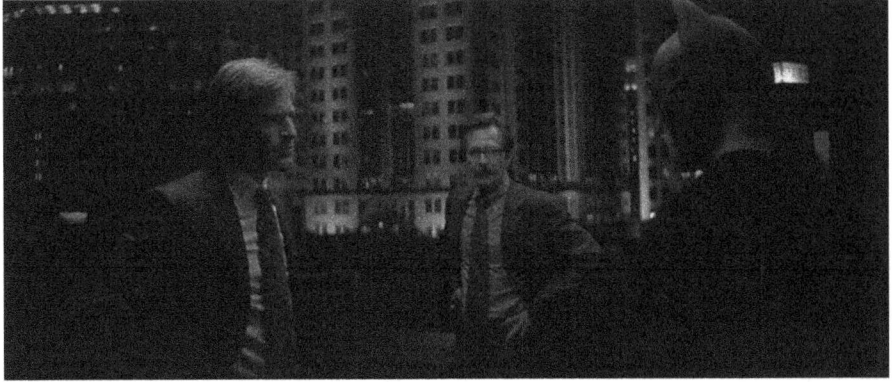

In *The Dark Knight*, Batman, James Gordon, and Harvey Dent are all figures of justice who deal in deception. Batman is the sanctioned super-hero, but all three must ultimately fight through the implications of their masks.

In turning to Christopher Nolan's Batman films, it should be emphasized that lies, deception, and counterfeit realities have always featured prominently within Nolan's filmography, but they are particularly entrenched within the storytelling of *The Dark Knight*.[12] What is noteworthy is that most of these lies function in pursuit of the theoretical "greater good" by the film's protagonists. For example, Gordon fakes his death as a part of the operation to trap the Joker, and does so to protect his family. Likewise, upon the realization that Dent is missing after the Gotham General Hospital explosion, Gordon instructs the detectives to keep this news to themselves. Also, Dent lies about his identity as the Batman in order to lure out the Joker, permitting Batman to "take him down." Moreover, Alfred, upon reading the note by Rachel that she will not wait for Wayne and will instead marry Dent, burns it knowing that the truth would break Wayne's heart and that vengeance for Rachel's death would spur him into action. And in the film's climax, Batman covers up Dent's murderous actions and takes the blame for them because "... the Joker cannot win. Gotham needs

---

[11] For a detailed study of *Watchmen*'s use of the noble lie, see Dwivedi.

[12] For a detailed study of Nolan's use of lies throughout his filmography, see McGown.

its true hero [...] Because that's what needs to happen. Because sometimes... the truth isn't good enough. Sometimes people deserve more. Sometimes people deserve to have their faith rewarded." At the film's end, the city of Gotham embraces Batman and Gordon's lie and the pair sees the lie as a necessity to stop Gotham from falling into anarchy.

These lies, their sources, and their advocates are particularly important due to their roles of power within society. Jim Gordon is a respected member of the Gotham Police Department, a lieutenant, and later named police commissioner, not to mention a beloved husband and father. Harvey Dent is the district attorney assigned to prosecuting Gotham's crime families, and has even been named "Gotham's white knight." Both of these men are powerful public figures of the law and justice system, one appointed and the other elected. However, it is undeniable that both of these men draw their inspiration and zeal from Batman's vigilante crusade against crime. In reflecting back to *Batman Begins* (2005), in his dialogue with Alfred upon his return to Gotham, Wayne claims, "People need dramatic examples to shake them out of apathy, and I can't do that as Bruce Wayne. As a man, I'm flesh and blood, I can be ignored, I can be destroyed, but as a symbol... as a symbol I can be incorruptible. I can be everlasting." In this universe, the super-heroic identity is a construct, a persona created in the imagination of its avatar. First and foremost, this persona serves a symbolic function. In looking at the initial events of *The Dark Knight*, it appears that Batman's symbolic function has been quite successful.

However, Batman has not just gone on to inspire law enforcement and justice officials; he also has inspired other vigilantes. Several normal, everyday citizens don capes and cowls akin to Batman's and, regardless of their well-meaning intentions, this is a turn of which Batman does not approve. Despite his hopes for the citizens of Gotham to be motivated in improving their city's justice system, he comments to Alfred: "That wasn't exactly what I had in mind when I said I wanted to inspire people." It is striking that, when Batman confronts these copycat Batmen about their vigilantism, they call his own into question, asking: "What gives you the right? What's the difference between you and me?"

In continuing this theme, during his double date with Dawes and Dent, Wayne asks, in a perhaps ironic twist, "Who appointed the Batman?" Dent's response to Wayne's question ("We did") is particularly powerful given how the people of Gotham are characterized throughout *The Dark Knight* and later in *The Dark Knight Rises*. As law professor John Ip obverses, "For much of *The Dark Knight*, Gotham City's citizens come across poorly, behaving like a self-serving, fearful mob once the Joker begins his campaign of terror."[13] For example, when the Joker begins to demand that Batman unmask himself or people will die, Gothamites begin to protest and demand that Batman turn himself in. Later, when the Joker threatens to blow up a hospital if the lawyer, Coleman Reese, is not promptly executed, citizens attempt to kill Reese themselves. During the ferry scene, the Joker instructs the passengers on each boat to blow up the other or he will blow them both up, and this results in cries on both ferries for the other to be destroyed. While there are a few notable exceptions, Gotham's masses are easily persuaded, enraged, frightened, and corrupted. Due to the masses' need for inspiration, Dent's moral demise within the film becomes paramount in establishing Batman's noble lie.

While inspired by Batman, Dent's public involvement in fighting crime is received by the public, and by Wayne, as far more powerful and significant. Because Dent's position is publically acknowledged and his crime-fighting activities legal, Dent is clearly a far greater symbol for hope and change within Gotham. This is crystalized in the emphasis on Dent's physical appearance throughout the film as "the face of Gotham's bright future." Dent is a hero with a face and a crime-fighter without a mask. Dent embodies the truth and honesty desired by Batman for Gotham. Dent can be authentic, because his identity is known and his role as district attorney sanctions him to fight crime, whereas Batman's identity must remain mysterious and his vigilantism forces him to be deceptive. However, even before his downfall, Dent is not all that he appears to be.

Unbeknownst to or ignored by the public, Dent displays several concerning character flaws. As film critic Benjamin Kerstein notes:

> He is self-confident to the point of arrogance, personally vain, and extremely ambitious. More importantly, his idealism is not as pure as his admirers believe. In his most telling scene, Dent refers to the ancient

---

[13] Ip, page 224.

Roman custom of appointing a dictator in circumstances of extreme danger, and wonders whether an enlightened tyranny may not be superior to the rule of law – indicating a secret lack of faith in the institutions he represents.[14]

Dent has even been given the nickname "Harvey Two-Face" from his work at Internal Affairs. He is also willing to interrogate one of Joker's henchmen at gunpoint, at which time Batman needs to remind him that he is "the symbol of hope [Batman] could never be. [Dent's] stand against organized crime is the first legitimate ray of light in Gotham in decades."

Regardless of what lies beneath the surface, it is Dent's visible and symbolic role that matters. The crucial hope in the film is that people will imitate Harvey Dent in the same way they have imitated Batman. In *The Dark Knight*, Batman, himself, is trying to break Gotham's society free of the heroic conventions that modern comic book readers and movie attendees are accustomed to – it is the politician who is the model hero and symbolic figure of justice, not the vigilante. Despite Dent's weaknesses, it is the symbol of Harvey Dent, public hero, and its functions that lead Batman and Gordon to construct their noble lie. In the face of Dent's moral corruption, Gordon, knowing what it will mean to the city, comments: "The Joker won. Harvey's prosecution, everything he fought for, undone. Whatever chance you [Batman] gave us of fixing our city dies with Harvey's reputation. We bet it all on him. The Joker took the best of us and tore him down. People will lose hope." Given how Gotham's masses have previously responded to the Joker's terrorist activities, Gordon's lack of faith is understandably well-placed. In order to uphold the city's sense of law and order, Batman assumes the death of Dent's victims and is cast as Dent's cold-blooded murderer. By becoming Gotham's scapegoat and upholding Dent's legacy as a just figure worthy of transformative power, civil order is restored to Gotham. Moreover, as we see in *The Dark Knight Rises*, Gotham is so moved by Dent's supposed sacrifice that it enacts a law which effectively wipes out organized crime in Gotham.

In further examining the noble lie constructed by Gordon and Batman and its powerful effect on the people of Gotham, there are notable

---

[14] Kerstein, pages 140-141.

similarities with the scapegoating theories of literary critic and philosopher René Girard. In brief, Girard's thesis is that there is a subconscious drive within human society which stems from humanity's desire to mimic the desires of others, and this desire turns violent. As Thomas Hobbes puts it in *Leviathan*, "if any two men desire the same thing, which nevertheless they cannot both enjoy, they become enemies."[15] Girard calls this drive "mimetic desire."

This generated desire naturally creates numerous conflicts and scandals, each one building upon the last, until there is so much tension that the only result of this "mimetic rivalry" is wide-scale violence. Because the community is at risk, in order to prevent this catastrophic outbreak of violence, Girard argues that these rivalling tensions are collectively focused on an individual. This individual becomes a scapegoat, a figure from which the fractured community can unite in projecting its troubles upon. The scapegoat becomes the enemy, the source of all of society's troubles, and once the community unites in exiling or destroying this figure, they experience a sense of relief and order is restored. Through this violent "scapegoat mechanism," a myth of social harmony is generated, and often, the once-demonized scapegoat becomes divinized for his or her ability to bring peace to the community.[16] As Girard explains, "The rite may stem from violence and be steeped in violence, but it still aspires to peace."[17]

One can clearly see this rising tension throughout *The Dark Knight*. As the Joker's reign of terror escalates, Gotham begins to blame Batman as the cause of the violence that he is trying to fight and repel. The city continually erupts into outbreaks of violence, in which Batman seems to be at the center. However, in the end, Batman's sacrifice to take the blame of the deaths of Harvey's victims allows the city to unite in their hatred of him and regain social order. In a very Girardian manner, Batman becomes a scapegoat for the people of Gotham, literally taking on the sins of Dent and

---

[15] Hobbes, page 87.

[16] For more on Girard's theory on mimetic desire, mimetic rivalry, and the scapegoat mechanism, see Girard, *I See Satan Fall Like Lightning*. See also Palaver; and Golsan.

[17] Girard, *Violence and the Sacred*, page 146.

the figurative sins of Gotham's masses in order to maintain social harmony.[18]

Through Batman's noble lie, Dent becomes a messianic figure. This is previously evoked within the film by Dent's campaign slogan "I Believe in Harvey Dent," in which the people of Gotham are asked to place their faith in Dent. However, Dent's death takes his power to transform the justice system to new heights. As we later learn in *The Dark Knight Rises*, Dent is seen as a martyr, and Gotham honors his sacrifice with the Dent Act. This legislation allows law enforcement in Gotham unprecedented powers and effectively wipes out organized crime within Gotham. Not only is social harmony achieved, but a new reign of peace and security seems to be in full effect. Thanks to the noble lie, Dent's death becomes redemptive for the people of Gotham. Dent's death creates a new mythological narrative for Gotham, as Batman is remembered a villain and Dent as a hero, so much so that Dent is privileged with his own memorial day. While Batman and Gordon have clearly suffered as a result of their lying in the opening of *The Dark Knight Rises*, their deception is believed to be well-placed because of its effects on the city. Deception, despite its moral questionability, is used by our heroes as a means of achieving long-lasting justice. According to Slovenian Marxist philosopher and cultural critic, Slavoj Žižek, "[*The Dark Knight's*] take-home message is that lying is necessary to sustain public morale: only a lie can redeem us."[19]

Because of these themes, many film and cultural critics have understood *The Dark Knight* to be a politically conservative, right-wing piece of cinema and a commentary on the War on Terror. Mystery author Andrew Klavan and political commentator and journalist Jeffery Lord have viewed *The Dark Knight* as an endorsement of the Bush administration's War on Terror and some of the tactics it used in counterterrorism.[20] Moreover, *The Dark Knight* was also rated as one of *National Review*'s best "conservative

---

[18] See Magnani and Bertolotti, pages 1-15.
[19] Žižek, "Good Manners in the Age of WikiLeaks," pages 9-10.
[20] Klavan, "What Bush and Batman Have in Common"; Lord.

movies" from the past 25 years.[21] Lord sums up Batman's conservative appeal to the American public as follows:

> Batman is the cinematic (and comic book) personification of the way Americans like to see themselves. He is a rebel against the Establishment (and likewise with the *Star Wars* crew and Spiderman). He is unafraid to act. He is willing to take risks. He could not possibly care less about what "feels good" or whether anything he says or does "makes sense" to a single other person. He runs on instinct. He is here to do the right thing. Nothing more, nothing less. He has a vision of Gotham City, a dream, that is not unlike the favorite phrase associated with his friend Superman (another movie sensation): Truth, Justice and the American Way.[22]

It should be noted that Ip and others are critical of these readings, arguing that, rather than endorsing these vigilante figures and their tactics, "The message of *The Dark Knight* is that society ideally should not rely on heroic vigilantes..."[23] However, given the film's popularity and critical acclaim, one should ponder with Žižek: "Does *The Dark Knight*'s extraordinary popularity not point towards the fact that it touches a nerve of our ideologico-political constellation: the undesirability of truth?"[24] *The Dark Knight* is far more tragic than its right-wing advocates acknowledge. By becoming the people's scapegoat, Batman proves right the Joker's claim that "To them, you're just a freak – like me. They need you right now. But when they don't, they'll cast you out. Like a leper. You see, their morals, their 'code' – it's a bad joke. Dropped at the first sign of trouble." Batman does not trust the people of Gotham and takes their fate into his hands; he does not trust them to act in their own best interest. Much like Caesar within Dent's parable, he suspends democracy and becomes a fascist figure. Rather than endorsing his own belief that Gotham is "full of people ready to believe in good," Batman takes the power of Gotham's justice system upon himself. He offers the people of Gotham a noble lie to have faith in, rather than trusting them to do the right thing in the face of the ugly truth.

---

[21] Klavan, "The Best Conservative Movies of the Last 25 Years, #12: *The Dark Knight*."

[22] Lord.

[23] Ip, page 229.

[24] Žižek, *Living in the End Times*, page 61.

As Girard notes within his writings on mimetic theory, the problem with the scapegoat mechanism is that it is based upon a lie and is hence always a temporary solution. Because the community's victim was never the true source of its problems, the problems that cause the original clashes are always bound to go unresolved and naturally resurface. In fact, given that this redemptive myth is built on a false belief, the very fabric that holds society in law and order is extremely tentative. For example, at the very end of *Watchmen*, the simple release of Rorschach's journal could completely undo Veidt's noble lie for world peace. As in *The Dark Knight Rises*, the revelation of the Dent cover-up from Gordon's speech totally reverses the grand mythology created by Batman, Gordon, and Gotham City in the eight years following. As Bane rightly states, "You have been supplied with a false idol to stop you tearing down this corrupt city."

This fragile foundation for peace is artistically represented by Bane's activities within Gotham's sewers. As journalist John Nolte observes through a distinctly right-wing lens:

> In Gotham's sewers, Bane recruits those like himself – the insecure thumbsuckers raging with a sense of entitlement, desperate to justify their own laziness and failure and to flaunt a false sense of superiority through oppression, violence, terror, and ultimately, total and complete destruction. No one in Gotham even suspects the cancer of dangerous childish resentment growing beneath their feet, and even those who dare remain vigilant are laughed at as relics of a bygone age.[25]

While organized crime may have been effectively removed from Gotham, the city's socioeconomic problems have continued to grow and fester, so much so that at-risk children are now going into the sewers to find work. Bane's army gathers beneath the city and his bombs at the Gotham football stadium destroy from the base up. Bane displays just how poor Gotham's foundations are.

In an ironic twist, Bane, despite being the villain of the film, acts as a profound "truth-bringer." Bane (literally) reveals the poor foundations of Gotham's social code, denounces the noble lie constructed by Batman and Gordon, and exposes how the Blackgate prisoners have suffered at the hands of society's injustices. Bane reveals Dent to be a false messiah and

---

[25] Nolte.

shows that Gotham's salvation was never truly achieved. As a flawed archetype for inspiration, Dent as Gotham's role model over the previous eight years had generated more figures essentially like him. Gotham's congressman, Byron Gilly, appears to be a family man and a law-abiding citizen on the surface, but underneath he is an adulterer and political player. Deputy Commissioner Peter Foley is more interested in his position and the possibility of becoming the new police commissioner than in upholding the law, as displayed when given the choice between tracking down Bane or Batman after the stock market heist. Regardless of how things appear, the reality is that the justice system is broken.

At its core, the essential problem addressed within *The Dark Knight Rises* is that false beliefs generate false hope. Batman himself experiences this firsthand within Bane's prison, the Pit. Bane gives Batman a dose of his own medicine. Bane explains that the Pit's deadliest feature is the false hope that it inspires. Because the prisoners hold onto the belief that they might one day make the climb and escape, they constantly feed on this hope, but time and time again they fail, crushing their ambitions. The Pit demonstrates that false hope is the most deadly poison of all, because it tortures the soul. Dent, uplifted as the false hope for Gotham, has corrupted the city's soul.

While comic book critic Julian Darius might argue that *The Dark Knight Rises* invalidates the message of *The Dark Knight*, I argue that it, in fact, critiques it.[26] As Alfred states, "Maybe it's time we all stop trying to outsmart the truth, and let it have its day." While *The Dark Knight* reveals the undesirability of truth, *The Dark Knight Rises* reveals the instability of lies. The message of *The Dark Knight Rises* is that lies, no matter how noble, cannot endure as a source for justice and a basis for moral inspiration. Gotham's prosperity and progress is an illusion, and everything Gordon and Batman have tried to bury literally and figuratively surfaces with the arrival of Bane. Batman and Gordon are forced to come to grips with the reality that their noble lie was only a shallow victory. A better mythology is required.

---

[26] Darius.

After returning from the Pit, Batman rallies the people and forms a last stand against Bane and his army. Batman fights for the people, with the people, in broad daylight. While Batman remains a faceless figure, the symbol of Batman becomes a public one. In doing so, Batman becomes a visible source for inspiration and a character by which anyone can be inspired. Selina Kyle, despite her jaded past, rallies behind the symbol of Batman, and so does the once-cowardly Foley, along with Gordon and John "Robin" Blake. In the end, the whole city sees Batman as a man who gave his life for them. Batman goes from scapegoat to savior, last seen transporting a bomb away from Gotham City and supposedly dying in the blast.

Although *The Dark Knight Rises* critiques the noble lie, it is debatable whether or not this sacrifice is authentic. As Wayne did not truly die, it seems that, once again, Batman has provided a falsehood to be upheld by the people of Gotham, transforming him from scapegoat to savior within the city's mythology so much so that they create a monument to him and his so-called noble sacrifice. However, one should note the differences between the ending scenes of *The Dark Knight* and *The Dark Knight Rises*. Rather than displaying a repetition of the noble lie from *The Dark Knight*, the ending of *The Dark Knight Rises* shows its reversal. At the end of *The Dark Knight,* Batman is deemed an outcast, but at the end of *The Dark Knight Rises,* he is honored as its true hero. Likewise, the Bat-Signal is destroyed in *The Dark Knight*, but it is restored in *The Dark Knight Rises*. As the people once believed in Harvey Dent, they now believe in Batman. At Wayne's funeral, Blake is dissatisfied with the fact that no one will ever know who saved the city. In response, Gordon points out to Blake that the people know it was the Batman who saved them, which confirms Batman's parting words to Gordon: "A hero can be anyone."

Because Batman did authentically save Gotham, he is remembered faithfully as a hero, and so his symbolic function can form a proper foundation for justice. Batman's sacrificial death, while a lie, is still a genuine act of heroism. Given that Wayne has authentically retired as Batman, there is the Jungian understanding that Wayne's "shadow side," the Batman, did die.[27] As it appears at the café in Florence, the day has indeed come when Wayne no longer "needs" Batman. As paradoxical as it seems, perhaps we could view this act as authentically deceptive or deceptively authentic. While these actions carry a sense of deception, they are genuine because they allow Wayne to live authentically and not hidden behind a mask or a false lifestyle. For Bruce Wayne, the death of Batman was a genuine death, or at the very least, a psychological separation, allowing Bruce Wayne to be resurrected to a better life. Wayne allows the authentic burial of his constructed identities, the Batman and "the playboy" Bruce Wayne, in order to pursue the life he has always desired.

In turning back to the ancient heroes, one might see Batman's final use of the noble lie as the solution to Achilles's dilemma within Homer's *Iliad*.[28] Upon hearing the call to war, Achilles must choose between staying home and living a long, happy life, only to die forgotten, or fighting and dying in battle, to be remembered forever as a hero.[29] Achilles chooses the latter, only to regret it later in the underworld, as depicted in *The Odyssey*. He says to Odysseus that he would rather be a living slave than a dead king. In *The Dark Knight Rises*, Bruce Wayne, in sacrificing his alter ego, provides the solution to the problem. Batman dies in a sacrificial act and is thus immortalized as Gotham's hero, and Bruce Wayne lives a happy, peaceful life, with the knowledge of his own heroism. True to his form, Batman remains deceptive in the name of heroism. In his final feat, he tricks not only the people of Gotham, but perhaps even death itself. However, Wayne leaves Gotham with a new mythology, to be inspired by a new, but this time authentic, noble lie to believe in, and perhaps – if need be – a new Batman.[30]

---

[27] See Walker.

[28] Homer, *The Iliad*.

[29] Homer, *The Iliad*, IX.499-506: "My mother Thetis tells me that there are two ways in which I may meet my end. If I stay here and fight, I shall not return alive but my name will live forever: whereas if I go home my name will die, but it will be long ere death shall take me."

[30] The author would like to thank Peter Bell for offering helpful and critical feedback. Special thanks are due to Kate M. Colby for her advice and support throughout the process of writing and editing this chapter. The author is also

Bibliography

Darius, Julian. "Why *The Dark Knight Rises* Fails." *Sequart Organization*. 23 July 2012. http://sequart.org/magazine/13903/why-the-dark-knight-rises-fails/.

Dwivedi, Neerav. "Deconstructing the Ideology of Superheroes: A Critical Examination of Alan Moore's *Watchmen*." *International Journal of English Language, Literature, and Humanities* Vol. 3, No. 1 (2015). Pages 448-459. http://ijellh.com/papers/2015/March/40-448-459-March-2015.pdf.

Fenik, Bernard. *Studies in the Odyssey*. Hermes Einzelschriften, 30 (Wiesbaden: Franz Steiner Verlag, 1974).

Girard, René. *I See Satan Fall Like Lightning* (Maryknoll: Orbis Books, 2001).

Girard, René. *Violence and the Sacred* (London: Continuum [1988] 2005).

Golsan, Richard. *René Girard and Myth: An Introduction* (New York: Routledge, 2002).

Hobbes, Thomas. *Leviathan* (Cambridge: Cambridge University Press, [1651] 1996).

Homer. *The Iliad*, trans. Samuel Butler (London: A. C. Fifield, 1900).

Homer. *The Odyssey*, trans. A. T. Murray (Cambridge: Harvard University Press, 1919).

Ip, John. "*The Dark Knight*'s War on Terrorism." *Ohio State Journal of Criminal Law* Vol. 9, No. 1 (2011). Pages 209-229. http://moritzlaw.osu.edu/students/groups/osjcl/files/2012/05/Ip.pdf.

Kerstein, Benjamin. "Batman's War on Terror." *Azure* No. 34 (Autumn 5769 / 2008). Pages 136-144. http://azure.org.il/download/magazine/az34kerstein.pdf.

Klavan, Andrew. "The Best Conservative Movies of the Last 25 Years, #12: *The Dark Knight*." *National Review Online*. 11 Feb 2009. http://www.nationalreview.com/corner/177153/12-best-conservative-movies-last-25-years-andrew-klavan.

Klavan, Andrew. "What Bush and Batman Have in Common." *The Wall Street Journal*. 25 July 2008. http://online.wsj.com/article/SB121694247343482821.html.

Lord, Jeffery. "Batman and Rush: Why McCain Will Win." *The American Spectator*. 19 Aug 2008. http://spectator.org/articles/43139/batman-and-rush-why-mccain-will-win.

Magnani, Lorenzo and Tommaso Bertolotti. "Christ, Batman and Girard: Perspectives on Self-Sacrifice" (Presentation, Colloquium on Violence and Religion, Tokyo, 2012).

McGown, Todd. *The Fictional Christopher Nolan* (Austin: University of Texas Press, 2012).

Montiglio, Silvia. *From Villain to Hero: Odysseus in Ancient Thought* (Ann Arbor: University of Michigan Press, 2011).

Nolte, John. "*Dark Knight Rises* Review: Nolan Slaps Obama With A Masterpiece." *Breitbart*. 21 July 2012. http://www.breitbart.com/big-hollywood/2012/07/21/dark-knight-rises-review-nolte/.

Palaver, Wolfgang. *René Girard's Mimetic Theory*, trans. Gabriel Borrud (East Lansing: Michigan State University Press, 2013).

---

grateful to Ian Boucher for his generous support and editorial assistance that enabled the completion of this chapter.

Plato. *The Republic* Vol. 1, Books I-V, trans. Chris Emlyn-Jones and William Preddy (Cambridge: Loeb Classical Library, 2013).

Scheub, Harold. *Trickster and Hero: Two Characters in the Oral and Written Traditions of the World* (Madison: University of Wisconsin Press, 2012).

Segal, Charles. *Singers, Heroes, and Gods in the Odyssey* (New York: Cornell University Press, 1994).

Walker, Steven F. *Jung and the Jungians on Myth: An Introduction* (New York: Routledge, 2002).

Watchmen #1-12. Alan Moore (writer), Dave Gibbons (penciler/inker/letterer), and John Higgins (colorist). Ed. Len Wein. DC Comics, Sept 1986-Oct 1987.

Žižek, Slavoj. "Good Manners in the Age of WikiLeaks," *London Review of Books* Vol. 33, No. 2 (2011). Pages 9-10. http://www.lrb.co.uk/v33/n02/slavoj-zizek/good-manners-in-the-age-of-wikileaks.

Žižek, Slavoj. *Living in the End Times* (London: Verso, 2011). Page 61.

Must There Be
Superman Movies?

by Paul Jaissle

The question "Must there be a Superman?" is raised in a story of the same name written by Elliot S. Maggin and penciled by Curt Swan.[1] In this tale, the Guardians of the Universe summon Superman to inform him that he may be unintentionally inhibiting social progress on Earth, since people rely on him to solve their problems rather than taking care of themselves. This obviously shakes Superman since he believes he is using his powers to benefit everyone, and the notion that he might be unintentionally hindering humanity's cultural advancement makes him question his role as a hero. After his meeting with the Guardians, Superman encounters a small village of farm workers confronting their oppressive boss over their poor living conditions. When one of the children in the village begs him to help, Superman tells the farmers that he cannot solve all of their problems for them and that they must stand up for themselves. Just then, an earthquake destroys the village, and Superman, realizing that this would be too much for the villagers to handle on their own, rebuilds it for them. Although they are delighted that he helped them, Superman explains his seemingly

---

[1] *Superman* Vol. 1 #247.

conflicting actions by saying, "You must not count on a *Superman* to patch up your lives every time you have a crisis... You don't need a *Superman*! What you *really* need is a *super-will* to be *guardians* of your *own destiny!*"[2]

The idea that Superman might inadvertently be causing more harm than good is an interesting one – and one that Maggin returns to in his prose novel *Superman: Miracle Monday*[3] – since it attempts to draw out some of the "real-world" consequences of super-heroes in general. Maggin's story challenges the criticism of Superman being "too powerful." Rather than relying on his seemingly limitless physical strength and super-human abilities, Superman's greatest power is his ability to inspire those around him – as well as his real-world audience – to be better. Even though we live in a world without a Superman, the character can still serve as an inspiration, since he embodies the qualities we admire in ourselves. This is one of the reasons the super-hero genre is often referred to as a form of modern mythology: characters and their stories are retold and serve as allegories for a type of altruism and commitment to helping others. In their purest forms, super-heroes, like the heroes of classical fiction, are exemplars of truth and justice.

Although the notion of super-heroes as moral exemplars has existed since the beginning of the genre – even as these characters became pop culture icons beyond comic book characters – the current trend of big-budget comic book and super-hero films demonstrates that this does not always translate well in mass market adaptations. The obvious appeal of these films, such as *The Avengers* (2012) and *Man of Steel* (2013), is to see familiar characters and stories presented in a new way, which is why fidelity to the source material is often expected by the fans and promised by the filmmakers. However, in order to appeal to a larger audience, these films strive for more "grounded" portrayals of the characters. In these modern portrayals, the characters must be flawed and conflicted in order to be "realistic," believable, and – supposedly – easier for audiences to identify with, which downplays their inherent altruism in favor of a more soap opera

---

[2] Ibid., page 16.
[3] Maggin, *Superman: Miracle Monday*.

take on their stories. Rather than an inspirational message about justice, these films focus on the personal struggles of the characters. On one hand, these modern takes on the characters are attempting to explore the characters' nuances in much the same way Maggin does in "Must There Be a Superman?" However, what they seem to be missing is the underlying theme of inspiration present in that story. In *Man of Steel* for instance, the audience witnesses Superman struggle with the meaning of his powers without ever being asked to confront their own "super-will." Instead of an inspiring story, it is simply a flashy action film with a familiar-looking lead character. Despite the lack of inspirational messages, these films have proven incredibly successful and popular, which begs the question of what audiences expect from the genre. If modern audiences find the current iteration of "gritty and grounded" heroes – as exemplified in contemporary super-hero films – appealing, does that mean that altruistic heroes are simply passé? If that is the case, what do audiences find appealing about super-heroes instead?

Of course, it must be acknowledged that not all super-heroes are the same, and their respective pop culture portrayals should obviously reflect that. However, there are common qualities that make them "super-heroes" rather than super-human fictional characters. For example, Superman is usually presented as an authoritative figure sure about the just and right course of action, while Spider-Man is a character who must overcome his self-doubt in order to succeed. In both cases, there is still an aspirational and inspiring message: Superman, with his abilities and conviction, is usually presented as a character we should emulate, while Spider-Man, although we may recognize ourselves in him, has nevertheless dedicated himself to juggling Peter Parker's daily obligations with his "great responsibility." What makes them similar is that they both use their "great power" to do the right thing. The difference between the characters – and what makes them interesting – is the way they approach the problems they face. Even a character like Batman, who is often presented as a vengeful and grim vigilante, is motivated by a sort of optimism and altruism. Bruce Wayne isn't driven by revenge following his parents' murder. Instead, he vows to make sure that no one else has to suffer the way he has, which suggests an altruistic and sympathetic motivation. His "never-ending war on crime" is never-ending because its goal is unattainable, yet this Sisyphean task has an optimism at its core.[4]

Like the characters on which they are based, super-hero films have a variety of tones and styles. However, there do seem to be a few common tropes among the current crop of big-budget super-hero films. The first seems to be that of a conflicted, self-questioning hero. In *Batman Begins* (2005), *Man of Steel*, and *The Amazing Spider-Man* (2012), the first act of each film centers around the main character questioning his[5] role or purpose. Obviously this is an important part of each hero's "journey."[6] However, the self-doubt seems to define each character's actions throughout each film: rather than something to be overcome, this doubt becomes a part of their motivation. In *Batman Begins*, for example, Bruce Wayne is portrayed as an aimless young man seeking vengeance for his parents. In fact, a key scene of the film sees him confront Joe Chill, the man who murdered his parents in Crime Alley, in a Gotham courthouse with the intent to kill him. As the film goes on, Bruce decides to become a masked vigilante to rid the city of crime and protect it from corruption. However, rather than a desire to prevent others from suffering as he did, Bruce's goal seems to be to compromise the influence of Gotham's crime families destroying the city his father had worked to make better. The distinction between the film and comic book versions of Batman seems to hinge on Bruce's vow to his parents. In the comics, the young Bruce is smart and compassionate enough to recognize he is not unique in his suffering, yet he is naïve enough to think that he can single-handedly "wage war" on crime. It

---

[4] Oddly enough, 1997's *Batman & Robin*, widely considered the nadir of super-hero films, summarizes this element of Batman better than any of the other films in the franchise. When Bruce expresses doubt about his mission and methods, Alfred reassures him by explaining, "Death and chance stole your parents. But rather than become a victim, you have done everything in your power to control the fates. For what is Batman, if not an effort to master the chaos that sweeps our world? An attempt to control death itself."

[5] For in none of these films is the main character female.

[6] In his book *The Hero with a Thousand Faces*, mythologist Joseph Campbell claims that the "adventure of the hero" must include a "road of trials" on which the hero's strength and resolve is tested. These trials are what make the hero's eventual victory satisfying. See Campbell, pages 36-38 and 97-109.

is a decision that can only be made by an idealistic eight-year-old, not a jaded adult. So, in an attempt to make the character more "believable," the filmmakers downplay the altruistic intent of young Bruce in favor of an emotionally tortured young man suppressing his desire for revenge. The result is a morally ambiguous and conflicted hero audiences may see themselves as, but not aspire to emulate.

Batman, of course, is a character who is usually seen as more "human" than his contemporaries, and his emotional nuance and fragility are key to the character. Bruce Wayne's initial temptation for revenge can be seen as a part of him learning that true justice cannot be motivated by vengeance: the vow he makes to his parents in the comics is not seen explicitly in Nolan's films, but the sentiment may be implied. Superman, on the other hand, is traditionally presented as self-assured and certain, and his confidence is both a result of his power and what makes him an inspiring figure. However, *Man of Steel* portrays a young Clark Kent filled with doubt about his role in life; his great power is useless without a sense of responsibility. Much of this doubt is the result of his adoptive father Jonathan Kent telling him that the world would not accept him, and that he will know when it is the right time to reveal his true nature to others. Again, this sort of self-discovery is intended to "humanize" the character and "ground" him in the "real world." The problem with this approach is that it mainly focuses on Kal-El's power, implying that it is his Kryptonian abilities that make him "super" rather than his unwavering commitment to justice. His abilities may be "beyond those of mortal men,"[7] but his virtues of altruism, trustworthiness, and justice are arguably more important to the character and his appeal. Although we might not be able to fly or be bulletproof, we can strive to help and protect others, and we should do everything in our power to do so. While our limits, both physical and emotional, allow us to only do so much to help others, Superman is able to

---

[7] The famous phrase, "Yes, it's Superman! Strange visitor from another planet who came to Earth with powers and abilities far beyond those of mortal men," was first used on the *Adventures of Superman* radio program in the 1940s, and later on the 1950s television show. See Weldon, page 81.

do nearly anything imaginable, which is why he serves as a moral exemplar: if we had those powers we should do the same.

Superman: Secret Identity[8] by Kurt Busiek and Stuart Immonen provides an interesting counter-example to the moral uncertainty of *Man of Steel*. Set in our reality, one in which super-heroes are only fictional, a young boy jokingly named Clark Kent discovers that he has the same powers as the character with whom he shares his name. Like the character in *Man of Steel*, he tries to keep his powers a secret and stays largely anonymous, working with the government to avert disasters and prevent crises. What makes Busiek's story different, however, is that this Clark Kent has no doubt what he must do, knowing that his powers come with a duty to use them to benefit humanity. The implication of course is that the fictional Superman in that story serves as a moral example, just like in our real world. *Secret Identity* offers an unironic and idealistic take on the Superman character that manages to feel grounded and believable without overlooking the intrinsic inspirational elements. Rather than speculating how the real world may react to the presence of Superman, Busiek recognizes the influence the character has already had on popular culture. The notion of using one's powers and abilities to benefit others out of purely altruistic concern is not as unrealistic or rare as *Man of Steel* might assume or imply, and the existence of stories like *Secret Identity* suggests as much. Inspirational Superman stories do exist in the real world, and they both reflect and influence the worldviews of readers and creators. By choosing to focus on moral ambiguity or uncertainty, *Man of Steel* and other contemporary super-hero films seem to confuse cynicism for realism.

Although *Man of Steel* does at points hint at the notion of Superman as an inspirational figure, it fails to capture the spirit of the comics that inspired it. For example, the film paraphrases Grant Morrison and Frank Quitely's modern classic *All Star Superman*[9] when Jor-El tells Kal that he will inspire those around him: "You will give the people of Earth an ideal to strive towards. They will race behind you, they will stumble, they will fall.

---

[8] Originally published as *Superman: Secret Identity* Vol. 1 #1-4.
[9] Originally published as *All Star Superman* Vol. 1 #1-12.

Secret Identity is an example of a Superman story that is as inspirational as it is grounded. Art by Stuart Immonen. © DC Comics.

But in time, they *will* join you in the sun, Kal. In time, you will help *them* accomplish wonders." Unfortunately, the film rarely shows Superman doing anything inspiring. There are brief scenes that are intended to be inspiring, but they are undercut by the film's focus on the character's uncertainty since they take place prior to Clark becoming Superman. For example, when the young Clark saves his school bus from sinking, he is chastised by his father for revealing his abilities. Later, an older Clark saves workers on a burning oil rig, which is again designed to showcase the character's noble intentions. However, the scene's effectiveness is challenged by another moment in which Clark vandalizes and destroys a trucker's big rig following a confrontation in a bar, showing the character is petty and vindictive.[10] Both of these scenes demonstrate the film's preoccupation with Superman's powers, which often have disastrous ends. The penultimate action scene, which has Superman and General Zod battling through Metropolis and leaving destruction in their wake, could be a literal take on the idea Elliot Maggin proposes in "Must There Be A Superman?" – that of Superman inadvertently causing more harm than good. However, the film lacks the subtlety or conviction of Maggin's story, and instead Superman appears oblivious to those around him. When a character standing in the rubble of the city says, "He saved us," it rings hollow.

Even in the rare instances that the film does show Clark deciding to use his powers to help others, his actions are largely shepherded by Jor-El. Superman does, as Lois Lane points out, have a desire to help people, but the uncertainty of how he can do this makes the character feel flawed in a way that diminishes his heroism. Instead of having an innate moral certainty, Superman must learn to do the right thing, and instead of showcasing the character's intrinsic concern or responsibility for others, the focus is on his history, specifically his relationship to his father Jor-El and General Zod. Obviously, Superman's ancestry is an important part of the character, and one that has been explored extensively in comics and other media. However, *Man of Steel* focuses on this past as a way of explaining

---

[10] This bar scene is also reminiscent of a scene in 1980's *Superman II*, in which Clark travels back to Alaska to show up a trucker who had humiliated him earlier. Both scenes seem out of character.

the character and his motivations rather than showing him act in a virtuous manner.

The result is a version of the character who slowly learns that he should use his powers for good, which – in previous versions of the character – is something Jonathan Kent teaches him as a child. In *Man of Steel*, the fear of being out of place or misunderstood overshadows the innate moral clarity and altruism Pa Kent instills in Clark. Instead of a character inspiring people by example, Superman's motivations and actions are the result of forces outside of his control, such as Zod's grudge against Jor-El or Jonathan Kent's insistence that Clark not reveal his powers. This is seemingly done to make the audience relate to the character, to make him more "human." Of course, this approach assumes that the audience must sympathize with or recognize themselves in the hero. Instead of a character whose actions should be admired and emulated, Superman is just another person struggling with moral ambiguity and relativism. The notion of a conflicted Superman who questions his purpose can make for a compelling story, but again, the character must still have a distinct and identifiable moral code that guides him. What makes him a "super" man is his commitment to the noble and virtuous principles that we would also like to see in ourselves. Unfortunately, by making Superman an ineffectual and doubting hero, *Man of Steel* makes Superman feel all too "human."

By contrast, the most widely recognized version of the character outside of the comics – Christopher Reeve's portrayal in Richard Donner's 1978 film *Superman* – is arguably more realistic and believably human than the character in *Man of Steel*. The key difference in the two versions of the character is the way they interact with other characters, and by extension the audience. Unlike the shy or aloof character in *Man of Steel*, Reeve's Superman is presented as a sort of charming, personable savior. When Lois Lane first meets him and asks who he is, his response says it all: "A friend."[11] Rather than the stern patriarchal authority figure of the early comics, this modern Superman was a comrade who was here to help humanity as well as protect it, to rescue kittens from trees with the same attention and focus

---

[11] Weldon, pages 188-189.

that he would battle Lex Luthor. The end of the film most strikingly expresses the character's moral resolve, in that while this Superman has learned to be "human" from his adopted parents, he strives to be the best possible person he can, as he ignores Jor-El's command to never interfere with humanity to travel back in time and rescue Lois Lane. In this case, his realism is rooted not in self-doubt, but in his unwavering commitment and love for humanity. Obviously, the main reason this particular take on the character works overall is Reeve's performance, which masterfully shifts from Superman's self-assurance to Clark Kent's nervous attempts to fit in. The duality of the character, and Reeve's ability to portray it, doesn't bring Superman down to a human level so much as it makes us want to be more like Superman – he is human, but he also aspires to something better. The result is a film and performance that does something all the big-budget effects and CGI of *Man of Steel* cannot: it makes us not only believe a man can fly, but also believe in ourselves.

Portraying Superman as morally conflicted, rather than a certain, if dualistic, character may make him more "realistic" in some sense, but it dramatically changes the inspirational element of the character. It also makes the film's climax – when Superman kills General Zod – especially troubling. That penultimate scene of the film attempts to show a situation in which Superman "has no other choice" but to snap Zod's neck. Setting aside the fact that, as a fictional character, Superman is accustomed to doing the seemingly impossible on a regular basis, the moral conundrum implied by the scene undermines the character rather than makes him more complex. In a defense of the ending, director Zack Snyder has claimed that the scene is necessary to establish Superman's moral stance. "If it's truly an origin story," Snyder said of *Man of Steel*, "his aversion to killing is unexplained."[12] This might be a convincing argument if Superman were a new character whose motivations and beliefs were unfamiliar to the audience. However, Superman's moral stance against killing seems to be common knowledge, and a central component of the character's 77-year history. Even if *Man of Steel* is in fact a "reboot" of sorts for the character,

---

[12] Franich.

the fact that the filmmakers felt the need to establish that murder is wrong raises some questions about their understanding of the character and what the audience expects from super-hero films.

The implication of the scene – and Snyder's explanation of it – is that Superman chooses not to kill because of a personal "aversion" to it, as if he tried it once and didn't like it. Even with that justification, it's hard to imagine that anyone – fictional or not – approaches moral issues in this manner, especially something as serious as taking a life. Obviously, in the real world there are situations in which death is unavoidable, but in a fictional film about a character with extraordinary powers, the notion that he "had no other choice" is undermined by the fact that Superman can always do the seemingly impossible – it's one of his defining traits as a character. There is always a choice to be made, and what makes Superman a powerful and inspiring figure is that he does have an unflappable moral code: he always finds a way to do the right thing. Despite the character's abilities and established "aversion" to killing, the filmmakers believed that Superman's moral code needed to be explained to the audience.

Of course, the character's unflappable moral code has at times been bent – if not flat-out broken – in both comics and film. The infamous story "The Price"[13] by John Byrne has Superman executing General Zod and two other Phantom Zone prisoners after they murdered billions of people in a parallel "pocket dimension." Even though Superman felt justified acting as judge, jury, and executioner in this instance, the decision haunts him long afterwards. In film, the end of *Superman II* (1980) shows Superman take away the powers of Zod, Ursa, and Non and push them into an abyss. Even though their deaths are not shown on screen, it is clear that Superman kills the Phantom Zone prisoners as punishment for their destructive rampage across Earth. These examples stand out because they feel so out of character – Superman simply does not act this way normally. There are also practical explanations for them: John Byrne was leaving DC Comics at the time and his frustrations with editorial oversight may have influenced "The

---

[13] *Superman* Vol. 2 #22.

Price" as an attempt to "break the character" on his way out,[14] and the ending of *Superman II* was likely just as affected by the removal of director Richard Donner from the production as the tone of the rest of the film, which departed a great deal from Donner's more character-driven vision.[15] These are examples of Superman killing due to a sort of narrative or creative expediency, which makes the scene in *Man of Steel* so much more egregious, since the filmmakers felt it necessary to establish Superman's reluctance to kill only after doing it the first time; rather than feeling out of character of that version of Superman, killing Zod is part of what defines Superman's morals. In the attempt to explain the character's motivations, the filmmakers end up directly contradicting what makes Superman an inspirational figure in the first place.

Of course, *Man of Steel* is not the only recent super-hero film that attempts to make its super-human lead character's motivations feel more "realistic." For example, the plot of Marvel's *The Avengers* requires its disparate cast of characters to join forces, but rather than starting from a point in which the team is working together for a greater purpose, the film stresses the tension between them. Obviously, the tension between the members is a defining characteristic of the Avengers, and the team's dynamic is part of the appeal of the comics and the film. However, in the film that personal tension or distrust seems to overshadow the characters' moral obligations. Despite the clear and present threats posed by Loki, the Avengers' response is hindered by their personal foibles. After S.H.I.E.L.D. agent Phil Coulson is killed by Loki, Nick Fury uses his death as a means of rallying the characters around a cause. It's a fairly shrewd move on Fury's part, since knows that the Avengers do not entirely trust him. Of course,

---

[14] Byrne explained his frustrations with DC in an interview years later: "DC hired me to revamp Superman, and then immediately chickened out. They backed off at the first whiff of fan disapproval, which came months before anyone had actually seen the work. During the whole two years I was on the project, although nothing happened that was not approved by DC editorial, there was no conscious support... After two years of this nonsense, I was just worn down. The fun was gone." See "John Byrne: The Hidden Answers."

[15] See *You Will Believe: The Cinematic Saga of Superman* (2006) and *Superman II: Restoring the Vision* (2006).

Loki had already killed innocent people before this, but the Avengers seemed too distracted by their personal issues to effectively respond. The fact that there must be a personal emotional appeal in order to bring the team together feels cheap, and it challenges the purpose of the Avengers as a team. They appear reactionary, only effectively following through with their mission when they lose something important. As Tony Stark tells Loki later in the film: "if we can't protect the Earth you can be damn well sure we'll avenge it." Like *Man of Steel*, this narrative choice may seem necessary in order to explain why these characters choose to work together. The Avengers can be seen as more of military group – they are sanctioned to operate under the guidance of the government agency S.H.I.E.L.D., after all – than a super-hero team like the Justice League. In either case, however, there does need to be an explanation for why the respective heroes choose to join, and the filmmakers offer a fairly cynical one. Rather than a responsibility or duty to work together, the Avengers are driven by a personal sense of vengeance. On one hand, this may seem "realistic," but it is far from the altruistic virtue we might expect from super-heroes. Although the Avengers may not normally be thought of as aspirational characters like Superman, showing them as inherently petty and selfish seems to undermine their heroism: they are no longer seen as examples, but equals.[16]

While both *Man of Steel* and *The Avengers* focus on the motivations of the characters, they seem to do so in ways that undermine the characters' intrinsic moral resolve, since their motivations to do the right thing are personal rather than altruistic. The desire to make super-heroes in these films more "realistic" ends up making them less interesting overall. Although all super-heroes are not created equally, and there are different types of stories that can be told with them, the underlying theme that connects them all is that they reflect recognizable and admirable human

---

[16] It should be noted that the 2015 sequel *Avengers: Age of Ultron* seemingly attempts to address this by having the characters state numerous times the importance of rescuing civilians during the battle sequences. This seems to be a direct statement about how the dynamic and purpose of the group has changed, as well as a sly critique of *Man of Steel*'s disastrous finale (pun intended).

traits and virtues. Like the characters from classical myths, super-heroes serve as metaphors, and the stories we tell about them are allegories that explore what it means to be human. Of course, like myths, these stories are retold over time to reflect the changing social and cultural zeitgeist. If the current iteration of super-heroes – as exemplified by these current films – are presented as being morally conflicted or ambivalent, and are another step in the ever-changing genre, then that may suggest how the audience and the creators view themselves: instead of looking up to Superman or Steve Rogers because they embody the qualities we admire, there now seems to be a temptation – driven by either creative choices or profit margins – to bring them down to our level and look them in the eye. Rather than wanting to see ourselves as these heroes, we want to see ourselves in them, flawed and frail like we are.

Characters like Batman, Superman, and the Avengers are not simply "comic book" characters: they became fixtures of popular culture decades ago through adaptations in other media and relentless marketing and licensing. While their pop culture ubiquity may not be new, the increasing number of stories being told and sold to a mass audience suggests that mass audiences enjoy these characters, or at least the visual spectacle they provide. Additionally, like any myth, these characters and their stories evolve and change through retelling. However, the modern trend of these films seems to include a focus on explanation and exposition: the characters must have explicit motivations and purposes for what they do, even if they are well-known.[17] Explanations of characters' behaviors are seemingly taken more seriously than their powers, as if altruism is less believable than super-speed or mutations. More importantly, these motivations must be "believable" and "realistic," and instead of bringing characters to the screen that exemplify the best qualities of humanity, they merely reflect the most basic and selfish. In some cases, these latter qualities are exactly what must be overcome in order for the hero to succeed, but the extent of these

---

[17] This seems to be a common thread among many pop culture franchises and genres. Even classic fairy tales like Snow White and Sleeping Beauty are now augmented with prequels chronicling their characters' origins. It may be a modern desire for certainty, but it may just as easily be driven by profits.

explanations seem to change the characters themselves. For example, if Bruce Wayne or Superman are driven to fight for justice out of a sense of guilt, then they are no longer exemplary moral heroes; instead of examples of what humans should be, they are examples of what they already are.

If the success of these films is due solely to their content – as opposed to the familiarity of the characters, the visual spectacle, or their massive marketing campaigns – then it could be assumed that audiences want these kinds of stories. If that is indeed the case, then the inclusion of established characters like Superman is obviously a part of the marketing instead of a central component of the film: *Man of Steel* could simply be about any "strange visitor from another planet" instead of an updated retelling of an already familiar origin with a new, more "realistic" sheen. Of course, these movies and their associated marketing campaigns are primarily driven by profit, which is why each film is designed to lead into its inevitable sequels and spin-offs. Using universally recognizable characters is a sure way to generate interest and viewers, and as studios scramble to adapt super-hero stories for the big screen (and continue to remake them lest the copyright expire), the stories must appear to be new in order to maintain the audience's attention. Perhaps the current trend for "gritty," "realistic" heroes is simply an example of marketing trends attempting to assure audiences that each new retelling is worth seeing. Regardless, these recent examples of super-hero stories seem to lack the inspiring message that is intrinsic to the characters. Maybe they are no longer super-hero films with mythological undercurrents, but action films that merely feature familiar-looking characters.

If these films are in fact a new interpretation of the super-hero genre, then they may say more about the current social culture than they do about their subjects. It might be that super-heroes are not as popular as assumed, but the experience of – and hype surrounding – these films is what attracts viewers. If so, the resulting films are not really about super-heroes at all, but rather us as viewers and consumers. Nevertheless, maybe super-heroes as inspirational moral exemplars have not become passé. Perhaps we have instead lost the "super-will" to see how we can achieve the qualities of altruism and justice for ourselves, and we want our heroes to reflect that doubt. If that is indeed the case, then there must be Superman movies – ones that remind us of what we can be rather than what we merely are.

Bibliography

All Star Superman Vol. 1 #1-12. Grant Morrison (writer), Frank Quitely (penciler), Jamie Grant (inker/colorist), Phil Balsman (letterer), and Travis Lanham (letterer). Eds. Brandon Montclare and Bob Schreck. DC Comics, 2006-2008.

Campbell, Joseph. *The Hero with a Thousand Faces* (Princeton, NJ: Princeton University Press, 1949).

Franich, Darren. "Zack Snyder and David Goyer Talk About Controversial *Man of Steel* Ending... That Christopher Nolan Didn't Want." *Entertainment Weekly.* 19 June 2013. http://www.ew.com/article/2013/06/19/zack-snyder-david-goyer-christopher-nolan-man-of-steel-ending.

"John Byrne: The Hidden Answers." Interview by Michael Thomas. *Comic Book Resources.* 22 Aug 2000. http://www.comicbookresources.com/?page=article&id=151.

Maggin, Elliot S. *Superman: Miracle Monday* (New York: Warner Books, 1981).

Superman Vol. 1 #247. Elliot S. Maggin (writer), Curt Swan (penciler), and Murphy Anderson (inker). Ed. Julius Schwartz. DC Comics, Jan 1972.

Superman Vol. 2 #22. John Byrne (writer/penciler/inker), Petra Scotese (colorist), and and John Costanza (letterer). Eds. Mike Carlin and Renee Witterstaetter. DC Comics, Oct 1988.

Superman: Secret Identity Vol. 1 #1-4. Kurt Busiek (writer), Stuart Immonen (penciler/inker/colorist), and Todd Klein (letterer). Eds. Joey Cavalieri, Dan DiDio, and Harvey Richards. DC Comics, Jan-Apr 2004.

Weldon, Glen. *Superman: The Unauthorized Biography* (Hoboken, NJ: John Wiley & Sons, Inc., 2013).

Shadows Prove the Sunshine

by Rebecca Johnson

How do we know something is dark?

C. S. Lewis contemplated that very question when he wrote that "if there were no light in the universe and therefore no creatures with eyes, we should never know it was dark."[1] It's a profound statement that makes sense, but is an impossible concept for me to wrap my brain around. I know light exists in our universe. I've seen it. If I became blind today, there would still be light despite my inability to see it. Imagining a world without light is an insurmountable task.

It wasn't until I heard his idea summarized into the shorter, more understandable phrase "the shadows prove the sunshine"[2] that I started to grasp his illustration of darkness. Shadows need two things to form: a light source and an object to block it. Objects can exist, but if there is no light, the objects won't produce a shadow and conversely, light can exist, but if there is no object to obscure the light, shadows won't occur. The best way to identify light is to observe a shadow. We want our super-hero stories to be full of light, but what they really need to be are full of shadows. Movies like

---

[1] Lewis, page 39.
[2] Via Frank Turek's radio show, *CrossExamined*: http://crossexamined.org/radio/.

the Dark Knight Trilogy, *Man of Steel* (2013), and television shows like *Arrow* are often criticized as being "too dark" as if that's a bad thing. While "grim" and "gritty" have become no-no words in the super-hero genre, I would argue that "dark" themes and tones make for some of the most inspirational and heroic stories.

> And why do we fall, Bruce? So we can learn to pick ourselves up.
> — Thomas Wayne, *Batman Begins* (2005)

The best example of a super-hero story incorporating shadows is of the hero who not only fights crime in them, but is trained by them. In *Batman Begins*, the first film of Christopher Nolan's Dark Knight Trilogy, a young Bruce Wayne witnesses the murder of his parents, filling him with a vengeful rage that he believes can only be quenched by shooting their killer. When the opportunity is taken from him by someone else, Bruce finds a purpose in training with the elite group of assassins known as the League of Shadows. The League teaches him how to overcome his fears and how he can "turn fear against those who prey on the fearful."

While the League of Shadows assists Bruce Wayne in becoming Batman, it is the lesson of his father, Thomas, that holds the Dark Knight Trilogy together. In *Batman Begins*, young Bruce falls down a bat-filled hole and needs his father's rescuing. Seeing this as a teachable moment, Thomas asks his son, "Why do we fall?" The heart of Bruce Wayne's cinematic journey lies in the answer to that question. Over the course of three movies, situations arise that require Bruce Wayne to pick himself back up in order to save Gotham City. In *Batman Begins*, Bruce thinks he's failed Gotham and the Wayne legacy, and Batman fails to stop Ra's al Ghul from unleashing Scarecrow's toxin. *The Dark Knight* (2008) opens with evidence of Batman inspiring the people of Gotham, but in the wrong way, with men wearing hockey pads and carrying guns to ensure their brand of justice, and ends with Bruce grieving the death of the woman he longed to build a life with. In *The Dark Knight Rises* (2012), Bruce must climb out of a physical and metaphorical pit after he is easily broken by Bane, who capitalizes on Batman's absence by terrorizing the citizens of Gotham with the threat of a nuclear bomb.

Even with all of his struggles and setbacks, Bruce Wayne and his caped identity of Batman continue to respond to the Bat-Signal whenever it lights up the sky. In the Dark Knight Trilogy, Batman transforms from costumed vigilante, to hunted criminal, into, as anticipated by Commissioner James Gordon in *The Dark Knight*, "the hero Gotham deserves." The Gotham City Police Department ceases combatting the Batman, and eventually fights and dies alongside him in war. Batman's actions in saving Gotham City from the likes of Scarecrow, Ra's al Ghul, the Joker, Two-Face, Bane, and Talia al Ghul earn him a statue, but more importantly, redemption in the eyes of the citizens who built it in his memory.

What makes Batman one of the most inspiring super-heroes is that he is just like us. Batman shows that yes, there will be catastrophes in our lives, but we can choose how we respond to them. Actor Matthew Modine, who played Foley, a character who ultimately gives his life for Gotham in *The Dark Knight Rises*, said this about Batman's relatability and why we look up to him:

> He's not a man with supernatural powers, he's not a mythological character – he's just a man who's damaged, who's broken like so many people in the world... trying to do good... I think that "broken person doing good" is something we all aspire to in our life, trying to overcome our fears and trying to fight evil in the world. He's a character we all relate to.[3]

In *Batman Begins*, Bruce Wayne hopes that the Batman will "shake" the citizens of Gotham "out of apathy." He tells Alfred, "I'm going to show the people of Gotham their city doesn't belong to the criminals and the corrupt." This goal was achieved, and on real-world display following the horrific events of 20 July 2012, when a gunman in Aurora, Colorado opened fire on an unsuspecting moviegoing audience at a midnight screening of *The Dark Knight Rises*. When survivors and family members gathered in a courthouse to witness James Holmes "be charged with 142 counts, including 24 counts of first-degree murder," they proudly wore Batman T-shirts to show their solidarity. One of them was Don Lader, who was with his wife in theater nine, row eight, about 15 yards from the exit when Holmes interrupted the movie, firing rounds into the seated audience. In the courtroom, Lader's T-shirt quoted the phrase "A Fire Will Rise" from *The*

---

[3] Campbell.

Dark Knight Rises, and Lader said that Holmes "attacked us out of cowardice but we will attack back in strength."[4]

Filmmaker Brett Culp directed a documentary film called *Legends of the Knight* (2013) that features stories of real extraordinary people who view the Caped Crusader as a source of courage. It's his hope that seeing their stories can impact those who watch, by galvanizing them to do what they can in their own communities:

> We're not billionaires like Bruce Wayne but you don't have to be a billionaire to make a difference, sometimes what's needed is just engagement and really going out and helping people. Maybe that's people who are strangers to you, maybe it's just your brother or sister or Mom or your Dad, or your son or your daughter, but engaging with the world, your world, the way Batman engages with Gotham, is what everyone of us has the potential to do.[5]

In *The Dark Knight Rises*, Bruce Wayne tells John Blake that "Batman could be anybody. That was the point." You could be Batman. I could be Batman. Even if he is the "Dark" Knight, Batman shines a light on what is good. He encourages us to pick ourselves up when something bad happens and endeavor to prevent it from happening to someone else.

> All these changes that you're going through... one day you're going to think of them as a blessing.
>
> — Jonathan Kent, *Man of Steel* (2013)

When *Man of Steel* hit theaters in 2013, critics found the film joyless and devoid of hope. *The Washington Post* wrote that it had a "dour tone" that was "more appropriate for a tortured hero brooding in his cave than for an all-American alien who is as much a product of the wholesome windswept Plains as a distant planet called Krypton."[6] *The New Yorker* wrote that "when forces that hold the world in the balance do battle, even the winners are losers."[7] David Edelstein of *Vulture* referred to it as "pleasure-free."[8] *Entertainment Weekly* described the movie as transforming

---

[4] Wheeler.
[5] "Interview: Brett Culp, Director of the Batman Documentary *Legends of the Knight*."
[6] Hornaday.
[7] Brody.
[8] Edelstein.

Superman into a "soul-searching super-brooder."[9] *Variety* thought that the entire movie seemed to be "afraid to crack a smile."[10] NPR's Glen Weldon wrote "What it [*Man of Steel*] fails to supply much of – surprisingly, it must be said – is fun," and that, "when the lights come up, we're still waiting" to cheer on the hero.[11]

Henry Cavill's Superman in *Man of Steel* was such a departure from previous cinematic Supermen who donned "S" curls, winked at the camera from space, and reiterated the safety statistics of airline travel that it caught critics and audiences off guard. But Cavill's soul-searching Clark Kent is arguably the first time the character's journey has been portrayed realistically and, most importantly, *accurately* on the big screen. Christopher Reeve's Clark Kent may have experienced teenage angst because he was unable to date Lana Lang, but *Man of Steel* explored what it would be like for young Clark's super-hearing to manifest in the classroom, to have arguments with his adoptive father, and to contemplate his choices. When he first appears to the public, Reeve's 1978 Superman is met with cheers and compliments from strangers about his "bad outfit," while Cavill's Superman is introduced to Smallville during a time of fear and skepticism about aliens. Henry Cavill's Superman may not be the morally grey and threatening figure of his comic book counterpart's early days,[12] but *Man of Steel* perfectly depicts what Five For Fighting's been singing about all these years: It's not easy being Superman.

Much like Batman's origin, Kal-El's story traditionally begins in tragedy. Embedded within comics, live-action and animated television shows, and on the big screen is the tale of Kal's parents launching him off of their dying planet so that he might have a chance at life. Even though Jor-El and Lara are successful, and Kal lands on a farm to be raised by a salt of the earth Smallville couple, Clark grows up feeling isolated and alone, knowing he is unlike other kids. In the *Man of Steel* official movie guide, Henry Cavill describes his character as "far more complex than people think," that "he's

---

[9] Nashawaty.
[10] Foundas.
[11] Weldon.
[12] Moss.

an incredibly conflicted, lonely, and lost person," and that he's "ultimately an outsider, at all stages of his life."[13] The "dour," "pleasure-free" tone of his story captures what would cause anybody in his situation to become a "super-brooder" who might be "afraid to crack a smile."

What *Man of Steel* exhibits so beautifully is that in spite of being the last son of Krypton, the victim of bullying, and a wanderer, lost in purpose, Clark Kent develops into a man who can't stop helping people. He risks exposing his powers to prevent his fellow classmates from drowning. He abandons ship to safeguard the lives of oil rig workers. He performs emergency surgery on Lois Lane. He flies in front of American soldiers when Kryptonians attack Smallville. Even when he is faced with the difficult choice to kill General Zod, he does it to save a family of four and inevitably, all of the human race, because he believes Earth is worth saving.

Whether he's ending Zod's global threat or standing up to a drunk trucker on behalf of a woman who has been sexually harassed in a small town bar, Superman in *Man of Steel* represents hope for the planet in times of despair. Just because *Man of Steel* made those moments seem or feel real doesn't make them dark in a negative sense. Henry Cavill's understanding of the Superman character comes through in his performance, highlighting the misunderstanding of the movie:

> Superman genuinely represents hope, struggle in the face of adversity as opposed to rolling over and giving up. Really facing up to seemingly insurmountable odds and, hopefully, winning. That's the point: the hope that one will win as opposed to turning one's back on hope and giving up. Or becoming the thing we initially disliked or felt strongly about. That's his place in this world, it's genuinely the representation of hope. You know, no matter how many times I told people this was not dark and gritty, people kept on saying it. I'm so glad that people are starting to see it now in the latest trailer that it's not dark and gritty at all, it's just more realistic than previous incarnations of Superman, but without losing the super powered wonder of what Superman is.[14]

In *Man of Steel*, Jor-El envisions Kal's motivational effect on humanity. He believes that his son can "give the people of Earth an ideal to strive towards," but recognizes that despite our best efforts, sometimes, we are

---

[13] Wallace, page 18.
[14] *"Man of Steel*: One-On-One With Henry Cavill."

going to "stumble" and "fall." What brightens this unfairly criticized and "dark" film is the idea that although he can fly around the world, lift school buses, and shoot fire from his eyes, Superman makes mistakes, feels lonely, and can be conflicted over painful decisions. David Goyer and Christopher Nolan crafted their *Man of Steel* story in the effort to make Superman relatable, and to them, "relatable doesn't necessarily mean grim and gritty."[15] Their movie reminds us that challenging moments in our lives can be reconstructed into blessings when we look back and remember what we've overcome. Critics may have wanted a flawless Man of Steel who cracks jokes with an eternal smile, but isn't it more hopeful to envision that if we keep pushing through our turmoil, we too, can join Superman in the sun?

> I'm not going to pretend that I've been through anything that you have. But one thing that I've learned in the past year is that these things... they don't break us. They make us who we are.
> — Laurel Lance to Sara Lance, "Streets of Fire" (*Arrow*, 2014)

The title of the CW's *Arrow* may make it seem like the story is about how Oliver Queen becomes Green Arrow, but the true hero of the series is Laurel Lance, better known as the Black Canary.

Laurel Lance has endured many trials. Her boyfriend cheated on her with her sister, who then both "died" when the yacht they were sailing on sank. She watched her mother walk away from the family when her father became an alcoholic. She blamed herself for the death of another man she loved. Because of her struggles, fans and television critics grew to dislike the character and showed their disdain through online listicles. *TV.com* awarded her Worst Female Character.[16] *HuffPost TV Canada* listed her among their "Five Most Annoying TV Characters of 2012."[17] *WhatCulture* put her on their list of "5 Characters We'd All Secretly Like *Arrow* to Kill Off."[18] *TV Fanatic* listed her among their "12 Characters That Make Us Want to Punch the TV."[19]

---

[15] "David Goyer Extended Interview - *Man of Steel* (*JoBlo.com*)."
[16] Grumpyclown.
[17] Wilford.
[18] Challies.
[19] Richenthal.

In the *Arrow* episode "Birds of Prey," Laurel Lance becomes a hero long before she becomes the Black Canary.

Due to her poor choices in how she responded to her agony during the second season of *Arrow* (2013-2014), Laurel descended into alcoholism and pill addiction. She was arrested and lost her job. She fought with her family and rejected any attempts to seek rehabilitation. Even Oliver Queen, her oldest friend, didn't want to run after her anymore. She had nobody in her corner. Nobody but herself. However, Laurel Lance's life began to turn around when she made the decision to attend an Alcoholics Anonymous meeting, and in the episode "Birds of Prey," she reclaimed her courage.

At the time that episode aired on 26 March 2014, I was undergoing chemotherapy treatment for Stage 3 HER2+ breast cancer, and the side effects had become my new normal. My hair fell out, my nose bled, and my damaged tongue made it difficult to eat. I was having trouble staying awake at work and falling asleep at night. The tops of my hands and the bottoms of my feet turned red. My fingernails got so brittle that I worried they'd fall off. Nausea caused me to run away from kitchen aromas. And my sworn enemy was a shot intended to boost my white blood count that would leave me in 24 (sometimes, more) hours of paralyzing bone pain. Chemo was physically challenging, but the most strenuous aspect of my seven cycles was maintaining a positive attitude. The slightest reminder of what I was going through brought me to tears. I would emotionally break down at the thought of how broken my body was. When people described me as strong and brave, I couldn't help but think it was a lie designed to make me feel better. If only they knew how powerless and frightened I really felt.

"Birds of Prey" revealed a Laurel Lance who would rise above her misery and embrace her strength. In the episode, Laurel is working to rebuild her career as an attorney, and before she enters the courtroom, crossbow-wielding Helena Bertinelli – otherwise known as the Huntress – takes hostages in an effort to kill the latter's father. When realizing she'd been used by her boss to serve as an "expendable decoration" to trap the Huntress, the 30-day sober Laurel Lance grabs for a bottle of alcohol. As she threatens to drink it, Laurel confesses to the Canary – her costumed sister, Sara – that she went back to work to show herself that she could be strong. When the Canary gives her the opportunity to display her willpower and self-control, Laurel puts the top back on the bottle and stands up. In that moment, Laurel Lance is transformed into a hero.

What inspired me that night *Arrow* first aired "Birds of Prey" was seeing a Laurel who rejected her demon, accepted the call to action, and utilized her tragedies as a way to help others. While tied up as a hostage, it is Laurel's afflictions that open up communication with the Huntress. In hopes of making peace, Laurel relates to Helena's heartache and sadness of losing a loved one, by admitting the mistakes she made during her period of mourning. In a tearful admission, Laurel explains, "I couldn't deal with it, so I became a drunk. Every problem I had, I solved with a pill or a drink. My friends and my family, they tried to help me, but I wouldn't let them. You don't have to do this, Helena. It's not too late." Despite Laurel Lance's impeccable skills as an attorney, she couldn't prevent Helena from incarceration for the laws the latter had broken and the lives she took, but through the lessons Laurel learned in her own life, she could present the Huntress with a redemptive perspective on life.

It could be argued that Laurel Lance doesn't begin her Black Canary journey until she puts on her sister's Canary jacket at the end of the season, but I would make the case that Laurel's destiny was cemented in "Birds of Prey." After everything she had been through, Laurel took charge of her life again, and from then on, during chemo, I could see myself in her. Instead of focusing on the pain and frustration of what I was going through, I was determined to concentrate on the things in my life I could control. I leaned on my faith, adopted a new diet and developed an exercise program, stayed in touch with my family on a daily basis, and relished moments with friends. When I stopped assuming people were just trying to be nice to me, I accepted the love and support from those who would offer it. Following a double mastectomy, 30 sessions of radiation, and a pathology report that read "no carcinoma present," I consider my scars a badge of honor because it's a reminder of what I've experienced. It makes me who I am.

Laurel's personal triumph over adversity blossoms the character into a hero who is quick to hug, values friendships, and maintains an unwavering faith. Laurel's example has had a powerful influence on me. She didn't let hardships break her. Rather, they drove her to become an attorney with City Necessary Resources Initiative (CNRI) in Season 1 (2012-2013), an organization for aiding people in need. Laurel would later use her abilities in the courtroom to put bad guys behind bars. Her law career is a recognition of the fact – in her words in the Season 3 episode "Corto Maltese" (2014) – "that the world isn't fair" and "it's a terrible place where people deserve to get punished and they don't," yet she continually yearns for improvement. It's not until Season 3 (2014-2015), after her sister is murdered and punishing the killer proves to be problematic in the courtroom, that Laurel starts devoting her time to becoming the Black Canary. Through fight training with both a world-class champion boxer and a formidable assassin, wearing a sonic-powered necklace, and concealing her identity with a mask of her own, Laurel has been able to become the justice criminals can't run from. Overcoming her addiction taught Laurel that her scars (both literal and metaphorical) didn't break her. They made her who she is: "Dinah Laurel Lance... always trying to save the world."[20]

> Human progress is neither automatic nor inevitable... Every step towards the goal of justice requires sacrifice, suffering, and struggle; the tireless exertions and passionate concern of dedicated individuals.
>
> — Dr. Martin Luther King, Jr., Stride Toward Freedom: The Montgomery Story[21]

---

[20] As Tommy Merlyn puts it at the end of Arrow's pilot episode.
[21] "MLK Quote of the Week: A Time for Vigorous and Positive Action."

The correlation between struggle and justice is not lost on real-life heroes. People who fight for causes they believe in don't do it because it's easy. Rather, they do it because they see a need and wish to fulfill it. When progress enhances our world, it's because a voice has been heard that has spoken louder than its persecution.

One such voice was that of Dr. Martin Luther King, Jr., who was no stranger to the strife of pursuing justice. His conviction that blacks and whites could and should live equally and peacefully would serve as the guidance and foundation of the American Civil Rights Movement. Events he participated in such as the Montgomery Bus Boycott and the March on Washington led to the Civil Rights Act of 1964 and the Voting Rights Act of 1965. Dr. King received the Nobel Peace Prize in 1964 and is now remembered each year on an American holiday in January. However, his days weren't always filled with delivering "I Have a Dream" speeches and waving to cheering crowds. He was arrested, sent to jail, and, eventually, would die a martyr's death.

One of Dr. King's most famous letters is one he wrote on 16 April 1963 from a jail in Birmingham, Alabama. In it, he explains "I am in Birmingham because injustice is here."[22] Like fictional super-heroes, Dr. King never shied away from trouble. In fact, he sought it out, knowing full well it might lead to physical violence and imprisonment. Problems happening elsewhere couldn't be ignored because in his mind, "injustice anywhere is a threat to justice everywhere."[23]

Martin Luther King, Jr.'s "Letter from Birmingham Jail" overflows with appeals for justice and how it might be accomplished. He contrasts just and unjust laws, quotes St. Augustine that "an unjust law is no law at all,"[24] and reminds his reader about historical instances of civil disobedience that brought forth change. Dr. King would be charged with breaking laws through his protests, but he continually dissuaded others from defying the law, and if he was going to be labeled an extremist, he urged those who would follow his example to ask themselves whether they would choose to

---

[22] King, Jr., page 188.
[23] Ibid., page 189.
[24] Ibid., page 193.

be "extremists for hate or for love."[25] For Martin Luther King, Jr., the method of nonviolent tension was "necessary for growth" to "help men rise from the dark depths of prejudice and racism to the majestic heights of understanding and brotherhood."[26] Incarceration didn't stop Martin Luther King, Jr. He didn't dwell on his circumstance in a discouraging time filled with segregation, prejudice, and bigotry. Instead, Dr. King stands out as an example of a mistreated yet optimistic man whose suffering produced courage about the future.

Another example of a real-life hero who refused to allow dreary settings to dictate his actions was Abraham Lincoln, who served as president of the United States during the deadliest conflict in American history. In 2011, Binghamton University historian J. David Hacker estimated that around 750,000 soldiers lost their lives when the country was at war with itself.[27] I can't fathom what it would have been like for President Lincoln to make the hard choices when so many were dying, but he was a man who understood the price that needed to be paid. Decades before our United States would be divided against themselves, Abraham Lincoln stood before the Illinois House of Representatives to deliver a speech about President Van Buren's subtreasury that would articulate so much about Lincoln's philosophy on struggle. He passionately said, "The probability that we may fall in the struggle ought not to deter us from the support of a cause we believe to be just; it shall not deter me."[28] Like any super-hero, Lincoln was determined, no matter the odds.

In one of his most famous speeches, the Gettysburg Address, President Lincoln reflected on the sacrifice of soldiers who gave their lives during the Civil War. He recognized that in order for their deaths to have meaning and propel the country forward, the living needed to press on:

> The brave men, living and dead, who struggled here, have consecrated it far above our poor power to add or detract. The world will little note, nor long remember what we say here, but it can never forget what they did

---

[25] Ibid., page 198.
[26] Ibid., page 191.
[27] Coker.
[28] Lincoln, page 178.

here. It is for us the living, rather, to be dedicated here to the unfinished work which they who fought here have thus far so nobly advanced.[29]

In addition to political anguish, President Lincoln endured tragedies in his personal life. He and his wife, Mary, mourned the death of their son, Willie, who died of typhoid fever at the age of 11, and for the president, it was a long process of recovery.[30] To some, President Lincoln's grief made him look like a "weak, passive child,"[31] but ultimately, the President couldn't ignore the war. He could only lock himself in a room to grieve for so long. He had to get back to work.[32] I often get lost in the iconography of "Honest Abe" and his stovepipe hat, but the truth is that times were tough for President Lincoln. It might have been tempting to give up. He once told a friend, "We are on the brink of destruction... and I can hardly see a ray of hope."[33]

Abraham Lincoln is considered to be one of the most important and influential American presidents because his undeterred attitude paved the way to emancipation and held the Union together in a time of war.[34] His experiences taught him not to quit when times became demanding and troublesome, because the struggle would be worth it in the end. President Lincoln's story ended with assassination in a theater, but his last public address at the White House is filled with optimism. He began his speech with "We meet this evening, not in sorrow, but in gladness of heart," and that's how I would like to memorialize him.[35] The 16th president of the United States was a man who, despite his hardships, found gladness in his heart and was faithful to his country's potential for change.

Men aren't the only ones able to uphold their ideals during oppression. Early on in her childhood, Susan Brownell Anthony observed that women were treated differently than men. In school, she was told that girls didn't need to learn long division. When working at her father's mill, she was told that a woman couldn't be the overseer even if she knew more than her

---

[29] Holzer, page 136.
[30] Burlingame.
[31] Dennis.
[32] Holzer.
[33] Ibid., page 106.
[34] Kelly.
[35] Holzer, pages 183-184.

male co-workers. These early bouts with sexism fueled Susan to appeal for women's rights through temperance, women's rights to own property, and, famously, for women's rights to vote. In addition to speaking out for women's rights, Susan B. Anthony was an abolitionist who worked with the Underground Railroad and the Anti-Slavery Society. Even though she would do many great things on behalf of black Americans, she would encounter disappointment when black men were granted the right to vote while women were still intentionally left out. Women would fill out voting ballots as protest, but they were never counted.[36] It was a disheartening realization that women remained less valuable than men, no matter the color of their skin.

While gathered with friends to celebrate her birthday, Anthony once said, "If this were an assembled mob opposing the rights of women I should know what to say."[37] The confidence in her principles drove her to become a symbol of the suffragette movement, but we tend to forget the harassment she would encounter to embody it. Susan B. Anthony faced down angry mobs, was pelted with rotten eggs and tomatoes, and figures made to look like her were dragged through the streets and burned.[38] After casting a vote, she was arrested by a deputy U.S. marshal.[39] In 1872, she was arrested for voting in the presidential election. When she was put on trial in 1873, she vowed to continue to "rebel against your man-made, unjust, unconstitutional forms of law, that tax, fine, imprison, and hang women, while they deny them the right of representation in the government."[40] Threats to silence Susan never stopped her from promoting her cause.

Sadly, Susan B. Anthony died on Tuesday, 13 March 1906, never having seen the day when women were granted the right to vote. It would take 14 more years for that day to come, but when it did, some referred to the 19th Amendment to the U.S. Constitution as the Susan B. Anthony Amendment.[41]

---

[36] Pollack and Belviso.
[37] Ibid., page 62.
[38] Pollack and Belviso.
[39] Ibid.
[40] Ibid., pages 64, 66.
[41] Pollack and Belviso.

It may appear unfair that Susan B. Anthony never got to relish in her successful campaign for a woman's right to vote. She certainly thought so when she told her friend, Anna Shaw, "To think I have had more than sixty years of hard struggle for a little liberty, and then to die without it seems so cruel."[42] No doubt Anthony was frustrated about not witnessing her dream realized, but when asked if she would make the same choices if given the chance to live it over, without hesitating, Susan answered, "Oh yes, I'd do it all again."[43]

Growing up, the only thing I knew about Susan B. Anthony was that she was a suffragette, but that fact only scratches the surface of her legacy. M. Carey Thomas, second president of Bryn Mawr College, spoke of Anthony's profound effect on future generations of women through the dedication she exhibited:

> Susan B. Anthony has given to the cause of women every year, every month, every day, every hour, every moment of her whole life, and every dollar she could beg or earn... To you, Miss Anthony, belongs by right, as to no other woman in the world's history, the love and gratitude of all women in every country of the civilized globe. We, your daughters in the spirit, rise up today and call you blessed...[44]

As a woman, the ability to vote and own property are rights that I've taken for granted. I've enjoyed the fruits of the laborious resolution of women like Susan B. Anthony. It was no simple task and came with mistreatment, but their commitment to justice on behalf of the female sex allowed women to have a voice.

> My best friend is a man who will get me a book I ain't read.
> — Abraham Lincoln, If You Grew Up With Abraham Lincoln[45]

Just as stories can inspire us to be our best selves today, Martin Luther King, Jr., Abraham Lincoln, and Susan B. Anthony were all influenced by what they read in the past. They were drawn to Scriptural heroes in Biblical times, real-life heroes who set examples, and poets who captured their

---

[42] "Susan B. Anthony."
[43] Harper, page 1421.
[44] Parker, page 32.
[45] Edward C. Papenfuse. "Reading With and About Abraham Lincoln " (The Janet and Roger Levin Lecture, Boys' Latin School, Baltimore, 15 Feb 2002). http://msa.maryland.gov/msa/educ/speeches/html/notes.html#2

ideals through the written word. The treasured literature that forged their belief systems weren't prized because of guaranteed happy endings. Instead, they testified to what human beings were capable of achieving in the face of obstacles.

Dr. Martin Luther King, Jr.'s actions were heavily emboldened by his Christian faith and the example of Jesus, but also by reading Henry David Thoreau's *Civil Disobedience* and Howard Thurman's *Jesus and the Disinherited*. It was Thoreau who introduced Dr. King to the theory of nonviolent resistance. King was so "fascinated by the idea of refusing to cooperate with an evil system" and "so deeply moved" that he reread *Civil Disobedience* several times.[46] It is also believed that Howard Thurman's *Jesus and the Disinherited*, which Dr. King reportedly carried with him during protests, served as another influence in King's adoption of "nonviolence as a way to overcome evil," which is one of the most remarkable aspects of his involvement in the American Civil Rights Movement.[47] How could a man who had suffered so much prejudice and oppression not physically fight back? Why would he even choose to reject the option? I wonder what Dr. King's road to equality would have looked like if he had not read *Civil Disobedience* or *Jesus and the Disinherited*.

Young Abraham Lincoln was an avid reader, excited by tales of exceptional leaders. While Abe read the Bible in its entirety, it was the Old Testament's account of the Jewish people's escape from slavery in Egypt that left a strong impression on him.[48] Lincoln was also motivated by a book recounting the life of his presidential predecessor, George Washington. It was a book he loved so much that he would take it to bed with him.[49] Through its pages, he began to understand that the battlefields, heroes, and hardships would lead to "something that held out a great promise to all the people of the world to all time to come."[50] At an early age, Lincoln was presented with examples of individuals who lived during strenuous times,

---

[46] Montford.
[47] Lawton.
[48] Holzer.
[49] Ibid.
[50] Ibid., pages 12-13.

believed that their situations could be reformed, and worked toward making life better, even if it meant giving their lives. Abe would grow up learning lessons that ultimately helped teach him how to hold America together in the midst of a deadly period in history that threatened to tear it apart.

Like Dr. Martin Luther King, Jr. and Abraham Lincoln, Susan B. Anthony was well-read. Not only did she keep up with current events by reading copies of William Lloyd Garrison's *The Liberator* and *The New-York Tribune*, but she also read Thomas Carlyle's *Sartor Resartus*, George Sand's *Consuelo*, Madame de Staël's *Corinne*, Frances Wright's *A Few Days in Athens*, and Elizabeth Gaskell's *The Life of Charlotte Brontë*.[51] However, it was Elizabeth Barrett Browning's *Aurora Leigh* that Anthony would "cherish above all other books."[52] She even donated her copy to the Congressional Library in "the hope that women may more and more be like Aurora Leigh."[53] Susan's love for the epic poem makes it easy to see how it informed her quest for women's rights:

> You misconceive the question like a man,
> Who sees a woman as the complement
> Of his sex merely. You forget too much
> That every creature, female as the male,
> Stands single in responsible act and thought,
> As also in birth and death. Whoever says
> To a loyal woman, "Love and work with me,"
> Will get fair answers, if the work and love
> Being good of themselves, are good for her – the best
> She was born for.[54]

Heroes, both fictional and real, teach us how to respond in trying times. They demonstrate how to pick ourselves up when we fall, that we can consider change a blessing, and that we are defined by perseverance. Real-world heroes who have made a difference are excellent representations of these characteristics, because no justice is earned and upheld without struggle. Martin Luther King, Jr., Abraham Lincoln, and Susan B. Anthony

---

[51] Lutz.
[52] Ibid., page 74.
[53] Ibid., page 74.
[54] Ibid., page 75.

were able to move past their misery and heartache because of the powerful inspirations they studied on the page that reminded them that justice was worth their strife. These historical figures aren't admired today because they lived carefree and pain-free lives. They are celebrated because they serve as illustrations for what we can accomplish when we push through difficulties. Why should our super-hero stories be any different?

Unfortunately, there is evil in the world and inevitably, obtaining justice requires struggle. C. S. Lewis correctly suggested that if our world had no light, "dark" would be "a word without meaning."[55] Our world *does* have light. I've turned it on. I've lit matches. I've seen the sun rise to bring it every day. The light in our world helps us overthrow darkness. By making the hero face conflict, "dark" super-hero stories show us what the character is made of. Characters placed in shadowy situations help us find the light and discover the heroes within ourselves.

Bibliography

Brody, Richard. "Superman and the Superego." *The New Yorker*. 21 June 2013. http://www.newyorker.com/culture/richard-brody/superman-and-the-superego.

Burlingame, Michael. *Abraham Lincoln: A Life* Vol. 2 (Baltimore: The Johns Hopkins University Press, 2008).

Campbell, Josie. "Matthew Modine Discusses *The Dark Knight Rises*." *Comic Book Resources*. 11 June 2012. http://www.comicbookresources.com/?page=article&id=39116.

Challies, Josh. "5 Characters We'd All Secretly Like Arrow to Kill Off." *WhatCulture*. 28 Feb 2014. http://whatculture.com/tv/5-characters-wed-secretly-like-arrow-kill.php/6.

Coker, Rachel. "Historian Revises Estimate of Civil War Dead." *Discover-e*. 21 Sept 2011. http://discovere.binghamton.edu/news/civilwar-3826.html.

"David Goyer Extended Interview - *Man of Steel* [*JoBlo.com*]." Interview by Jimmy O. *YouTube* video, 6:49. Posted by JoBlo Movie Trailers on 10 June 2013. https://youtu.be/sJXt3E-Yr5A.

Dennis, Brady. "Willie Lincoln's Death: A Private Agony for a President Facing a Nation of Pain," *The Washington Post*. 7 Oct 2011. http://www.washingtonpost.com/lifestyle/style/willie-lincolns-death-a-private-agony-for-a-president-facing-a-nation-of-pain/2011/09/29/gIQAv7Z7SL_story.html.

Edelstein, David. "Edelstein on *Man of Steel*: A Movie So Heavy, Superman Would Have Trouble Picking It Up." *Vulture*. 12 June 2013. http://www.vulture.com/2013/06/movie-review-man-of-steel.html.

---

[55] Lewis, page 39.

Foundas, Scott. "Film Review: *Man of Steel*." *Variety*. 10 June 2013.
    http://variety.com/2013/film/reviews/film-review-man-of-steel-
    1200493929/.

Grumpyclown. "The Blowies 2014: TV.com's Worst of the Year Awards (Users
    Edition) - WINNERS!!" *TV.com*. 2 Jan 2015.
    http://www.tv.com/topics/general-tv-discussion/community/post/the-
    blowies-2014-tvcoms-worst-of-the-year-awards-users-edition—winners-
    1420231116/.

Harper, Ida Husted. *The Life and Work of Susan B. Anthony* Vol. 3 (New York: Arno
    & The New York Times, 1969).

Holzer, Harold. *Lincoln: How Abraham Lincoln Ended Slavery in America* (New
    York: HarperCollins Publishers, 2012).

Hornaday, Ann. "*Man of Steel*. Henry Cavill stars as Superman in this bombastic
    reboot." *The Washington Post*. 13 June 2013.
    http://www.washingtonpost.com/goingoutguide/movies/man-of-steel-henry-
    cavill-stars-as-superman-in-this-bombastic-
    reboot/2013/06/12/6d77d5d0-d36c-11e2-a73e-
    826d299ff459_story.html.

"Interview: Brett Culp, Director of the Batman Documentary *Legends of the
    Knight*." Interview by Martin Deer. *Flickering Myth*. 15 Aug 2013.
    http://www.flickeringmyth.com/2013/08/interview-brett-culp-director-of-
    batman.html.

Kelly, Martin. "Abraham Lincoln – 16th President of the United States." *About
    Education*. Accessed 30 May 2015.
    http://americanhistory.about.com/od/abrahamlincoln/p/plincoln.htm.

King, Martin Luther, Jr. *The Autobiography of Martin Luther King, Jr.*. Ed.
    Clayborne Carson (New York: Warner Books, Inc., 1998).

Lawton, Kim. "The Legacy of Howard Thurman: Mystic and Theologian." *Religion &
    Ethics Newsweekly* video, 7:39 (PBS). 18 Jan 2002.
    http://www.pbs.org/wnet/religionandethics/2002/01/18/january-18-
    2002-the-legacy-of-howard-thurman-mystic-and-theologian/7895/.

Lewis, C. S. *Mere Christianity* (New York: HarperCollins Publishers, [1942, 1943,
    1944] 1980).

Lincoln, Abraham. *The Collected Works of Abraham Lincoln* Vol. 1 (New
    Brunswick, N.J.: Rutgers University Press, 1953).

Lutz, Alma. *Susan B. Anthony: Rebel, Crusader, Humanitarian* (Boston: Beacon
    Press, 1959).

"*Man of Steel*. One-On-One With Henry Cavill." Interview by Ed Gross. *I Am Media
    Geek*. 15 Nov 2013. http://www.iammediageek.com/2013/11/man-of-
    steel-one-on-one-with-henry-cavill.html.

"MLK Quote of the Week: A Time for Vigorous and Positive Action." *The King
    Center*. 26 Dec 2012. http://www.thekingcenter.org/blog/mlk-quote-week-
    time-vigorous-and-positive-action.

Montford, Christina. "8 Books That Inspired Dr. Martin Luther King Jr." *Atlanta
    Blackstar*. 20 Nov 2014. http://atlantablackstar.com/2014/11/20/10-
    books-inspired-dr-martin-luther-king-jr/.

Moss, Charles. "Superman's Dark Past." *The Atlantic*. 24 May 2015.
    http://www.theatlantic.com/entertainment/archive/2015/05/supermans
    -dark-days/393998/.

Nashawaty, Chris. "*Man of Steel*." *Entertainment Weekly*. 25 June 2013.
    http://www.ew.com/article/2013/06/25/man-steel-movie.

Papenfuse, Edward C. "Reading With and About Abraham Lincoln " (The Janet and Roger Levin Lecture, Boys' Latin School, Baltimore, 15 Feb 2002). http://msa.maryland.gov/msa/educ/speeches/html/notes.html#2.

Parker, Barbara Keevil. *Susan B. Anthony: Daring to Vote* (Brookfield, Connecticut: Millbrook Press, 1998).

Pollack, Pam and Meg Belviso. *Who Was Susan B. Anthony?* (New York: Penguin Group, 2014).

Richenthal, Matt. "12 Characters That Make Us Want to Punch the TV." *TV Fanatic.* 20 Feb 2014. http://www.tvfanatic.com/slideshows/11-characters-that-make-us-want-to-throw-out-tvs-out-the-window/.

"Susan B. Anthony." *Bio.* Accessed 30 May 2015. http://www.biography.com/people/susan-b-anthony-194905.

Wallace, Daniel. *Man of Steel: Superman Takes Flight - The Official Movie Guide* (San Rafael, CA: Insight Editions, 2013).

Weldon, Glen. "'Steel' Trap: Snyder's Superman, Between Worlds." *NPR.* 13 June 2013. http://www.npr.org/2013/06/13/189284063/steel-trap-snyders-superman-between-worlds.

Wheeler, Sheba. "Colorado Shooting Victims Wear Batman T-Shirts to James Holmes Court Hearing." *The Hollywood Reporter.* 30 July 2012. http://www.hollywoodreporter.com/news/colorado-shooting-james-holmes-hearing-victims-batman-shirt-355850.

Wilford, Denette. "The Five Most Annoying TV Characters of 2012." *HuffPost TV Canada.* Last updated 23 Feb 2013. http://www.huffingtonpost.ca/denette-wilford/5-annoying-tv-characters-2012_b_2359183.html.

Honing Our Senses: Remembering the Vibrancy of Super-Hero Justice

by Ian Boucher

It reconfirms their *faith* in the *big city myth*... a *mugger* in *every* alleyway. It's nice to know *Neil Simon* was right.
— *Power Man* Vol. 1 #28[1]

"And, for the truth or particulars of any fact, it is safer to depend on common traditions than upon their best recollections."
— *Gulliver's Travels*[2]

"I took responsibility for my *own* acts; humanity should do the same."
— *The Spectre* Vol. 3 #22[3]

"My parents taught me... to hone my senses, Zod."
— *Man of Steel* (2013)

---

[1] Page 5.
[2] Page 203.
[3] Page 23.

Being a super-hero is generally tough, but as we know, their greatest challenge isn't giant robots, regular-sized crime lords, or even appointments – it's themselves, even without those bothersome symbiotes. To help the multiverse, their section of town, or the astral plane, super-heroes must assess and hone themselves every step of the way. No hero embodies this more than Superman. For one thing, his nemesis Lex Luthor is the ultimate critic. Secondly, there is a lot of information out there, and Kal-El can hear most of it at once. Superman must focus through constant cacophony on what will give him the best answers for helping others. While he has had more time to develop this skill than his cousin Kara Zor-El, it's no wonder he gets tricked all the time.

Super-hero comics play a similar role for readers. Like any form of storytelling, they are internal as well as external. With their layered combinations of words and images concentrating on hero figures, they help us make sense of our own intertwining personal and societal struggles, to hone our own senses, reinforcing and challenging what we tell ourselves and one another as we grow as individuals and as a culture.[4] With the explosion of super-hero media into mainstream Western discourse, super-hero comics, the wellspring of it all, are more central to Western culture than ever before. However, using super-hero comics to navigate the internal and external is not much easier on super-hero fans than focusing is for Superman, even before movies and TV come into the mix.

As with anything, the culture of super-hero comics has its own dominant ideological frameworks shaped over time by fans and creators. Unfortunately, many of the current frameworks in super-hero comics are severely limiting, for, although they may appear to be enthusiastic about progressive thinking, what they ultimately do rather than drive change is promote contentment and the status quo, sometimes to the point of creating dogma. With super-heroes, this is especially problematic because of the added concept of justice, which is not only a cornerstone question for culture, but an organic endeavor. Although figures for entertainment first,

---

[4] For a fascinating analysis of the roles of popular culture in our development, see Gerard Jones. *Killing Monsters: Why Children Need Fantasy, Super Heroes, and Make-Believe Violence* (New York: Basic Books, 2002). PDF e-book.

super-heroes are inherently about illuminating justice on some level and contributing to society's discourse about it. Consequently, the current dominant frameworks in super-hero culture contribute to the reinforcement of larger cultural delusions, while in fact not even adequately reflecting the comic book stories actually being published. Two prominent frameworks that are especially representative of super-hero comic book discourse have been built around *Watchmen*[5] and the *Green Lantern/Green Arrow* series.[6]

As with any cultural discourse, super-hero enthusiasts must always remember to keep asking themselves questions as they listen to the statements of others. What are we, as spectators and creators, focusing on with what we consume? What facts do we inform our culture with? What is being reinforced and what are we challenging? Although super-heroes are so often about justice, do we truly care about justice, at least when it comes to super-heroes? In answering questions like these, super-hero fans must remember that super-heroes, with all their fascinating points of focus, have in fact fulfilled their fundamental roles in justice, utilizing their potential as the diverse beacons of hope they have set out to be. But this precedent is not being utilized in the cultural stream[7] between super-hero aficionados and the rest of society, and the ostensibly vibrant presence of super-heroes in current pop culture makes this even more important. We must remember to keep honing our senses, for all our sakes. Superman, as is his wont, is just the beginning.

There is Life after *Watchmen*

Watchmen is consistently hailed as one of the most influential works of sequential art ever published.[8] Its analysis of the appeal of super-heroes is the gold standard for super-hero enthusiasts and detractors alike, and an essential part of every comic book collection, with many viewing it as the

---

[5] Originally published as *Watchmen* #1-12.

[6] Published in *Green Lantern* Vol. 2 #76-87, and 89 (1970-1972) and *The Flash* Vol. 1 #217-219, and 226 (1972, 1974).

[7] I would like to think we can be a step above the Madness Stream of Vertigo's Shade, the Changing Man.

[8] Grossman.

be-all and end-all of super-hero stories. In a pivotal scene, the infamous antihero the Comedian sardonically cuts right to the heart of his fellow costumed adventurers: "You people are a *joke*. You hear [the super-villain] Moloch's back in town, you think 'Oh, *boy*! Let's *gang up* and *bust* him!' You think that *matters*? You think that *solves* anything?"[9]

When the story begins, the only heroes allowed to remain active in the United States are those who work for the higher justice of a dystopian Cold War government. Told through traditional panels, diverse in-world documents at the end of each chapter, and the comic-within-a-comic "Tales of the Black Freighter" – written by a diegetic author who in turn helps necessitate a fiction – *Watchmen* is certainly one of the richest comic book stories, much less super-hero stories, yet written. Three core explorations of *Watchmen* are the reasons for super-hero appeal, the efficacy of institutions, and the value of life itself, culminating most prominently in the super-man Dr. Manhattan and the vigilante Rorschach. *Watchmen* is an essential part of building discourse about super-heroes as crime-fighting stories.

But *Watchmen* is commonly viewed as so much of a gold standard that it can never be surpassed,[10] and more than that, its insights are used to justify the real-world status quo as a necessary truth[11] – a truth to merely point out rather than inspire. In the fall of 2014, I wrote an article for Sequart Organization about the lack of diversity in the justice of super-hero media – how often do we see anything beyond villains being put in jail or dropped off of cliffs? I compared super-hero storytelling conventions with justice in real life, and contemplated the potential for Wonder Woman, as a hero pursuing harmony, to inspire change.[12] Justice in super-hero comics is in fact spectacularly diverse, but where super-heroes exist culturally is up to

---

[9] *Watchmen* #2. DC Comics, Oct 1986. Page 11.
[10] Richard Corliss at *Time* referring to it as a "sacred text" comes as no surprise.
[11] According to a *Cinemablend* review of the film adaptation, the film is able to "focus in on the real heart of the matter, the people who make up *Watchmen*'s world and the desperately dark path their society, and in a way our society, is on," and a review of the book by *The Mary Sue* alludes to an appeal to readers for whom cynicism is "a selling point."
[12] Boucher.

people. Instead of harnessing what comics have done, the notions of super-hero justice that creators, readers, and certainly movie executives bring to the surface largely reinforce the same antiquated notions, irrational fears, and stereotypes that the current American justice system is structured around, and the discourse around *Watchmen* is a big part of this.

If super-hero stories were significantly helping Western culture understand justice, the conventions of super-hero storytelling would have changed decades ago in response to the effects of the United States of America's War on Drugs. As the mainstream is increasingly becoming aware, the world has more to worry about than shadowy purse snatchers, or, as *Captain America: The Winter Soldier* (2014) would have us think, Hydra. In the United States, which in turn has enormous influence on laws around the world,[13] the criminal justice system is not driven by crime rates,[14] or research about the causes and solutions to crime,[15] but by politics and business, marginalizing some people to gain the support of others.[16] Due to the War on Drugs, the offender population in the United States has skyrocketed to the largest in the world,[17] and this rogues gallery of "some people" is not actually comprised of the likes of the Joker or Norman Osborn, but rather low-level, nonviolent drug offenders,[18] rounded up primarily from low income, nonwhite neighborhoods.[19] The current system worsens more problems than it solves.[20] When primary praise around *Watchmen* frames the book as merely a scathing truth, a dreary, nihilistic final word about super-heroes, this status quo becomes "academically" justified. It equates enlightenment with acceptance, while countless people

---

[13] Reynolds; Risse.

[14] Alexander; Campbell; Cox; Harcourt; Massoglia, Firebaugh, and Warner; Sampson and Loeffler; Wildeman and Western.

[15] Alexander; Arrigo, Bersot, and Sellers; Campbell; Reynolds; Vuong et al.

[16] Alexander; Campbell; Reynolds.

[17] Campbell; Massoglia, Firebaugh, and Warner; Nichols and Loper; Vuong et al.

[18] Alexander; Bush-Baskette; Cox; Gaudio; Moore and Elkavich; Reynolds; Wildeman and Western.

[19] Alexander; Campbell; Cox; Gaudio; Geller et al.; Harcourt; Massoglia, Firebaugh, and Warner; Moore and Elkavich; Sampson and Loeffler; Wildeman and Western.

[20] Alexander; Arrigo, Bersot, and Sellers; Bush-Baskette; Campbell; Gaudio; Madsen; Moore and Elkavich; Nichols and Loper; Reynolds; Wildeman and Western.

in real life continue ad nauseam to be thrown under the bus for the sake of a few.

No character in *Watchmen* demonstrates this paradox better than Rorschach. Any reader of *Watchmen* knows of this character's extraordinary representation of America's popular standard of super-hero justice as reflected by the violence of Batman and the Punisher. Yet he is also an incredibly popular character, his "necessary" anger at his society a catharsis along the same lines of Bruce Wayne and Frank Castle.[21] This anger is actually intensified as a result of the expertly-crafted, critical nature of the story – readers who identify with Rorschach can feel justified in venting their frustrations, because they are "in the know." The 2009 film adaptation of *Watchmen* is of no help, with Batman comic book covers appearing in the opening credits – despite Superman comics inspiring the adventurers in the book – and the role of Rorschach's therapist Dr. Malcolm Long reduced to an oblivious coward. Yet in the book, although Rorschach's inkblot mask is heartbreakingly inspired by the real-life atrocity of the murder of Kitty Genovese, and Rorschach eventually finds no hope in people at all, Rorschach, Dr. Manhattan, and Dr. Long all decide to help others anyway. For all of *Watchmen*'s sadness, like all good social commentaries, there is so much more to it.

Ironically commenting on the state of the world because we've read *Watchmen* does nothing to help our understanding of society. Like the "Takers" and "Leavers" of Daniel Quinn's *Ishmael*,[22] it ultimately co-opts a criticism, to accept and reinforce the status quo rather than consider it. *Watchmen* is indeed a revelation, but it is much more than simply a final confirmation of what we already do. *Watchmen* is a snapshot in history, a statement to build upon, and anyone concerned with super-heroes should remember that.

---

[21] According to *IGN*, ranking him as the 16th top comic book hero, "One has to admire his determination, if not necessarily his methods."

[22] Quinn argues that the absorption of hunter-gatherer society ("Leavers," who viewed themselves as part of the natural world) by agricultural society ("Takers," who viewed themselves as owners of the natural world) resulted in that curious paradox of the Genesis story where Western culture both cautions against and validates itself.

Laurels' Lance

As Harvey Dent would readily acknowledge, however, there is another side to this coin. In addition to reinforcing living with a dreary status quo, mainstream comic book culture repeatedly touts its social accomplishments in a positive way – as countless documentaries[23] and DVD special features about super-hero comics demonstrate – to reinforce the view that society is better, which starkly contrasts with the laws that have been adopted by that very society. This is an essential part of justifying a society's status quo. One of the most prominent of these comic book achievements is the landmark but short-lived *Green Lantern/Green Arrow* series by Denny O'Neil and Neal Adams.

This series begins with one of the truly greatest openings in super-hero comics. Hal Jordan is flying around Star City as the Green Lantern, hoping to visit Oliver Queen, the Green Arrow. Jordan notices a teen threatening an affluent middle-aged man, and immediately spirits the former away to incarceration with his ring. The affluent man thanks Green Lantern heartily, but a can hits Jordan in the head, heralding a barrage of garbage from every direction. When Jordan threatens to quell what he sees as a riot, it is Oliver Queen who leaps in his way, explaining with his signature intensity that Hal needs to look past the surface before literally flying in and judging things. Sure enough, the affluent man turns out to be a slumlord evicting his tenants, and an elderly man, notable at that time for being an African American, approaches Hal, famously stating:

> I been readin' about you... how you work for the *blue skins*... and how on a planet someplace you helped out the *orange skins*... and you done considerable for the *purple skins!* Only there's *skins* you never bothered with – ! ... The *black* skins! I want to know... *how come?!* Answer me *that*, Mr. *Green Lantern!*[24]

This is indeed one of the proudest moments in super-hero comics culture. The *Green Lantern / Green Arrow* series went on to similarly explore other real-life problems with the complexities they deserved, such as the environment, overpopulation, and religious fundamentalism, climaxing with Green Arrow finding his ward Roy Harper, a.k.a. Speedy, addicted to heroin.

---

[23] PBS's *Superheroes: A Never-Ending Battle* (2013) is a significant example.
[24] *Green Lantern* Vol. 2 #76, page 6.

Roy is involved with the very drug addicts Green Arrow and Green Lantern are trying to take down, and Green Arrow, the most left-wing super-hero of all, must come to terms with the implications of that.[25] These stories did not solve the problems they captured, but only addressed them, as writer Denny O'Neil told SuperMOOC2 in 2014, to get children thinking about them.[26] Like any good story, the themes were fundamentally linked to their characters, most prominently Hal and Oliver, the ultimate police officer and ultimate protestor. This was quintessential reality-informed, if hyperbolic, poetic entertainment using super-heroes, and instrumental in the struggle for super-hero comics to be taken seriously by American culture.[27]

However, much like with *Watchmen*, the popular comic book cultural narrative focuses too much on praising triumphs such as these, patting itself on the back with its milestones without taking the time to consider them within the context of the present. Pointing to the past in this regard not only downplays the ever-continuing work in super-hero comics, but it also justifies the status quo by overlooking that there is more to understand about the world. Like *Watchmen*, the *Green Lantern/Green Arrow* series is not just a triumph at which to point, but a blueprint *that has been* built upon. In fact, if he were self-aware like She-Hulk and Deadpool, Ollie would be flabbergasted at how many of the same issues in his series are still invisible today to pop culture's awareness, despite the continued exploits of his fellow heroes. How much have readers really learned from Roy? If our super-hero comics have come so far, why have justice systems around the world gotten so much worse? Regardless – whatever is said, there is never 'nuff said.

Cultivating Justice

With the growth of super-hero media, these two dominant ideologies are only getting stronger. Consider one of the most popular super-hero

---

[25] *Green Lantern* Vol. 2 #85-86.

[26] "Denny O'Neil Final Interview."

[27] Not only did the series garner several awards, but it gained a lot of attention outside the comics industry, including being famously praised in a letter by John Lindsay, the mayor of New York City. See the above interview and *Green Lantern* Vol. 2 #86.

adaptations today, CW's *The Flash*.[28] For Cisco Ramon of S.T.A.R. Labs, tracking down and naming villains is, more often than not, the coolest thing in the world. For at least the majority of the first season (2014-2015), Cisco is not reined in by the other characters, but is rather meant to represent the ever-growing audience – fans thrilled by the status quo. The market is growing, and this is who is buying. Yet the paradox is that in this case, continuing to condone this status quo condones ignorance, and ignorance is bliss for only so long.

Super-hero comics certainly need to be entertaining first. That's why they were created. Martian Manhunter is just as fun when he eats Chocos as when he uncovers sociopolitical conspiracies. But super-heroes are also part of what culture says about justice. Why continue to promote the stories that have permeated the mainstream, painted with ignorance rather than facts? Why are portrayals of society immune to the standards we hold for portrayals of people? Kids and adults alike may not care about every single technicality in the real-life justice system, but the current idea of justice in the United States is the equivalent of kookaburras in Hollywood jungles, and in this case, to say that the kookaburras hurt people is an understatement. Super-hero culture is shifting, but we need to be aware of how it is shifting. As *Man of Steel*'s Pa Kent might say, what kind of society do we want to grow up to be?

As we think about these things, there are scores of outstanding super-hero comic book stories to remember, both inside and outside the main cultural narrative – stories that continue to give us greater insight and inspiration on many aspects of justice, in terms abstract and concrete, in strokes broad and precise, from core themes to fleeting moments. The problem isn't which heroes we promote, it's what we say about them. What follows are just a few reminders. The deeper we delve, the more we find. Justice systems around the world can be like Wonder Woman, and a lot more. We need only hone our senses to cultivate it. It's not about individual issues that point out current events. Each new comic can be cultivated and built upon, to keep connecting the dots.

---

[28] O'Connell.

Forgive me, reader, because I'm definitely leaving out a lot. Like the Runaways as children in a flawed societal structure.[29] Or Kelly Sue DeConnick's Captain Marvel wrestling with questions of interplanetary diplomacy.[30] Or the Black Spectre having a corrupt parole officer.[31] Or Gail Simone's Batgirl, buttressed with crime statutes, gentrification, the bias of law enforcement and media, the ineffectiveness of Arkham Asylum, the Occupy movement, and wealthy murderers free to party with athletes and business leaders.[32] Or Simon Baz being subjected to government torture.[33] Even the 1966 Batman has talked about low-income housing, living by example, and not confusing justice with revenge.[34] John Ostrander's Spectre, on the verge of judging humanity as a whole, learns that it's not the injustice of the world, but his own grief, driving him – by being tied to the human soul of Jim Corrigan, the very embodiment of vengeance must learn that "without mercy, there is no justice."[35] Or take "Evil Incarcerated,"[36] where Norman Osborn is sent by the United States government (and ultimately society) to a top-secret prison without a trial. Or Green Lantern and Green Arrow, teaming up once again, when Kyle Rayner and Connor Hawke respond to racial conflict orchestrated by a super-villain posing as two different media personalities.[37]

And counting.

Wonder Woman and Restorative Justice

Gail Simone's work on Wonder Woman, the inspiration for this book, immediately stands out from the core tenets of the American criminal justice system by bringing out restorative justice, a notion seldom seen in the rise of super-hero films but increasingly utilized in the real world to help heal communities. It's a fact that simply punishing an offender is largely

---

[29] *Runaways* Vol. 1 #1.
[30] *Captain Marvel* Vol. 9 #1-6.
[31] *Moon Knight* Vol. 5 #15-16.
[32] *Batgirl* Vol. 4 #1-6.
[33] *Green Lantern* Vol. 5 #0.
[34] *Batman '66 Meets the Green Hornet* Vol. 1 #1-6.
[35] *The Spectre* Vol. 3 #18, page 23.
[36] *Osborn* Vol. 1 #1-5.
[37] *Green Arrow* Vol. 2 #125-126; *Green Lantern* Vol. 3 #92.

On this page from *Wonder Woman* Vol. 3 #14, Wonder Woman's method is very reminiscent of the concept of restorative justice. Art by Terry Dodson (pencils) and Rachel Dodson (inks). © DC Comics.

ineffective, hurting the community as well as the offender.[38] Furthermore, unlike the Joker, vast numbers of former offenders legitimately want to improve their lives after release, but are unable to overcome the unreasonable amount of restrictions that make it extraordinarily difficult to meet basic living expectations.[39] Restorative justice strives to work with victims and offenders to help communities overcome crime,[40] and whatever the intentions, Gail Simone's Wonder Woman furthers Diana's tradition as a character who is very much an ambassador to that.

In the first part of "The Circle,"[41] Wonder Woman is attacked by a group of hyper-intelligent gorillas. As Diana overpowers her attackers, she uses her strength to determine that they were sent under false pretenses, and mediates an agreement for the resolution of the problem.[42] In the subsequent issue, she subdues a neo-Nazi with her Lasso of Truth, forcing the latter to not only tell the truth, but to also see the truth about himself. To be sure, this lasso is a handy tool, but Diana is a hero in that moment because she takes it upon herself to make that most difficult first step, to be there objectively, "even for him," the ultimate category of villain.[43] In Gail Simone's two-parter "Expatriate," Wonder Woman defends conquering aliens from a vengeful Green Lantern, because justice, she maintains, is not revenge.[44] This is true to a character that, almost since her inception in 1941,[45] has been an ultimate example of a super-hero. Diana's goal is frequently not just to stop a crime, or to bring offenders to authorities, but to look past symptoms to get to the roots of offenses. Simone's Wonder Woman is strong, funny, and kicks butt, but also distinctly delivers justice in

---

[38] Arrigo, Bersot, and Sellers; Reynolds; Vuong et al.

[39] Alexander; Campbell; Cox; Gaudio; Geller et al.; Massoglia, Firebaugh, and Warner; Moore and Elkavich; Rose and Rose; Schrader.

[40] Arrigo, Bersot, and Sellers.

[41] *Wonder Woman* Vol. 3 #14.

[42] She notes of her former adversaries: "Misguided, rather than blackhearted" (page 12).

[43] *Wonder Woman* Vol. 3 #15, pages 12-14.

[44] *Wonder Woman* Vol. 3 #18-19.

[45] See "Wonder Woman" in this essay's bibliography.

a way that contrasts with the most prominent narratives we tell one another as a culture.

Daredevil, She-Hulk, and the Law

As counselors by day, these two super-heroes have seen in their own ways that the justice system is more than dropping criminals off at the police station. "Born Again" is a Daredevil story that powerfully explores the machinations behind society, depicting a world where, despite all that Matt Murdock can do as a lawyer and Daredevil as a super-hero, the rules governing both of them are in reality subject to a higher, ruling class, represented in the story by the Kingpin. What counts in the end is Matt's spirit, the people he loves, and the voices of citizens, the latter personified through *Daily Bugle* reporter Ben Urich.[46] In recent years, Mark Waid's Matt Murdock has shown that people are not only affected by the justice system, but can *affect it*, as Murdock has trained clients to defend themselves in court.[47] Daredevil has even decided to fight crime in a red suit and tie, literally becoming a lawyer super-hero.[48]

Charles Soule and company have used Jennifer Walters and her alter ego She-Hulk to create immensely fun comic book premises based around legal concepts. In the first issue of the series, Jennifer contends with Tony Stark's stoic legal department to save the widow of a C-list super-villain from years of litigation over a patent claim, while battling both Tony Stark's and the former super-villain's robots.[49] In the third issue, Jennifer fights through legions of Doombots to get the son of Victor von Doom to an immigration judge for last-minute asylum in the United States.[50] There is also an affecting scene in the fifth issue where she talks to a former criminal – Shocker (yes, the villain Shocker, and he's just as surprised) – as a normal person to help her solve a case.[51]

As agents of the law who are also vigilantes, Daredevil and She-Hulk's equally legal and super-heroic adventures work magnificently. As much as

---

[46] *Daredevil* Vol. 1 #227-233.
[47] *Daredevil* Vol. 3 #1-6.
[48] *Daredevil* Vol. 4 #14.
[49] *She-Hulk* Vol. 3 #1.
[50] *She-Hulk* Vol. 3 #3.
[51] *She-Hulk* Vol. 3 #5.

the law is their arena, both characters have repeatedly shown that lawyering is many times just as outside the lines of textbook protocol as being a super-hero, and indeed, as with any good literary character, their being super-heroes is largely why they are able to be successful.

The Green Hornet and Citizenship

It's the 1940s. The Green Hornet and Kato have just stopped a group of Nazi saboteurs while toppling organized crime in Chicago, tying everything together into a beautiful package for the police and the media. On the night Britt and Kato plan to finally retire, Kato discovers that someone has stolen their costumes. Their search for the culprit culminates with an imposter Green Hornet shockingly revealed as none other than Lenore Case, Britt's secretary by day and super-librarian by night. She deliberately gets herself arrested to provide Britt and Kato with information from inside prison. When Britt attempts to use his legal resources to get her out, Lenore refuses, driving home in a few hard-hitting panels that Britt can never walk away from the status quo he helped create, no matter how trying it may be, especially by playing the role of a criminal.

This is the masterful finale of Mark Waid and Ronilson Freire's *The Green Hornet*,[52] very much a deconstruction of conventional super-hero storytelling. By having Britt directly use his dual influence over society, Waid has Britt not only cross the line by posing as a criminal, but also by going further than super-heroes normally do overall in trying to change their worlds. Britt is equally preemptive as he is reactionary, and more than asking Britt, Lenore is asking the reader – what is up to us and what is up to others? What do we have a role in shaping?

The Martian Manhunter and the X-Factor

No, we're not at the X-Men quite yet, but "x-factor" is very much in the spirit of the Martian Manhunter. Malcolm X is a real-life hero because he consistently strived to bring to light the subtle, deep-seated frameworks taken for granted in American society. To truly improve, a society needs to be able to verbalize the structures supporting it – the meanings and

---

[52] *The Green Hornet* Vol. 5 #12-13.

foundations behind its actions, and the law is no exception.[53] One comic book story that puts this idea into action, and, much like Malcolm X, is still very much on the outskirts of American society's awareness, is the Gerard Jones and Eduardo Barreto story *Martian Manhunter: American Secrets*.[54]

Ever the objective, self-reflexive observer, J'onn J'onzz, the telepathic, phasing alien super-hero detective is superbly positioned to delve into society's deepest chasms, and in *American Secrets*, the last Martian leaps into a thrilling conspiracy that takes him there. In the 1950s, aliens are attempting to control the world through cultural conformity in media, from television to music, and they are succeeding, keeping humans' mouths shut on pain of a mysteriously involuntary, fiery death – the Manhunter's greatest weakness. But unlike most stories about the 1950s, it's not just the sanitized quiz shows and suburbs that are put in the hot seat, as it were, but all media is called into question, even rock and roll – typically hailed as a liberation of a new decade, but just as co-opted and controlled a machination. In such an environment, where even super-hero comics, as Doctor Mid-Nite points out in the story, can only go so far, how much can justice really be achieved? *American Secrets* is thus a fascinating super-hero thriller, and best of all, although the story may possibly uncover some secrets about the framework of American society, it leaves the reader with many more to think about.

The X-Men, Law Enforcement, and Justice for All

The X-Men have faced challenges intimate and intergalactic, but at the end of the day, their primary conflict is that of equality for all, further brought out by the seminal work of writer Chris Claremont. Arguably his most powerful and inspirational X-Men story in this regard is *God Loves, Man Kills*,[55] partially the basis for the film *X2* (2003) and most certainly part of the mainstream comic book cultural narrative. In this version, Stryker is a televangelist leading an organization against mutants. The book begins with two mutant children – who happen to not be white – pursued and hung by Stryker's covert soldiers from a school swing set. In the end, the X-Men

---

[53] Arrigo, Bersot, and Sellers.
[54] *Martian Manhunter: American Secrets* #1-3.
[55] *Marvel Graphic Novel #5 - X-Men: God Loves, Man Kills*.

confront Stryker in front of a live television audience at Madison Square Garden, appealing to the very people who are trying to marginalize them through policies, and worse. This story is quintessential X-Men.

But *God Loves, Man Kills* contains another powerful reminder. The X-Men, although paradoxically acting outside the law, are ultimately just citizens, because it's a particular handful of audience members – law enforcement – who save the day. When the police officers at the event observe Stryker attempting to attack the X-Men, they incapacitate him and keep Stryker's followers from retaliating, reminding them of the law. The police officers use logic and training to protect and serve – "even" mutants, those on the margins. Stryker is left alive to face justice, while those on the margins aren't as on the margins. By so exceptionally putting this moment of tension and decision in the police officers' point of view, *God Loves, Man Kills* not only reminds the reader of the crucial fact that average people must enforce the law every single day, but also that it can in fact be done well for all citizens, even under the most difficult of circumstances. At the very least, we can aspire to it. Members of law enforcement in this story aren't just figures to show up when needed for staring dumbfounded, or for driving a criminal away to prison. They are people in a field that must require infrastructure, expertise, and equipment. They are as much a part of the equation as anyone else, and need to be considered as such, by themselves and everyone else. Their decision is our decision.

Luke Cage: Black Lives Matter

The world of super-heroes is largely a white one. Even in casts with characters of diverse racial backgrounds, the white characters are most often the focus, at the cost of many great characters, especially African American characters. The list is long and does no one any favors. That's why at his worst, he represents pandering and perpetuation, but at his best, Luke Cage, a.k.a. Power Man, encapsulates a breath of fresh air. The early Luke Cage stories written by Don McGregor, Chris Claremont, and at times Marv Wolfman have largely been forgotten in mainstream comic book discourse, but their depictions of American society are just as important now to understanding criminal justice as they were in the 1970s, and, appallingly, are just as overlooked.

Their Luke Cage is a deeply layered leading man. On one hand, he is passionate about social justice, much like Denny O'Neil's Green Arrow, yet his primary focus is survival. He is a "hero for hire," and his reality, despite its critical role in society's infrastructure, is just as parallel to the mainstream as Blade's or Dr. Strange's are to Spider-Man's. Except instead of vampires or sorcery, Luke Cage lives in a world where prison is a part of life[56] even for innocents,[57] money buys freedom,[58] research is ignored,[59] respected corporations back illegal activities,[60] and, simultaneously, criminals can clean up.[61] This is a world where people's homes can be set ablaze while their white neighbors passively encourage the criminal vigilante who started the fire. This is a world where the kids don't always make it and justice itself is called into question.[62] Luke Cage is incredibly strong, but not more powerful than his secret identity, which in his case is a secret *label* as a convict. Much like the real world, Power Man is not overtly framed as a public menace like Spider-Man, nor is he feared like the X-Men. Instead, he is completely expected – invisible unless white society wants to confirm to themselves that he is a screw-up. But reflecting his namesake, Luke Cage powers through it, always asking questions along the way.[63]

If mainstream society continues to fail to think about how society functions in its *entirety* – how it is constructed for *everyone* – it will fail to understand and overcome its problems, and Luke Cage can be a central character to help more super-hero fans keep up with that. At this point, it is indeed up to comic book fans to leave the apparent safety of Spider-Man's panels more often and make more representative figures like Luke Cage more prominent in their discussions. Comic book culture loves to point to a handful of black characters as groundbreaking, but in the decades following

---

[56] *Power Man* Vol. 1 #39.

[57] *Power Man* Vol. 1 #43.

[58] *Power Man* Vol. 1 #35.

[59] *Power Man* Vol. 1 #28.

[60] *Power Man Annual* Vol. 1 #1.

[61] *Power Man* Vol. 1 #39.

[62] *Power Man* Vol. 1 #32-33.

[63] As he tells an attacker in #28: "Nuthin' *wrong* in askin' questions, you beef jerky – only way you can *learn* anything!" (page 16).

Cage's early stories, Marvel has largely squandered Luke's incredible potential, even relegating him to busting low-level crack dealers,[64] a problem Cage would know much better to solve elsewhere. Luke Cage can be a much more nuanced reminder to readers and beyond.

A Better Vision

When this chapter was written, the most recent super-hero theatrical release was *Avengers: Age of Ultron* (2015). Being a Marvel movie, it was particularly indicative of mainstream super-hero culture at that point in time. It includes great commentary about the status quo – the perpetuity of war, the corruption of officials, and the extension of structures beyond nations. The film also demonstrates that S.H.I.E.L.D. can protect, and that the Avengers must reconsider their place in the world.

However, the film ultimately sidesteps everything it sets up, keeping itself, as Bruce Banner acknowledges, in a "time loop." Tony Stark is depicted as being wrong to bring about artificial intelligence, until he isn't. Conveniently, not only can the Avengers ask the Vision, depicted as a deterrent of higher understanding, if he is on their side, but this deterrent is also worthy of Thor's hammer Mjolnir. This is like asking the atomic bomb its opinion before using it to win World War II. The Vision actually does in fact serve as the ultimate vision – the self-fulfilling prophecy – that Western culture creates for itself, for the film ends with the Vision acknowledging to Ultron that humanity is doomed, reinforcing an earlier line about "the end times." And then the Vision kills Ultron. From the Ralph Wolf and Sam Sheepdog nature of the film's combat, to the clichéd character roles of Hawkeye's family, to the end credits' fetishization of the Avengers in a marble statue invoking Greek mythology, *Avengers: Age of Ultron* is a reinforcement of what Western culture has told itself for thousands of years.

Luckily, responses to the film have been increasingly mixed. This, however, needs to be cultivated – the more representative ideas in super-hero comics need to take root and grow in mainstream discourse.

---

[64] *The Pulse* Vol. 1 #4.

Progression is a balance between listening to others and remembering what we know, analyzing the best information possible to make our own honest decisions, and never taking any worldviews for granted. While considering super-hero justice, it is crucial to remember that, as much as super-hero media and discourse have kept the nuances of justice in the background, the super-hero comics at the heart of it all have also continued to live up to their namesakes and used their expansive universes to explore justice in incredible ways, strengthening their foregrounds with informed backgrounds – informing their fantasies with larger questions and verified facts of life rather than perpetuations of ignorance.

Super-hero comics are part of the realities we construct. When a culture sanctions something, it gives it weight. And what we tell each other can change laws. The last few thousand years may have been just fine for some people, but, as the mainstream is confronting more and more in today's headlines, it certainly has been far less for most. Don't listen to the Vision. Be self-aware. Keep your experiences with you. Build. Inspire interests, professions, research, activism, and policy. To borrow from Charles Xavier in *X-Men: Days of Future Past* (2014), if we allow ourselves to feel and embrace all of what super-hero comics have to offer, we can make the discourse better. Channel Superman. Hone your own senses and fill in those gaps. Otherwise, no one else will.

Bibliography

Alexander, Michelle. *The New Jim Crow: Mass Incarceration in the Age of Colorblindness* (New York: The New Press, 2012). Kindle edition.

Arrigo, Bruce A., Heather Y. Bersot, and Brian G. Sellers. *The Ethics of Total Confinement: A Critique of Madness, Citizenship, and Social Justice* (Oxford: Oxford University Press, 2011). PDF e-book.

Batgirl Vol. 4 #1-6. Gail Simone (writer), Ardian Syaf (penciler), Vicente Cifuentes (penciler/inker), Ulises Arreola (colorist), and Dave Sharpe (letterer). Eds. Eddie Berganza, Bobbie Chase, Bob Harras, and Katie Kubert. DC Comics, Nov 2011-Apr 2012.

Batman '66 Meets the Green Hornet Vol. 1 #1-6. Kevin Smith (writer), Ralph Garman (writer), Ty Templeton (penciler/inker), Jon Bogdanove (penciler), Madpencil Studio (inker), Vicente Cifuentes (inker), Andres Cruz (inker), Roberto Flores (inker), Ted Keys (inker), Carlos Muñoz (inker), Tony Aviña (colorist), and Wes Abbott (letterer). Eds. Jim Chadwick and Aniz Ansari. DC Comics and The Green Hornet, Inc., May-Oct 2014.

Boucher, Ian. "Overcoming the Status Quo: Wonder Woman, Superheroes, and the American Criminal Justice System." *Sequart Organization*. 10 Sept 2014.

http://sequart.org/magazine/49664/overcoming-the-status-quo-wonder-woman-superheroes-and-the-american-criminal-justice-system/.

Bush-Baskette, Stephanie. "The War on Drugs and the Incarceration of Mothers." *Journal of Drug Issues* Vol. 30, No. 4 (Fall 2000). Pages 919-928. http://connection.ebscohost.com/c/articles/4000940/war-drugs-incarceration-mothers.

Campbell, Michael C. "Politics, Prisons, and Law Enforcement: An Examination of the Emergence of 'Law and Order' Politics in Texas." *Law & Society Review* Vol. 45, No. 3 (Sept 2011). Pages 631-665. http://onlinelibrary.wiley.com/doi/10.1111/j.1540-5893.2011.00446.x/abstract.

Captain Marvel Vol. 9 #1-6. Kelly Sue DeConnick (writer), David López (penciler/inker), Lee Loughridge (colorist), Virtual Calligraphy (letterer), and Joe Caramagna (letterer). Eds. Axel Alonso, Sana Amanat, Devin Lewis, Nick Lowe, and Stephen Wacker. Marvel Comics, May-Oct 2014.

Corliss, Richard. "*Watchmen* Review: (A Few) Moments of Greatness." *Time.* 4 Mar 2009. http://content.time.com/time/arts/article/0,8599,1883200,00.html.

Cox, Robynn J. A. "The Impact of Mass Incarceration on the Lives of African American Women." *The Review of Black Political Economy* Vol. 39, No. 2 (June 2012). Pages 203-212. http://link.springer.com/article/10.1007/s12114-011-9114-2.

Daredevil Vol. 1 #227-233. Frank Miller (writer), David Mazzucchelli (penciler/inker/colorist), Christie Scheele (colorist), and Joe Rosen (letterer). Ed. Ralph Macchio. Marvel Comics, Feb-Aug 1986.

Daredevil Vol. 3 #1-6. Mark Waid (writer), Paolo Rivera (penciler), Marcos Martin (penciler/inker), Joe Rivera (inker), Javier Rodriguez (colorist), Muntsa Vicente (colorist), Virtual Calligraphy (letterer), and Joe Caramagna (letterer). Eds. Axel Alonso, Ellie Pyle, and Stephen Wacker. Marvel Comics, Sept 2011-Jan 2012.

Daredevil Vol. 4 #14. Mark Waid (writer), Chris Samnee (penciler/inker), Matthew Wilson (colorist), Virtual Calligraphy (letterer), and Joe Caramagna (letterer). Eds. Axel Alonso, Sana Amanat, Charles Beacham, and Nick Lowe. Marvel Comics, May 2015.

DeMarco, Joseph P. *Moral Theory: A Contemporary Overview* (Boston: Jones and Bartlett Publishers, Inc., 1996).

"Denny O'Neil Final Interview." Interview by Christy Blanch and Jason Pierce. *YouTube* video, 1:00:11. Posted by Christy Blanch on 8 Apr 2014. http://www.youtube.com/watch?v=yom94UuO3to.

Gaudio, Christina M. "A Call to Congress to Give Back the Future: End the 'War on Drugs' and Encourage States to Reconstruct the Juvenile Justice System." *Family Court Review* Vol. 48, No. 1 (Jan 2010). Pages 212-227. http://onlinelibrary.wiley.com/doi/10.1111/j.1744-1617.2009.01302.x/abstract.

Geller, Amanda, Carey E. Cooper, Irwin Garfinkel, Ofira Schwartz-Soicher, and Ronald B. Mincy. "Beyond Absenteeism: Father Incarceration and Child Development." *Demography* Vol. 49, No. 1 (Feb 2012). Pages 49-76. http://link.springer.com/article/10.1007/s13524-011-0081-9.

Green Arrow Vol. 2 #125-126. Chuck Dixon (writer), Doug Braithwaite (penciler), Will Rosado (penciler), Robert Campanella (inker), Robin Riggs (inker), Allen Jamison (colorist), Lee Loughridge (colorist), and John Costanza (letterer). Ed. Darren Vincenzo. DC Comics, Oct-Nov 1997.

The Green Hornet Vol. 5 #12-13. Mark Waid (writer), Ronilson Freire (penciler/inker), Márcio Menyz (colorist), and Troy Peteri (letterer). Ed. Joseph Rybandt. Dynamite Entertainment, May-June 2014.

Green Lantern Vol. 2 #76. Denny O'Neil (writer), Neal Adams (penciler/inker), Cory Adams (colorist), and John Costanza (letterer). Ed. Julius Schwartz. DC Comics, Apr 1970.

Green Lantern Vol. 2 #85-86. Denny O'Neil (writer), Neal Adams (penciler/inker), Dick Giordano (inker), Cory Adams (colorist), and John Costanza (letterer). Ed. Julius Schwartz. DC Comics, Aug/Sept and Oct/Nov 1971.

Green Lantern Vol. 3 #92. Ron Marz (writer), Darryl Banks (penciler), Terry Austin (inker), Rob Schwager (colorist), and Chris Eliopoulos (letterer). Eds. Eddie Berganza, Kevin Dooley, and Dana Kurtin. DC Comics, Nov 1997.

Green Lantern Vol. 5 #0. Geoff Johns (writer), Doug Mahnke (penciler), Christian Alamy (inker), Keith Champagne (inker), Mark Irwin (inker), Tony Aviña (colorist), and Alex Sinclair (colorist). Eds. Bob Harras, Matt Idelson, and Wil Moss. DC Comics, Nov 2012.

Grossman, Lev. "All-*Time* 100 Novels: *Watchmen.*" *Time*. 11 Jan 2010. http://entertainment.time.com/2005/10/16/all-time-100-novels/slide/watchmen-1986-by-alan-moore-dave-gibbons/.

Harcourt, Bernard E. "From the Asylum to the Prison: Rethinking the Incarceration Revolution." *Texas Law Review* Vol. 84, No. 7 (June 2006). Pages 1751-1786. http://www.law.uchicago.edu/files/file/harcourt_institutionalization_final.pdf

Madsen, Frank G. "International Narcotics Law Enforcement: A Study in Irrationality." *Journal of International Affairs* Vol. 66, No. 1 (Fall/Winter 2012). Pages 123-141. http://jia.sipa.columbia.edu/international-narcotics-law-enforcement-study-irrationality/.

Martian Manhunter: American Secrets #1-3. Gerard Jones (writer), Eduardo Barreto (penciler/inker), Steve Oliff (colorist), and Pat Brosseau (letterer). Eds. Brian Augustyn and Ruben Diaz. DC Comics, Aug-Oct 1992.

Marvel Graphic Novel #5 - X-Men: God Loves, Man Kills. Chris Claremont (writer), Brent Anderson (penciler/inker), Steve Oliff (colorist), and Tom Orzechowski (letterer). Eds. Danny Fingeroth, Louise Simonson, and Jim Shooter. Marvel Comics, 1982.

Massoglia, Michael, Glenn Firebaugh, and Cody Warner. "Racial Variation in the Effect of Incarceration on Neighborhood Attainment." *American Sociological Review* Vol. 78, No. 1 (Feb 2013). Pages 142-165. http://asr.sagepub.com/content/78/1/142.abstract.

Moon Knight Vol. 5 #15-16. Mike Benson (writer), Charlie Huston (writer), Javier Saltares (penciler/inker), Mark Texeira (penciler/inker), Dan Brown (colorist), and Joe Caramagna (letterer). Eds. Axel Alonso and Daniel Ketchum. Marvel Comics, Apr-May 2008.

Moore, Lisa D. and Amy Elkavich. "Who's Using and Who's Doing Time: Incarceration, the War on Drugs, and Public Health." *American Journal of Public Health* Vol. 98, No. 5 (May 2008). Pages 782-786. http://ajph.aphapublications.org/doi/abs/10.2105/AJPH.98.Supplement_1.S176.

Nichols, Emily Bever and Ann Booker Loper. "Incarceration in the Household: Academic Outcomes of Adolescents with an Incarcerated Household Member." *Journal of Youth and Adolescence* Vol. 41, No. 11 (Nov 2012). Pages 1455-1471. http://link.springer.com/article/10.1007%2Fs10964-012-9780-9.

O'Connell, Michael. "TV Ratings: *The Flash* Premiere Gives CW a 5-Year Best." *The Hollywood Reporter.* 8 Oct 2014. http://www.hollywoodreporter.com/live-feed/tv-ratings-flash-premiere-gives-739170.

Osborn Vol. 1 #1-5. Kelly Sue DeConnick (writer), Emma Ríos (penciler/inker), Becky Cloonan (penciler/inker), José Villarrubia (colorist), Matthew Wilson (colorist), Virtual Calligraphy (letterer), and Clayton Cowles (letterer). Eds. Axel Alonso, Alejandro Arbona, and Stephen Wacker. Marvel Comics, Jan-Feb and Apr-June 2011.

Power Man Vol. 1 #28. Don McGregor (writer), George Tuska (penciler), Vince Colletta (inker), Petra Goldberg (colorist), and Dave Hunt (letterer). Ed. Marv Wolfman. Marvel Comics, Dec 1975.

Power Man Vol. 1 #32-33. Don McGregor (writer), Frank Robbins (penciler), Vince Colletta (inker), Janice Cohen (colorist), and Karen Mantlo (letterer). Ed. Marv Wolfman. Marvel Comics, June-July 1976.

Power Man Vol. 1 #35. Marv Wolfman (writer), Don McGregor (writer), Marie Severin (penciler), Frank Giacoia (inker), Joe Giella (inker), Phil Rachelson (colorist), and Karen Mantlo (letterer). Ed. Archie Goodwin. Marvel Comics, Sept 1976.

Power Man Vol. 1 #39. Marv Wolfman (writer), Bill Mantlo (writer), Bob Brown (penciler), Klaus Janson (inker), Roger Slifer (colorist), Jim Shooter (colorist), and Denise Wohl (letterer). Ed. Archie Goodwin. Marvel Comics, Jan 1977.

Power Man Vol. 1 #43. Marv Wolfman (writer), Lee Elias (penciler), Alex Niño (inker), Janice Cohen (colorist), and John Costanza (letterer). Ed. Marv Wolfman. Marvel Comics, May 1977.

Power Man Annual Vol. 1 #1. Chris Claremont (writer), Lee Elias (penciler), Dave Hunt (inker), Bonnie Wilford (colorist), and Denise Wohl (letterer). Ed. Archie Goodwin. Marvel Comics, 1976.

The Pulse Vol. 1 #4. Brian Michael Bendis (writer), Mark Bagley (penciler), Scott Hanna (inker), Pete Pantazis (colorist), and Cory Petit (letterer). Eds. Andy Schmidt and Nicole Wiley. Marvel Comics, Sept 2004.

Quinn, Daniel. *Ishmael: An Adventure of the Mind and Spirit.* New York: Bantam Books, 1995.

Reynolds, Marylee. "The War on Drugs, Prison Building, and Globalization: Catalysts for the Global Incarceration of Women." *NWSA Journal* Vol. 20, No. 2 (Summer 2008). Pages 72-95. http://muse.jhu.edu/journals/ff/summary/v020/20.2.reynolds.html.

Risse, Mathias. *On Global Justice* (Princeton, NJ: Princeton University Press, 2012). PDF e-book.

"Rorschach: #16 Top Comic Book Heroes." *IGN.* Accessed 10 Dec 2016. http://www.ign.com/top/comic-book-heroes/16.

Rose, Kristin and Chris Rose. "Enrolling in College While in Prison: Factors That Promote Male and Female Prisoners to Participate." *Journal of Correctional Education* Vol. 65, No. 2 (May 2014). Pages 20-39. http://connection.ebscohost.com/c/articles/99273293/enrolling-college-while-prison-factors-that-promote-male-female-prisoners-participate.

Runaways Vol. 1 #1. Brian K. Vaughan (writer), Adrian Alphona (penciler), David Newbold (inker), Brian Reber (colorist), and Paul Tutrone (letterer). Eds. C.B. Cebulski, Stephanie Moore, and Joe Quesada. Marvel Comics, July 2003.

Sampson, Robert J. and Charles Loeffler. "Punishment's Place: The Local Concentration of Mass Incarceration." *Daedalus* Vol. 139, No. 3 (Summer 2010). Pages 20-31. http://www.mitpressjournals.org/doi/pdf/10.1162/DAED_a_00020.

Schrader, John Benjamin. "Reawakening 'Privileges or Immunities:' An Originalist Blueprint for Invalidating State Felon Disenfranchisement Laws." *Vanderbilt Law Review* Vol. 62, No. 4 (May 2009). Pages 1285-1314. http://www.vanderbiltlawreview.org/articles/2009/05/Schrader-Reawakening-_Privileges-or-Immunities_62-Vand.-L.-Rev.-1285-2009.pdf.

She-Hulk Vol. 3 #1, 3, 5. Charles Soule (writer), Javier Pulido (penciler/inker), Ronald Wimberly (penciler/inker), Muntsa Vicente (colorist), Rico Renzi (colorist), Virtual Calligraphy (letterer), and Clayton Cowles (letterer). Eds. Axel Alonso, Tom Brennan, Frankie Johnson, and Jeanine Schaefer. Marvel Comics, April, June, Aug 2014.

The Spectre Vol. 3 #18. John Ostrander (writer), Tom Mandrake (penciler/inker), Digital Chameleon (colorist), Carla Feeny (colorist), and Todd Klein (letterer). Eds. Dan Raspler and Peter J. Tomasi. DC Comics, May 1994.

The Spectre Vol. 3 #22. John Ostrander (writer), Tom Mandrake (penciler/inker), Digital Chameleon (colorist), Carla Feeny (colorist), and Todd Klein (letterer). Eds. Jenette Kahn, Dan Raspler, and Peter J. Tomasi. DC Comics, Sept 1994.

Swift, Jonathan. *Gulliver's Travels* (London: HarperCollins Publishers, 2010).

Tyler, Josh. "*Watchmen* Movie Review." *Cinemablend.* Accessed 10 Dec 2016. http://www.cinemablend.com/reviews/Watchmen-3755.html.

Vuong, Linh, Christopher Hartney, Barry Krisberg, and Susan Marchionna. "The Extravangance of Imprisonment Revisited." *Judicature* Vol. 94, No. 2 (Sept-Oct 2010). Pages 70-80. http://scholarship.law.berkeley.edu/cgi/viewcontent.cgi?article=2720&context=facpubs.

Watchmen #1-12. Alan Moore (writer), Dave Gibbons (penciler/inker/letterer), and John Higgins (colorist). Ed. Len Wein. DC Comics, Sept 1986-Oct 1987.

Wildeman, Christopher and Bruce Western. "Incarceration in Fragile Families." *The Future of Children* Vol. 20, No. 2 (Fall 2010). Pages 157-177. http://www.princeton.edu/futureofchildren/publications/docs/20_02_08.pdf.

"Wonder Woman." *DC Comics.* Accessed 1 June 2015. http://www.dccomics.com/characters/wonder-woman.

Wonder Woman Vol. 3 #14-19. Gail Simone (writer), Terry Dodson (penciler), Ron Randall (penciler/inker), Bernard Chang (penciler/inker), Rachel Dodson (inker), Jon Holdredge (inker), Lee Loughridge (colorist), Alex Sinclair (colorist), Pete Pantazis (colorist), I.L.L. (colorist), Travis Lanham (letterer), John J. Hill (letterer), and Rob Leigh (letterer). Eds. Nachie Castro and Matt Idelson. DC Comics, Jan-June 2008.

Empowerment Through Their Shoes: Mark Waid on Super-Hero Justice

IAN BOUCHER: What super-hero comics have been the most inspirational to you throughout your life and why?

MARK WAID: In general, the super-hero comics that've been most inspirational to me are the ones where it's all about the heart, or it's all about characters being inspirational – characters not just punching bad guys or righting wrongs, but inspiring other human beings, inspiring the people around them, and sort of raising the level of the people around them. Any number of Superman stories, any number of Captain America stories are the ones that resonate most with me in terms of being inspirational.

There's one Superman story in particular that's my favorite Superman story of all time. It's gonna sound goofy and corny and childlike, but then again, if you remember that these stories were written for nine-year-olds, then you take that into account. It's from *Superman* #148,[1] and it's called "Superman Owes a Billion Dollars." The setup of the story is that some

---

[1] *Superman* Vol. 1 #148. Robert Bernstein (writer) and Curt Swan (penciler). Ed. Mort Weisinger. DC Comics, Oct 1961.

eager beaver IRS agent has decided that, even though Superman gives all the wealth and rewards he receives or creates to charity, it still counts as income. Therefore, he still owes back taxes, on all the diamonds he's ever created for charity, all the gold bullion he's dug out of the ground, or radium he's obtained for hospital research. Since it's a story for eight and nine-years-olds, it's not Superman just laughing this guy out of his IRS offices. The guy calls Superman in, and Superman is presented with a bill for, like, a billion dollars in back taxes. *(Boucher laughs)*

So the main part of the story of course is Superman running around the Earth trying to unearth riches that will pay that back tax, and it's a series of bizarre coincidences; like he'll unearth some ancient artifact only to realize that it belongs to a lost civilization, and he'll then rescue the people of the lost civilization and give the artifact back. Or he'll unearth some rare mineral from Atlantis only to realize that it can be used to wipe out a certain disease so it's better off donated to a hospital rather than sold. But the inspirational part to me is the end, where the IRS agent's boss comes in – and shuts the whole thing down.

BOUCHER: Oh wow.

WAID: He says you don't understand. If you're playing by the rules of the IRS – this is like 1961 or whatever so the figures obviously would have to be adjusted for inflation *(Boucher laughs)* –

He says if you're talking about the rules, then by the IRS code everybody gets a $600 exemption for dependents – and the whole world is dependent on Superman. So if anything, he has two billion dependents and we owe him money. And as silly and as goofy as that sounds, it just moved me so much as a kid, that idea that Superman has done such good things and he's been so selfless that the entire world feels indebted to him. Of course Superman is too humble to ever accept that that was true, except in this story – but still I just love that sentiment.

BOUCHER: In what ways do you think super-hero comics have matured the most, and where do you think they should grow the most, both in terms of storytelling and the processes of the industry?

WAID: Well in terms of storytelling, the good news is I think they've matured quite nicely. 1986 was the kickoff year. 1986 was the year where we saw *Watchmen* and *Maus* and *The Dark Knight Returns*, so you have the holy trinity of "comics no longer just for kids," and since that time, they set the pattern that super-hero comics don't have to be just simple child's fare, and we've proven it. There's still plenty of super-hero comics out there too for younger readers, stuff that's more punch 'em up and less sophisticated, but in terms of themes, in terms of subject material, I think they've matured quite a bit.

I think that in terms of process of the industry, the room for growth is still in trying to reach outside the genre, or try to broaden the genre a little bit. I mean super-hero comics, for all of their sophistication, all of their gravitas, are still largely written and drawn by a white male audience, for a white male audience, and that's changing very quickly. I don't think it's changing fast enough, but social change doesn't happen by fiat, it happens because people are demanding it. And more and more, there's more diversity both within super-hero comics and the subject matter, and diversity among the creators themselves, and I think that's the growth area because that's where you end up coming up with new stories and new concepts and new themes that are not obvious to the current audience and the current batch of creators.

BOUCHER: In an interview a few years ago with Blastoff Comics,[2] you talked about the diversity of motivation, and I think that's a point that's not discussed nearly enough. It does play into things beyond super-hero storytelling, like who's writing and what their motivations are.

WAID: *Absolutely*. Absolutely. The place you always start with super-heroes is a fairly clear-cut simplistic childish motivation, which is "you're gonna go punish bad guys." And then everything that you do to make a super-hero have some weight and heft and longevity to it means adding something to it that has some real emotional resonance for people of all ages, and that's harder to do than it looks because the fallback position is always, "Well why does he do this?" "Well, 'cause he's a super-hero." That's a terrible answer. *(Boucher laughs)*

---

[2] Interview by Amy Ratcliffe. "The Blastoff Video Interview - Mark Waid, Part 1." *YouTube* video, 9:30. Posted by Scott Tipton on 24 Jan 2012. https://www.youtube.com/watch?v=GX4KtJ68H_U.

You got to flip the question. Why is he a super-hero? Why does he choose to deal with his problems as a vigilante as opposed to within the system? That's a more interesting question and there's a lot more room for different answers in there if you just let your imagination go.

BOUCHER: I don't know the specifics exactly, but I do know that you weren't a fan of the movie *Man of Steel*.

WAID: Well, that's an understatement, yeah. *(laughs)*

BOUCHER: What do you think about the current paths of super-hero comic adaptations to film and TV in general?

WAID: I think if you'd asked me two years ago when I saw *Man of Steel* I would've made choking noises, but I'm really impressed with the adaptations to film and television since. I think that with each succeeding attempt, especially with stuff that seems off-brand like *Guardians of the Galaxy* or [Netflix's] *Daredevil* – stuff that doesn't seem like household name material – that there continues to be less and less of a sense of embarrassment on the part of the TV and movie people. With each successful project like that, they're more confident in embracing the trappings of a super-hero comic without feeling mortified by it, a repudiation of the famous *Smallville* approach of "no flights no tights," no costumes, no capes. Conversely, I don't know if you've seen [CW's] *The Flash*, but that's the ultimate in terms of embracing the tropes of comic book super-heroes and making them fun and making them not shameful. For every *Gotham* which is dark, grim, and embarrassed of its roots, you have a *Flash*; with every *Man of Steel*, you have an *Avengers: Age of Ultron*. I'm not saying that the path always has to be a light, breezy, goofy one, but there needs to be more of a range to the material that isn't just, "Wow, we're really embarrassed about comics, how do we make this appeal to a mass audience?" – when in fact, that is the mass audience now, we won the culture war. Guess what? Comic books aren't a tiny sliver of pop culture, we are pop culture now, so embrace it.

BOUCHER: Have you watched the *Daredevil* show [Season 1] on Netflix or are you going to watch it?

WAID: I have watched it, I'm about halfway through, and it's darker than I would've approached the material but I don't feel at any point like they're embarrassed about the source material; it seems like it has the integrity of the source.

BOUCHER: So many of your super-hero stories challenge their characters as people and as super-heroes. They're equally engaging, thought-provoking stories for characters, but also for super-heroic themes. Can you talk about how some of these stories came about for you, starting with the Legion of Super-Heroes struggling with their new alliance with the established adult power structure of the United Planets?[3]

WAID: That actually ties into Matt Murdock training clients as well.[4] That all came from two things at play. I don't write super-heroes just as people with costumes. I mean, I do in the sense that they have to be real to me; they have to feel real. You apply all the same rules that you do to writing ordinary people in fiction, but I can't stop there, because whether they've got powers, or whether they've just got a funny costume, or whatever it is that makes them a super-hero, I have to filter that part in. I have to make that a lynchpin for myself, and it has to be a part of their personality, and key to how they view the world. I have to write the character from the inside out.

Take Cosmic Boy for example. I ask myself, "What is it like to detect electromagnetic radiation wherever you go, and to be able to sort of sense that the same way we feel sunlight?" Saturn Girl is a better example. The fact that she's a telepath has to inform her personality, it has to affect her actions, it has to affect her speech – in her specific case, she doesn't speak at all, because why would a race of telepaths have to speak? I don't write Daredevil and Matt Murdock any different, I don't write Wally West or the Flash any different whether they're in or out of costume. I just concentrate on how their abilities allow them to see the world.

---

[3] Beginning with *Legion of Super-Heroes* Vol. 5 #14. Mark Waid (writer), Adam DeKraker (penciler), Ken Lashley (penciler), KWL Designs (inker/colorist), Rodney Ramos (inker), Sno-Cone Studios (colorist), and Travis Lanham (letterer). Eds. Harvey Richards and Stephen Wacker. DC Comics, Mar 2006.

[4] *Daredevil* Vol. 3 #1-6. Mark Waid (writer), Paolo Rivera (penciler), Marcos Martin (penciler/inker), Joe Rivera (inker), Javier Rodriguez (colorist), Muntsa Vicente (colorist), Virtual Calligraphy (letterer), Joe Caramagna (letterer). Eds. Axel Alonso, Ellie Pyle, and Stephen Wacker. Marvel Comics, Sept 2011-Jan 2012.

Specifically about the Legion of Super-Heroes, this gets back to the "inspirational" question. What appealed to me about flipping the script on the Legion was that in previous incarnations, they were always the hyper-obedient junior arm of the United Planets. They were always Establishment, which was really weird for a bunch of teenage kids, 'cause that's exactly what teenage kids aren't. As the biggest the Legion fan in the world, I'm not in any way knocking the approach that was taken before, but I thought, "Well, we need to do something drastic to let people know that this is not the same Legion that you're used to." So my creative partner Barry Kitson and I flipped the paradigm, and they became rebellious, as teenagers would be. They were rebelling against a conformist society and an established power structure but doing so in a way that was wrapped around a message of inclusiveness. They declared loudly that anyone their age could be a Legionnaire. All they had to do was believe in what the Legion believed in. You didn't have to have super-powers. If you wanted to call yourself a Legionnaire, you were a Legionnaire, which means that you're young either in body or in spirit and you're against the Establishment and you want to make change, you want to create waves, and you want to make a splash. So the idea of the Legion as an inspiration to the young and young at heart across the galaxy is what I was trying to get at there.

BOUCHER: But then you took a huge next step with the United Planets saying, "Okay well you know what? You guys are with us now, we're sanctioning you, and now what're you going to do?" I think that's a huge step.

WAID: Thank you, and it was intended because, honestly, that's the way governments work. The way the smart systems work is to say, "We're not going to continue to fight you, we're going to subsume you, and turn you into part of the Establishment," and that was the next phase of the book – watching the rabble-rousers and the agitators suddenly have to work within a system, and how that sort of tore the Legion leadership apart.

And the transition of Matt Murdock training clients to defend themselves was much the same thing. I was kind of caught in a box from a visual standpoint. There's nothing duller in comics than watching a guy in a courtroom, page after page after page, so if you're going to do Matt Murdock as a lawyer, I really wanted to try and find some new take on that.

Once I sort of settled in on this idea that, because his identity was public now, and Matt would in no way shape or form be able to stand in a courtroom without it being a mistrial every time, I came up with the idea of him training his clients to defend themselves – which again I think plays into that theme of trying to inspire others and help other ordinary people raise their game.

BOUCHER: Have you read Gerard Jones's book *Killing Monsters*[5] [a book about the positive, empowering role of "violent" media such as super-heroes in the development of children]?

WAID: Oh yeah.

BOUCHER: Foggy Nelson meeting with the children in the hospital where they're drawing their own comic book[6] reminded me of that a lot and I loved it.

WAID: Thank you. It just seemed to me that's how you engage kids, you empower them. You can either make them feel like victims or you can empower them through encouraging them to let their imagination run wild and use comics as an analogy for how they feel and what they want. It's funny, I didn't really think about it until you posed the questions this way, but I guess that sense of conveying empowerment to ordinary people really is a standing theme in my work.

BOUCHER: Especially your Daredevil work right now is very inspirational to a lot of people.

WAID: I'm getting a lot of positive feedback about the depression angle specifically, the idea that here's a guy dealing with depression, dealing with it in a realistic way – I gotta tell you, that's very gratifying and very flattering that people are responding to it on a real emotional level.

BOUCHER: And all of these themes blur and combine with the stuff that's going on fictionally. Like in the hospital, to Foggy and the kids, when they talk about super-heroes, they're talking about real people, yet they're also

---

[5] Gerard Jones. Killing Monsters: Why Children Need Fantasy, Super Heroes, and Make-Believe Violence (New York: Basic Books, 2002). PDF e-book.
[6] *Daredevil* Vol. 3 #26. Mark Waid (writer), Chris Samnee (penciler/inker), Javier Rodriguez (colorist), Virtual Calligraphy (letterer), and Joe Caramagna (letterer). Eds. Axel Alonso, Ellie Pyle, and Stephen Wacker. Marvel Comics, July 2013.

writing fiction in their own comic book. Yet we know that Iron Man and the Hulk aren't real, but can still be stand-ins for elements of real life, and it all intertwines together into fantastic storytelling.

WAID: I'm going to hire you as my publicist.

BOUCHER: *(laughs)* Okay, fair enough. And Daredevil's newest costume – he's a lawyer now essentially, fighting crime in a red business suit!

WAID: *Yeah!* That actually comes from a completely different place. Near the end of the previous run of that book, when Matt admits on the stand that he's Daredevil, he's just tired of secrets. I think Matt thinks to some degree that part of the woes he's withstood over the years and part of the trouble he goes through is thanks to some sort of karma for being so secretive. This gave me the opportunity to really blow out the doors with a super-hero who is unmasking himself one step at a time, to the point where he just starts wearing a maskless business suit. Frankly, that's a little more flamboyant than I think I would've taken the chance on if artist Chris [Samnee] weren't having so much fun with it – but the theme we're dealing with is that honesty is a virtue and yet everything about super-heroes, everything about the tropes of super-heroes, is wrapped up in secrecy and masks and protecting your secret identity from the people you love, and not admitting who you really are.

On a meta level there's nothing wrong with that because that's one of the tropes of being a super-hero. But if you take a microscope to that stuff – which we can with a character like Daredevil, where the status quo is a little more flexible because he's not Superman or Spider-Man or a character who is merchandized around the world, so Marvel's not as protective of the status quo – what does keeping secrets from the people around you really mean? How does it affect your life? How does it affect how you deal with other people? A lot of the last year and a half or so of our run is Matt very slowly dropping all of those tropes and sort of shedding himself of all those typical super-hero conveniences like masks and secret identities and secret hideouts and all that sort of thing. The transparency – and the irony is not lost on me – of a blind man letting the whole world see him is where we've been going with this and that's the theme of the entire run of the book.

BOUCHER: I'm a big fan of the original Green Hornet TV show, and your work on the Green Hornet has been the closest thing I've seen to that original show. It was fantastic to see Britt and Kato back, and Lenore Case. Lenore gets herself arrested on purpose at the end of Volume 2 and tells Britt how he helped create this status quo, that he has resources and needs to be able to live with the consequences, to keep working, and how we all have a part.[7] To me, it came across like we all have a part in the justice system. That might be a leap, but that's sort of what it said to me. It's a super-hero we're talking about here, but again it's intertwined with such real stuff, and the whole story is told in such a way that when you get to those last few panels, it just hit me so hard, and I would love to hear your thoughts about how that whole thing came about.

WAID: Thanks. The Green Hornet was a really interesting experiment for me in terms of storytelling because to my mind it was never a super-hero book, it was a crime comic, so I didn't to want give Green Hornet or Britt Reid the same sort of outs or easy pass that a lot of traditional super-heroes have. I wanted there to be real weight and consequence to the fact that if you're going to play the part of a villain, sometimes you have to play it very well, and there are consequences to that. You see some of that in the earlier issues where Kato has some cross words with the Hornet or some bad feelings about watching the Hornet perhaps cross boundaries that Kato wouldn't want to cross.

But the finale with Lenore really was being able to fold two ideas in at once: one that again, there is an inspirational nature of super-heroes to those around them. That in a weird way, this is Lenore taking a hit for the team, but doing it for a greater good. And then you fold that in with the idea that I also needed there to be some genuine consequence for Britt Reid, for crossing some lines that perhaps he shouldn't have crossed. But since I knew that was the last issue, and I knew that I wasn't going to do anything that'd permanently upend the status quo of the Green Hornet in the last issue of his own series, like put him in jail – because that would seem to be a very weird place to end a series – I just wanted there to be a sense of

---

[7] *The Green Hornet* Vol. 5 #13. Mark Waid (writer), Ronilson Freire (penciler/inker), Márcio Menyz (colorist), and Troy Peteri (letterer). Eds. Hannah Gorfinkel, Molly Mahan, and Joseph Rybandt. Dynamite Entertainment, June 2014.

Lenore Case's final words in *The Green Hornet* Vol. 5 #13 reach far beyond their powerful panels. Art by Ronilson Freire. © The Green Hornet, Inc.

consequence, and the Lenore stuff just seemed to be the right note to hit. It clearly will haunt him.

BOUCHER: Yeah, and what it made it even more hard-hitting for me was that I thought the plan where they wrapped everything up was very nice and neat and all done and then it's like, oh my gosh, there's *so much* more to this!

WAID: *(laughs)* Yeah!

BOUCHER: What feedback has stood out the most to you about your work over the years, positive and negative?

WAID: I think the most positive has always been when I get lucky enough to write something that seems to touch people on an emotional level. Dealing with depression with Matt, or last year writing a story about postpartum depression with his own mother,[8] I've been getting a lot of positive feedback about that from people for whom it seems to have touched a nerve. That's really a good feeling, because that gives what I do a little more urgency on a day-to-day level, than just guys in costumes running around. The negative stuff that stands out – and it will always stand out, and there's nothing I can do about it except just roll my eyes and keep moving forward – is that, because I tend to write characters that are not relentlessly dark and ugly and bitter and grim, I don't care how many thousands of comics I write, there will still always seem to be a wide swath of comics fans who think that all I write is silly Silver Age stuff, which just makes me insane, but I've reached the point where there's nothing you can do about it except just let them have their say.

BOUCHER: Do you feel like that sort of feedback is greater than the positive feedback in terms of the amount?

WAID: No, not really. Now it's easy for me to say because if you come at me on Twitter just to insult me I'll block you, so to some degree I've set up a little bubble for myself, but, I think overall, the positive outweighs the negative. Either way you kind of gotta let it go when you sit down at the keyboard. At the end of the day, all that really matters is I have to feel like I

---

[8] *Daredevil* Vol. 4 #7. Mark Waid (writer), Javier Rodriguez (penciler/colorist), Álvaro López (inker), Virtual Calligraphy (letterer), and Joe Caramagna (letterer). Eds. Axel Alonso and Ellie Pyle. Marvel Comics, Oct 2014.

did a good job and I was honest on the page. If I come away from a story feeling like I was honest, and the characters were honest, and I was hitting emotional beats that were genuine, then if haters come at me on Twitter, fine, I can live with that.

BOUCHER: What are the two most interesting precedents for you in terms of super-hero justice and why?

WAID: The Superman IRS thing is definitely one of them. Another one is just the very basic tenet that was drilled into me in super-hero comics that I read as a kid, which is that super-heroes don't kill. And it is something that I cannot get away from. It gets back to part of my issues with the *Man of Steel* movie. The counterargument to Superman killing his enemy in that film from fans is often, "Well yes, but in the real world – " Well this isn't the real world. This isn't the real world. These aren't documentaries [laughs]. Yes, I'm sure if I worked hard at it I could construct a Batman story in which the only solution to the Joker was to kill the Joker to save innocent lives, but that's a disservice to what a super-hero story is. The characters behave in certain ways because you as the writer have set them up to behave in that way. The precedent for me that was always set, the grounding principle that was always set was that super-heroes don't kill. In part that's because it's just basic human morality, "Thou shalt not kill," but also on a more meta level, it's that super-heroes were created specifically to do the impossible. And to overcome challenges that ordinary people can't overcome.

The very first time we ever saw a super-hero was on the cover of *Action Comics* #1,[9] and he was picking up an automobile and smashing it against a cliffside. That was impossible. Nobody'd ever seen anything like that before. The very first image of a super-hero was of doing the impossible, and that's what super-heroes do. That's what they are designed to do, things that ordinary people can't do, and so my job as a writer is not to try to drag them down to a human level, and ask what they would do if they were in our shoes. I don't care what they would do if they were in our shoes. I want to know what we would do if we were in their shoes.

---

[9] Referring, of course, to the first appearance of Superman in *Action Comics* Vol. 1 #1. Jerry Siegel (writer) and Joe Shuster (penciler/inker). Ed. Vincent Sullivan. DC Comics, June 1938.

BOUCHER: Wow! Jumping off of that, in super-hero comics, both in the storytelling and the process of selling them, how much of a factor are accurate, more representative, or more expansive depictions of criminal justice and related topics like law, government, or citizenship for you and why?

WAID: Everything is in service to the story, so while, especially with Daredevil, I try to be as accurate with matters of law and government as I can, I'm also willing to bend those rules if I need to, to tell a good story. You have to bear in mind the fact that in super-hero comics, you're dealing with characters whose entire existence is illegal and based on vigilante action, so if you're willing to accept a world in which Superman is able to fly people into jail and Batman is able to roam the streets without being put in prison, then you kind of have to assume that the rule of law is a little more flexible in the super-hero universe. So that's not the most common priority, but it does factor thematically in that again they are agents of the law.

That said, I think we're reaching an interesting tipping point. I'm going to be dealing with this as I write *The Avengers* starting this fall. With Captain America being a part of that, and Captain America being, of course, Sam Wilson, the black Captain America, we really want to get into the issue of how, for Captain America Sam Wilson, there are at least two Americas, and that's something that Steve Rogers, the 1940s Captain America, would never say, because he comes from a place and a time and a white heritage that says that everything is inclusive and that everybody is an American. I think that, as more of the creators embrace a diversion of voice, this sort of idea that super-heroes are enforcers and agents of the status quo has a good chance of changing, and I would love to see that. I would love to see us lean into that a little bit more.

BOUCHER: Do you think that current events have been affecting things like that within the industry?

WAID: I think so. Especially in the last couple of years, with Ferguson and with the Trayvon Martin case, with Charleston — you can't look at those incidents, you can't be aware of them as somebody who is writing ostensibly heroic characters that deal in morality, and not be aware of how the world is changing. It's a little tricky because if you're writing super-heroes for DC and Marvel, they're still corporate entities, and so there's only so far you can go with social statement where Disney or Warner Bros. will not feel a little bit nervous, because they cater to all people of all audiences. The last thing in the world Marvel Comics wants on any given morning is some character's comment on Tea Partiers or whatever taken out of context and placed on Fox News where Marvel has to play defense for something that shouldn't have to be defended. So that said, it's a little bit of a minefield to get into heavy social commentary in mainstream super-hero comics, but I think that we're all interested in doing it, I really do. We want to write about the world in which we live.

BOUCHER: In that Blastoff Comics interview, you said that you consult with Marc Guggenheim sometimes because of his law expertise. Is that sort of a common thing in the industry to do, or are people's routines as vastly different as each creator?

WAID: I think they're a little different with each creator but, between the easy access to people in other professions, and frankly, the ease of internet accessibility in terms of research, I think that all of us are trying to be a little bit more mindful of the fact that sometimes you have to write toward the expert in the audience so your story doesn't completely fall down.

BOUCHER: Do you think with the internet that things have changed significantly since back in the '90s or even before your time, like in Denny O'Neil's days?

WAID: Yeah, I think so because I think there's a lot less excuse for being sloppy or mistaken in detail – not that Denny ever was, but not everyone was as diligent as Denny. There is no excuse for being sloppy in your detail or for fudging just because you weren't able to find something out or look it up. All information is available to us at all times now.

BOUCHER: Are there any particular ideas about super-heroes and villains that you consistently run into conflict with in your work and have trouble actually bringing to the shelves, whether internally within yourself, people you're working with, or externally via other organizations? We're not living in the Code age anymore but...

WAID: Right, but I think the only answer that I have to that is what I said before, which is this idea that the more socially active and the more of a social justice warrior I want my characters to be, the more mindful I have to be of the fact that I'm writing for corporations who may not share my views, and ultimately it's their toys. So the trick then is to find some way to take a social issue that you feel strongly about, for example the Trayvon Martin case, and "Marvelize" it if you will – create a bigger sort of super-hero story that is more of an analogy, more of a sort of disguised form of that story. You still have the emotional beats, but you're doing it sort of on a bigger stage.

BOUCHER: Why do you think that Wonder Woman's brand of justice, where she sort of thinks about the bigger picture and is a diplomat in a lot of ways – she's very much like a restorative justice mediator in some ways – hasn't caught on as much in the mainstream as Batman and the Punisher?

WAID: Because it's hard to draw. *(Boucher laughs)* It sounds like a glib answer but that's really the answer. Diplomacy is harder to draw in an interesting way that is compelling and uses the comics medium to its fullest extent. I'm not saying it can't be done. It can be done by really smart, talented people, but by and large most comics writers and artists are a lot more interested in watching somebody turn over a tank or punch Doctor Psycho in the face than they are trying to do peacekeeping stories. Wonder Woman as an agent of peace makes perfect sense to me, but I understand how that is harder to get across the printed page because comics deal with external conflict better than internal conflict. That's what novels do, they deal with internal conflict. I'm making broad stroke generalizations, but by and large super-hero comics, whether you're talking about violence which is a fight, or just action which is people doing things on the page that are interesting to look at – you can have both, but neither of them tend to lend themselves very much to being an agent of peace.

BOUCHER: Yeah and in that sense I find Gail Simone's *The Circle* very inspirational, because there's a scene where Wonder Woman is fighting hyper-intelligent gorillas, but while she's fighting them, in self-defense mostly, and trying to subdue them, she's trying to figure out why they're upset, and in the end they're her friends.[10]

---

[10] *Wonder Woman* Vol. 3 #14. Gail Simone (writer), Terry Dodson (penciler), Rachel Dodson (inker), Lee Loughridge (colorist), Alex Sinclair (colorist), and Travis Lanham (letterer). Eds. Nachie Castro and Matt Idelson. DC Comics, Jan 2008.

WAID: Yeah, right exactly, but it would be hard to do that month after month after month after month and it would be hard to extend that to other characters too. I stand by my original answer: because it's hard to draw.

BOUCHER: Do you think that kids' favorite comic book super-heroes, in names or their actions, seem very different to you now from when you were a kid?

WAID: Yeah they do. We live in a society where each next generation is angrier than the last, and that is not without good reason, especially this time around. The most recent young generation is the first generation to grow up less better off than the previous generation economically and socially, and it's that anger that has turned everything around.

When I was growing up, for children, Superman was their main super-hero. He's all about fantasy and flying through the air and doing incredible things. Then, as they got older, they began to think of Batman as cooler because he's more reflective of kids' natural rebelliousness. Batman speaks to that because he's an agent of anger, an agent of vengeance rather than an agent of childlike hope and brightness.

I know I'm overgeneralizing, but the world gets darker and the world gets angrier and people learn anger at a younger and younger age. I think we've reached a point now where kids get in touch with the darker emotions earlier, so that is why I think we've sort of reached a point where even young kids think of Superman as goofy and silly and they all love Batman and Wolverine because they do badass things.

BOUCHER: And I feel like there's just so much more openness in the world. It's not just that they're being exposed to things that aren't real, it's also that you see more how things work, and where the flaws and the cracks are in things.

WAID: That's true, that's a good point, there's a lot more transparency in the world, there's a lot more understanding. Yes.

BOUCHER: Kind of like during the Vietnam era in a way.

WAID: It's just what it is. I would sound like Abe Simpson standing on his front lawn *(Boucher laughs)* yelling at the clouds if I were to say, "And comics were better back then," or "Super-heroes weren't like that in my day." That's not what I'm saying at all, I'm giving just a straightforward emotion-free answer to the question, which is that right or wrong, I think that yes they've changed. Whether that is for good or bad, that's above my paygrade to say.

BOUCHER: Where do you hope super-hero comics will be in another 10-20 years in terms of justice and related topics, and why?

WAID: I think that the greater influx of diversity you get both with creators and with characters – but especially with creators – I think that's gonna be the change in terms of the themes of justice and related topics. I think that as more non-male white people make their way into comics – and they are – I think that you'll get a much different variety of flavor when it comes to what justice is and I think that's great.

BOUCHER: Do you have any particular recommendations for creators and readers just in terms of how the industry works in this progression?

WAID: You really have to write from what you feel is an honest place. You've really got to write what you feel is important. You have to say something with a story and if it's not saying something about the world around us, or if it's not saying something even allegorically about the justice system or society or human emotion or where we are as a people, then you may as well be creating a crossword puzzle or building a Sudoku puzzle, all pieces of plot and action and tropes and capes and punches. If that's what you're doing, then why are you bothering? Go work at a Burger King. If you're gonna write a story, whether it's a super-hero story, or any kind of story, but especially a super-hero story, think about what justice means today, think about what the law means, think about what the role of a vigilante in today's society means, and what people are looking towards for salvation. Don't default to thinking it's an authority figure.

As this book went to print, you could read Mark Waid in titles such as S.H.I.E.L.D., Archie, and All-New, All-Different Avengers. You should also immediately check out his innovative – and incidentally, empowering – digital comics platform, Thrillbent.

The Personal, the Societal, and the Canonical: Gerard Jones on Super-Hero Justice

IAN BOUCHER: I love *Martian Manhunter: American Secrets*[1] – its words and its images. I love how it's equally a quintessential J'onn J'onzz story and "more." While being an exciting sci-fi noir story, it's also an intense commentary, constantly peeling back layers on reality. It takes the typical story beats about 1950s America and encourages the reader to reconsider them further as a puzzle. How did that story come about?

GERARD JONES: It was a direct outgrowth of a monthly series I'd been writing, *The Shadow Strikes*.[2] The editor of that, Brian Augustyn, wanted to do another history-based project with me and the artist, Eduardo Barreto. I

---

[1] *Martian Manhunter: American Secrets* #1-3. Gerard Jones (writer), Eduardo Barreto (penciler/inker), Steve Oliff (colorist), and Pat Brosseau (letterer). Eds. Brian Augustyn and Ruben Diaz. DC Comics, Aug-Oct 1992.

[2] Starting with *The Shadow Strikes!* Vol. 1 #1. Gerard Jones (writer), Eduardo Barreto (penciler/inker), Anthony Tollin (colorist), and David Cody Weiss (letterer). Ed. Brian Augustyn. DC Comics, Sept 1989.

In *Martian Manhunter: American Secrets* #1, J'onn J'onzz reflects in solitude on his world. Art by Eduardo Barreto. © DC Comics.

don't remember for sure, but I think the use of the Martian Manhunter was my idea. I'd always had a strange fascination with him – such an odd character, who'd gone through so many transmutations. Somehow Brian and I together worked out the idea of setting a story in that in-between period in DC's internal history, after the Golden Age heroes faded and before the new Flash. From there I think I went off and started thinking about what I might be able to say about America in the '50s using a super-hero as the viewpoint.

The thing about me is that I've always been interested in comics, but I've always been much more interested in American history. I only got into writing comics because I'd made connections with people in the business while writing *The Comic Book Heroes*,[3] a history of the super-hero genre with a social-cultural background. One of the things that made my Shadow stories most interesting, I think, was the way I related them to social history. So this was right in my wheelhouse, as they say.

BOUCHER: What was the process like?

JONES: It started off wonderfully, but then it got choppy. Which is basically the story of my whole relationship with the comics industry. Brian and I had conceived it as an imaginary story, like the *Gotham by Gaslight* graphic novel he'd done with Mike Mignola,[4] that didn't require any fidelity to DC continuity. But after I'd nearly written the whole thing, word came down that DC was backing away from that kind of story – that we couldn't contradict the canon. Originally, I'd conceived the Justice Society, or members of it, as the bad guys. Don't ask me what the details were, because I honestly don't remember. But I know there was a riff on McCarthyism in there, the paradox of tyranny being employed to protect freedom, and there was something about the anti-comics crusade, about super-heroes having been chased to the shadows and trying to reclaim their

---

[3] Will Jacobs and Gerard Jones. *The Comic Book Heroes: The First History of Modern Comic Books - From the Silver Age to the Present* (New York: Crown Publishing Group, 1985).

[4] *Gotham by Gaslight: An Alternative History of the Batman*. Brian Augustyn (writer), Mike Mignola (penciler), P. Craig Russell (inker), David Hornung (colorist), and John Workman (letterer). Eds. Bob Harras, Denny O'Neil, Kelley Puckett, and Mark Waid. DC Comics, 1989.

power in darker ways. Whatever the story was though, I was told that I couldn't have evil super-heroes.

So I had to make up a new ending on the fly, with the first issue ready for the printer and the second one, I believe, entirely penciled – and I'm a writer who really believes in foreshadowing and setup. Instead of a corrupt version of super-heroes, I went with a corrupt version of the Manhunter himself, an evil Martian. Brian gave me a chance to rewrite a few balloons in the second issue to change some setups, which helped. I came out of the whole experience pretty frustrated – although I have to wonder if the evil Martian might actually have been a better idea than my first one. In either case, though, it would have been nice to be able either to pay off my original setups or foreshadow the right ending.

BOUCHER: How was the reception of fans and the industry when it was first published?

JONES: It was good right from the start. For a while I went around telling people they should have seen it as I originally wrote it, but then I caught on that it's kind of ungracious to tell people who are complimenting you that they shouldn't be. I started allowing myself to think that it was good after all, and maybe the unwanted changes even helped me. Or maybe Eduardo's art was so good that it just didn't matter what I did.

BOUCHER: Have you gotten any particularly surprising feedback about it over the years?

JONES: I was pleasantly surprised when Darwyn Cooke told me it was one of his inspirations in creating his *New Frontier* series,[5] which I liked quite a bit. In general, it's turned out to be one of the comics I hear the most mentions of as the years go by. The one I get most of the nice comments on, by far, is *Green Lantern: Mosaic.*[6] But I'd say *Martian Manhunter, The Shadow*

---

[5] *DC: The New Frontier* Vol. 1 #1-6. Darwyn Cooke (writer/penciler/inker), Dave Stewart (colorist), and Jared K. Fletcher (letterer). Eds. Mark Chiarello and Valerie D'Orazio. DC Comics, Mar-May, July, Sept, Nov 2004.

[6] The 18-issue title that began with *Green Lantern: Mosaic* Vol. 1 #1. Gerard Jones (writer), Cully Hamner (penciler), Dan Panosian (inker), Steve Mattsson (colorist), and Albert De Guzman (letterer). Ed. Kevin Dooley. DC Comics, June 1992.

Strikes, and *The Trouble with Girls*[7] come next. I don't know that that's surprising, but it's gratifying, since I put a lot of myself into those.

BOUCHER: What super-hero comics continue to inspire you?

JONES: I don't actually read comics anymore. Sorry. I always feel a little awkward saying that. Nothing against comics or super-heroes, but they just stopped meaning anything to me. I haven't read a new comic book in years, super-hero or otherwise.

I have been reading some old comic strips, though. So let's say Little Orphan Annie continues to inspire me. If I have any pluck or spirit in me, it's no doubt due to Annie.

BOUCHER: When you were working in super-hero comics, how much of a factor were accurate or more representative depictions of criminal justice among you and your colleagues, and why?

JONES: Okay, now we get to the part where I have to think. Honestly, I was not thinking much consciously about issues of criminal justice. It was clear that I was working within a genre that called for bad guys to be handed their just deserts, but I also knew that justice in real life was capricious – guilty people get away with things, innocent people get convicted. Of course, one of the original functions of crime stories, not just super-heroes but whodunits and all the rest, is to create a reassuring fiction that justice will somehow always be done. I didn't want to subvert that, but I was interested in playing with the tension between the fantasy and the reality.

As for depictions of the actual criminal justice system – police, courts, jails – I don't recall really doing much. A cop character here and there, but no guiding philosophy to their depictions.

BOUCHER: Were there particular ideas about super-heroes and villains that you consistently ran into the conflict with in your work, during production or through fan reception? Did conflicts arise more internally within yourself, the industry, or externally via other organizations?

JONES: I suppose the issue with the original *American Secrets* plot fits into that question. The Justice Society was, explicitly, a representation of justice,

---

[7] Which began with Vol. 1 #1. Will Jacobs (writer), Gerard Jones (writer), Tim Hamilton (penciler), Dave Garcia (inker), and Diane Valentino (letterer). Ed. Chris Ulm. Malibu Comics, Aug 1987.

and I wanted to use them to show how justice can be politically and socially perverted, but the editors wouldn't allow it. Although I don't think that was really about conflicting ideas about heroes and villains so much as conflicting ideas about canonical and noncanonical portrayals of the company's characters.

Otherwise I can't remember any external conflicts. As far as internal conflicts go, I don't know that I can say I experienced them as conflicts per se – but I did play with some ambiguities and internal contradictions. In *Mosaic* I made John Stewart confront some questions about the extent to which he should manage and adjudicate different societies with clashing standards, to what extent there can be a common standard of law or justice. I don't think I developed those issues in particular depth, though. And of course with the Shadow I was charged with valorizing his particularly bloody style of vigilantism, although I don't personally believe in that kind of justice at all. And I did soften it – I worked the plots so that he rarely killed anyone as an act of punishment but did it out of exigency or needing to save someone. But that's more about a writer's relationship with genre expectations.

BOUCHER: What are the two most interesting precedents for you in terms of super-hero justice and why (comics, TV, movies, or otherwise)?

JONES: Well, at a cultural history level, I've always been intrigued at how Batman used a gun early on but complaints from parents – at least according to the usual story – drove Jack Liebowitz or someone else with authority to adopt a no-gun, no-kill policy for their comics. This being in Batman's first year, and so at a very formative moment in the development of super-heroes. That policy was later adopted by most other publishers of super-hero comics, and of course it was eventually embedded in the Comics Code, so for decades you have super-villains being carted off to jail, from which they inevitably escape – in that way making it a very convenient rule for the writers. When someone did want a villain to die, as the Marvel guys often did, then the cosmos had to be drafted to help. Villains falling ironically off rooftops and all. Gravity became a great purveyor of both irony and justice.

That, in turn, brings up another interesting moment, when Superman killed the villain at the end of his most recent movie.[8] I have to admit I didn't really follow that closely, but I was struck by how many people in the comics community, not just fans, but writers and editors, felt that as a genuine emotional blow. I found it interesting how this company code, which was originally a corporate self-protective maneuver – I don't think Jack Liebowitz gave a damn about the ethics of justice, he just didn't want trouble – had become such a part of the emotional experience of being a super-hero fan. There's clearly a deep, intuitive sense of what constitutes justice here, shaped by super-heroes; although I'd be interested to know more about the range of opinions on the real-life death penalty among fans who objected to that scene. How much is this about justice and how much is it about fidelity to a fictional icon?

BOUCHER: In *Killing Monsters*,[9] you seemed to view super-heroes primarily – for young people at least – as providing ways to learn how to function in the world on a personal level. Super-hero comics are indeed full of empathy, but criminal justice in them is not meant to be depicted as accurate or otherwise representative of the real world, and may not even be a point of focus for a story. If super-heroes, like any media creation, help young people learn symbols, where should the symbols being learned fit into super-hero storytelling?

JONES: The super-heroes themselves are symbols. And every story is a symbol, or a series of symbols. Every conflict is a symbol, and so is every outcome. All I'll say about placing symbols is that they should help the organic whole of the idea and the story hold together – they shouldn't be interjected as pedagogy.

BOUCHER: Do you think the pieces have been fitting together accurately enough for children? We can learn to be strong through our stories, but are the depicted facts in the periphery, which are informing our perceptions and values, on an adequately progressive path?

---

[8] *Man of Steel* (2013).
[9] Gerard Jones. Killing Monsters: Why Children Need Fantasy, Super Heroes, and Make-Believe Violence (New York: Basic Books, 2002). PDF e-book.

JONES: As I think about this, I'm wondering how relevant children are to the discussion, at least relative to comics. Kids know super-heroes through cartoons, movies, and Halloween costumes, not so much comics. And in terms of super-heroes as children experience them — I stumble over the word "accurately." Do we necessarily want an accurate depiction of criminal justice for children? Is that of any use in childhood? Children usually want the depiction of justice to make sense within their own worldviews, because what they're working with every day isn't the criminal justice system, it's day-to-day consequences, things being "fair," outcomes being somewhat dependable in the home, school, and friendships. For them, crime-fighters and criminals are symbolic of those issues — which makes the depiction innately inaccurate, if we're talking about social realism.

BOUCHER: At the end of the day, super-heroes are technically supposed to be delivering some notion of justice. Should super-hero comics portray elements of justice in a more accurate, representative, or otherwise expansive manner, and progress notions of justice, at least peripherally? Within the bounds of the super-hero action story, should more comics and movies explore what happens after the criminal is dropped off at the police station? Or does learning the facts that are informing the background come later? Does society need to change its views first?

JONES: One huge shift in nearly all popular narrative over the past few decades is toward the individual and psychological, away from the societal and philosophical. Super-hero stories now are almost entirely about how the characters deal with their own conflicts, angers, and fears. The defeat of the villain is usually about the eradication of someone who had brought personal grief to the hero — not justice in any larger sense but personal vengeance. Or if vengeance is too negative a word, let's say a leveling of the scales. The social aspect of super-heroes, in which they enacted dramas about larger issues of rules, conformity, judgment, and punishment — or about recompense or balance at a level broader than the personal — has been pretty much abandoned.

To some extent, that feeds into a new model of justice that's more about retribution and emotional satisfaction, which parallels some things in the larger society — some elements of the victims' rights movement, like the consideration of victims' emotions in sentencing decisions. In another way, though, it just pulls super-heroes entirely out of the realm of societal and legal justice and makes them purely psychological symbols. Which isn't necessarily a bad thing – but it's a different thing.

BOUCHER: Adults use media to reinforce their worlds, whether that media is fiction, nonfiction, or fiction purporting to be nonfiction. What once helped us release stress as children becomes our reality. Media stays with us throughout our lives. Especially since super-hero comics are geared more toward adults, what potential can super-hero comics have in helping adults understand what cultural connections they value?

JONES: Super-hero comics create a theater where thoughtful storytellers can take their time exploring the nuances of stories that are hurled at us in high speed and with hardly any complexity in movies. In comics you can stop and raise a question for people to chew on. I don't know that that actually happens much in comics, but it certainly has sometimes. Back in my day, I remember Alan Moore and Neil Gaiman asking some very interesting questions about the ideas of violence and justice contained in super-hero stories. Right about the time I was drifting away from the field, I noticed Ed Brubaker doing some interesting things with real-world criminality.

BOUCHER: Do you check in on the comics world often?

JONES: I go to San Diego Con to see friends. I have a vague idea of what people are working on and how well different companies and genres are doing. That's about it.

BOUCHER: What are the biggest general differences within the industry from when you worked in it?

JONES: It's full of people I don't know. And all the people I do know are turning wrinkly and grey.

What else? It seems to be getting by on smaller sales than ever, which I suspect translates into an even greater dependence on a small, esoteric audience. I get the feeling that marketing drives editorial more than it used to, that publishing "events" are more essential than ever, that centralized company control of the stories is greater. More women, more people whose ancestors weren't all from the western tip of Eurasia. But in some ways it's hardly changed at all. Hordes of nerdy young writers and artists getting all excited at the chance to rework these characters they've read about all their lives. Slightly older writers and artists bitching about publishers and how the whole business is going to hell. That's what we were doing 25 years ago.

BOUCHER: What changes do you especially like, and what changes are you especially not a fan of?

JONES: I don't think I have much to contribute about these questions. Except I'm not a big fan of the wrinkly, grey part.

BOUCHER: Out of general curiosity, not necessarily for this anthology, have approaches to violence in the media changed a great deal for the better since you wrote *Killing Monsters*?

JONES: I think the discussion of violence is much more nuanced, compassionate, and realistic. No one seems to be paying much attention to the old, linear, media-effects crowd anymore. I think when the NRA started using the violence-in-media argument as a political smokescreen after mass murders – a pretty cynical moment even for that cynical group – it was a sort of death knell to the argument. For now. One thing the history of moral battles over media shows is that the same arguments keep coming back around in new clothes.

BOUCHER: Where are you hoping super-hero comics will be in another 10-20 years, in terms of justice or otherwise? What recommendations do you have for creators and readers in this progression?

I haven't thought much about this and don't know that I have strong opinions. But now that we're talking about it, I think it would be a good thing if super-heroes were used more to explore the meanings and subtleties of all these issues – crime, justice, the relationship of individuals to society, heroism – and at a more general, less private and emotional, plane.

Keep your eyes peeled for Gerard Jones's latest work with his books My Pal Splendid Man – a humorous look at super-heroes, co-written with Will Jacobs, from Atomic Drop Press – and, as this book went to press, Nation of Faith and Flesh, a history of "America's first moral war," for Farrar, Straus, and Giroux!

About the Contributors

With a background in television production, film studies, and communication theory, **Ian Boucher** earned his Master of Library and Information Science at Kent State University to become a librarian to advocate for information literacy. He is fascinated with the stories cultures tell themselves, and writes about film and comics in that regard. Continue the conversation with him on Twitter @Ian_Boucher.

Daniel N. Gullotta is a graduate student at Yale University. He is currently completing his Master of Arts in Religion at Yale Divinity School. He holds a Master of Theological Studies from the Australian Catholic University and a Bachelor of Theology with Honours from the University of Newcastle. His research focuses on Christian origins, the intersection of religion and pop culture, and the reception history of religious and mythological studies. He is married to creative writer Kate M. Colby.

Paul R. Jaissle is a philosopher and writer living in Grand Rapids, Michigan, who first discovered his love for super-heroes while watching the *Super Friends* cartoon and reruns of *Batman* as a kid. He later rediscovered his passion of comic books while earning his master's degree in art and philosophy from Stony Brook University in 2009. Since then, he has written about the super-hero genre and the comic book medium in general, including an essay for the *Green Lantern and Philosophy* anthology, and has spoken at presentations and philosophical conferences. He currently contributes to the pop culture blogs DestroyTheCyborg! and Sequart.

Rebecca Johnson is a video editor, encoder, and podcaster who received a degree in Telecommunications and Film from the University of Alabama. In addition to working in the television industry for over ten years, she shoots and edits videos for her YouTube channel, and her voice can be heard on *Supergirl Radio*, a podcast that discusses Kara Zor-El and CBS's *Supergirl* television series.

John Loyd lives in Binghamton, NY with his wife, Hilary, and their dog Crash. He owned a turtle named Slash, but had to leave it in South Korea after living and working there for several years as an English teacher. He continues to work as an English tutor for Korean students. He has been a contributor for *The Buffalo News*, and wrote about the Comedian's role in *Watchmen* for Sequart's *Minutes to Midnight* anthology. He was formerly a reporter for the *Olean Times Herald*, and has a Bachelor of Arts in Communication from Roberts Wesleyan College.

Ross May has written for comics, including *Tales of the Teenage Mutant Ninja Turtles*, and the original graphic novel *Devil Dealers* with artist Brett Wood. He lives and writes in Saskatchewan, Canada. His website is RossMayWriter.com and he's on Twitter at @rossmaywriter.

Colby Pryor graduated from the University of Central Florida in 2012. He grew up a lifelong fan of science fiction, fantasy, and horror, and has read more comics than what can deemed safe by the Geneva Conventions. This is his first published work and he hopes many more will follow.

Jaime Infante Ramírez was born in Madrid in 1989, and has lived in Alcorcón ever since. He earned a bachelor's degree in Audiovisual Studies at URJC (Universidad Rey Juan Carlos). Later, he obtained a Master in Cultural Theory and Criticism of Culture at UCIIIM (Universidad Carlos III de Madrid) with a study on Frank Miller's *The Dark Knight Returns* and Alan Moore's *Watchmen*. He is currently writing his Ph.D. on Alan Moore's comics. He earns his living as an anatomy illustrator for medical textbooks. He also writes and draws comic strips. He would like to acknowledge Jessica, Susana, and his family in this, his first published work.

By day, **Michał Siromski** works as a psychologist and coordinator of projects helping socially excluded people. By night, he transforms into a researcher of comics. He specializes in topics such as the psychology of super-heroes, mechanisms of comic book perception, and autobiographical comics. He has been published many times in Poland. Since 2004 he has been a member of the editorial board of *KZ Magazine*, the most important Polish magazine devoted to comics.

ALSO FROM **SEQUART**

THE BRITISH INVASION: ALAN MOORE, NEIL GAIMAN, GRANT MORRISON, AND THE
    INVENTION OF THE MODERN COMIC BOOK WRITER
CLASSICS ON INFINITE EARTHS: THE JUSTICE LEAGUE AND DC CROSSOVER CANON

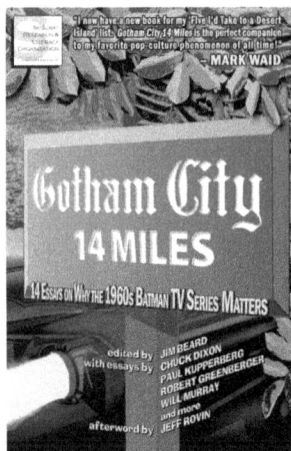

GOTHAM CITY 14 MILES: 14 ESSAYS ON WHY THE 1960S BATMAN TV SERIES
    MATTERS
NEW LIFE AND NEW CIVILIZATIONS: EXPLORING STAR TREK COMICS
A LONG TIME AGO: EXPLORING THE STAR WARS CINEMATIC UNIVERSE

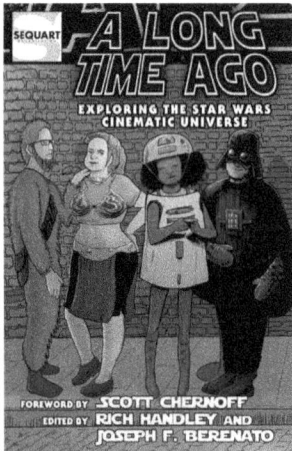

BOOKS ON GRANT MORRISON:

GRANT MORRISON: THE EARLY YEARS

OUR SENTENCE IS UP: SEEING GRANT MORRISON'S *THE INVISIBLES*

CURING THE POSTMODERN BLUES: READING GRANT MORRISON AND CHRIS WESTON'S *THE FILTH* IN THE 21ST CENTURY

THE ANATOMY OF ZUR-EN-ARRH: UNDERSTANDING GRANT MORRISON'S BATMAN

BOOKS ON WARREN ELLIS:

SHOT IN THE FACE: A SAVAGE JOURNEY TO THE HEART OF *TRANSMETROPOLITAN*

KEEPING THE WORLD STRANGE: A *PLANETARY* GUIDE

VOYAGE IN NOISE: WARREN ELLIS AND THE DEMISE OF WESTERN CIVILIZATION

WARREN ELLIS: THE CAPTURED GHOSTS INTERVIEWS

OTHER BOOKS:

A GALAXY FAR, FAR AWAY: EXPLORING STAR WARS COMICS

THE SACRED SCROLLS: COMICS ON THE PLANET OF THE APES

THE WEIRDEST SCI-FI COMIC EVER MADE: UNDERSTANDING JACK KIRBY'S *2001: A SPACE ODYSSEY*

THE DEVIL IS IN THE DETAILS: EXAMINING MATT MURDOCK AND DAREDEVIL

TEENAGERS FROM THE FUTURE: ESSAYS ON THE LEGION OF SUPER-HEROES

MINUTES TO MIDNIGHT: TWELVE ESSAYS ON *WATCHMEN*

AND THE UNIVERSE SO BIG: UNDERSTANDING *BATMAN: THE KILLING JOKE*

IMPROVING THE FOUNDATIONS: *BATMAN BEGINS* FROM COMICS TO SCREEN

WHEN MANGA CAME TO AMERICA: SUPER-HERO REVISIONISM IN *MAI, THE PSYCHIC GIRL*

THE FUTURE OF COMICS, THE FUTURE OF MEN: MATT FRACTION'S *CASANOVA*

THE BEST THERE IS AT WHAT HE DOES: EXAMINING CHRIS CLAREMONT'S X-MEN

MUTANT CINEMA: THE X-MEN TRILOGY FROM COMICS TO SCREEN

MOVING PANELS: TRANSLATING COMICS TO FILM

DOCUMENTARY FILMS:

DIAGRAM FOR DELINQUENTS

SHE MAKES COMICS

THE IMAGE REVOLUTION

NEIL GAIMAN: DREAM DANGEROUSLY

GRANT MORRISON: TALKING WITH GODS

WARREN ELLIS: CAPTURED GHOSTS

COMICS IN FOCUS: CHRIS CLAREMONT'S X-MEN

For more information and for exclusive content, visit Sequart.org.

www.ingramcontent.com/pod-product-compliance
Lightning Source LLC
Chambersburg PA
CBHW030917090426

42737CB00007B/223